Praise for EMPIRES OF FOOD

"*Empires of Food* deals with a subject of grave importance and profound implications for the political economy of the world. Although the subject is serious, it is written in a compelling and readable style. While not pedantic or ponderous in any way, it is of impressive academic rigor. This book needs to be read and thoughtfully considered by policy-makers and citizens everywhere. And if you enjoy lunch, don't fail to read it!"

—John Manley, former Deputy Prime Minister of Canada

"With a breathtaking sweep, *Empires of Food* takes us on a rollicking culinary journey through the ecological history of civilization. The result is a rare treat: hard-hitting analysis cooked to read like a captivating novel. For pure pleasure or a deeper understanding of why civilizations rise and fall, it's a perfect choice for any curious mind."

—Peter Dauvergne, Professor and Canada Research Chair in Global Environmental Politics, University of British Columbia; author of *The Shadows of Consumption*

"*Empires of Food* is a panoramic and prescient book which presents the challenges that civilizations have faced with agricultural production and societal fashions for food. The authors approach the issue with refreshing pragmatism and urge us to move towards a 'glocal' approach to consumption norms. Their compelling narrative recognizes the value of efficient global food systems while also appreciating the importance of local connections to reduce ecological impacts. Such a vision for our palates holds much promise in balancing the debate on food ethics and sustainable development."

—Saleem H. Ali, author of *Treasures of the Earth: Need, Greed, and a Sustainable Future*

Empires of Food

Feast, Famine, and the Rise and Fall of Civilizations

Evan D. G. Fraser

and

Andrew Rimas

FREE PRESS

NEW YORK LONDON TORONTO SYDNEY

fP
FREE PRESS
A Division of Simon & Schuster, Inc.
1230 Avenue of the Americas
New York, NY 10020

Map by Jason Snyder

First Free Press hardcover edition June 2010

FREE PRESS and colophon are trademarks of Simon & Schuster, Inc.

Manufactured in the United States of America

1 3 5 7 9 10 8 6 4 2

Library of Congress Cataloging-in-Publication Data

Fraser, Evan D. G.
Empires of food : Feast, famine, and the rise and fall of civilizations /
Evan D. G. Fraser and Andrew Rimas.
p. cm.
Includes bibliographical references and index.
1. Food—History. 2. Food supply—History. 3. Agriculture—
History. I. Rimas, Andrew. II. Title.
TX353.F77 2010 641.309—dc22

ISBN 978-1-4391-0189-6
ISBN 978-1-4391-1013-3 (ebook)

To Gabrielle and Paloma

Contents

Introduction

The two authors of this book have never gone hungry. We've never even lacked an embarrassment of dried pasta choices. This is important to know because, while this book is about food as a historical—and environmental, economic, and political—force, the act of eating is a highly personal one. Every family has its culinary DNA. Ours were Scots Canadian (Fraser) and Lithuanian American, undercut by the influence of an ancestor from Alsace (Rimas). In the one case, this meant tuna casserole, sweet and sour spareribs, and stir-fried beef with broccoli and carrots; the other was stuffed cabbage and chicken crepes Mornay. But growing up, both of us knew the comfortable expectation of the ice cream quart, the ham sandwich on white, the stuffed tortilla bag. Eating connects us to our histories as much as it connects our souls to our bodies, our bodies to the earth. So it's useful to consider that we mean "sustenance" when we write the word "food."

Historically, sustenance has taken the form of the gritty, bland grains that kept humanity alive for ten thousand years. Yet eating is never merely the care and maintenance of cells. No species would invent chocolate *ganache au crème fraîche* for the sake of cellular health. As well as triggering at least two of the more enjoyable stimuli, eating is about society. It's about fellowship and memory, about Proust's madeleine, about our culinary hooks in the reflecting pool. At its most evolved, it's the second glass of port, the bite of Camembert assessed alongside the nibble of Stinking Bishop, the fresh-shucked oyster in a porcelain dish. Eating is what all animals do, but humans do it beautifully.

But we didn't write this book as a celebration of gastronomy. The libraries of the world are full of prose dedicated to the dripping sensuality of the table, and long tracts of our previous book, *Beef: The Untold Story of How Milk, Meat, and Muscle Shaped the World,* are unabashedly epicurean. But while writing *Beef* we began to mull over the topics that formed the skeleton for this book: how climate change will alter our menus; why obesity and hunger coexist in the world with such seeming inevitability; whether the Earth's soil will burn away into dust. And whether our beloved Western supermarkets will someday lock their sliding doors, their refrigerators humming over aisles shorn of meat.

These are very old questions. They were asked, in a form, by laborers hoeing at the sandy runnels off the Euphrates five thousand years ago. They were asked again by Mayan farmers watching the parched skies of the medieval Yucatán. The Romans asked them, as did the Mycenaean Greeks. And so did Californians before the arrival of movie cameras. Now, in this age of designer fertilizers and test-tube crops, we're forced to ask them again. But today, we need to find new answers.

Our ten-thousand-year-old urban civilization could be summed up in the throwaway line "We are what we eat." From Jericho to Manhattan, cities have been founded on the creation and exchange of food surpluses. Food is wealth, and so food is art, religion, government, warfare, and all the potent, sometimes stinking blossoms of culture. We've built complex societies by shunting corn and wheat and rice along rivers, up deforested hillsides, and into the stewpots of history's anonymous generations.

These societies, these food empires, can only exist if three things happen: Farmers need to grow more food than they eat; they need a means of trading it to willing buyers; and they need a way to store it so it doesn't dissolve into sludge before reaching its economic apotheosis. When these three premises are met, urban life flourishes.

Which is, in itself, the seed of a problem. Food empires, like the crops on which they're founded, have a tendency to grow. Unlike wheat stalks, though, they have a tendency to swell past sustainable boundaries until they implode. For instance, a food empire might stretch out during a period of mild sun and soft rainfall, but when the weather turns foul a few centuries down the line, it hastily shrinks on account of the cold. Or it may throw its economic heft behind a particular crop, using specialist producers to feed its hungry cities. But this makes the food empire vulnerable to droughts, floods, and pests, leading it to topple when the crop fails. Or it may expand in a furrow of fresh soil, breaking virgin ground, exhausting it, then breaking virgin ground again until the hillsides stand bare.

Or all of the above.

When a food empire fails, mobs tear apart the marketplaces, angry over the cost of bread. Governments raise armies to conquer greener, more fertile valleys. People uproot. Forest creeps back over the old fences. Arable land falls into disuse, and society contracts. It happens again and again. And it's happening now.

This book is about how food, economics, agriculture, and human empires are all strands of the same narrative. In following these strands, we've traced two journeys. The first took place at the turn of the seventeenth century, at the dawn of the global marketplace. This was the first time that a merchant could make a circuit of the Earth, jumping on and off ships, buying and selling merchandise in the hope (usually deluded) of getting fabulously rich. Using the journal of one of the first people to ever attempt such a journey, we trace the beginnings of the modern "food empire," the mesh of human arrangements, technology, and land that binds farmers in Indonesia to banks in Holland, Peruvian fishermen to bureaucrats in Europe.

The second journey takes place four hundred years later, in 2008. It's a trip down the Yangtze River in central China, through the heart of an industrial food empire. Many of the themes from the first journey—erosion and transport, the price of fish in one place and of chickens in another—repeat in the second. Large and complex civilizations expand and contract, breathing out and pulling back in a sequence that's been repeating itself since the agricultural revolution. Today, the fertilizers are better, but that's just going to make the contraction all the more abrupt. The shape of the pattern—a gradual rise in comestible wealth, ending in an unpleasant plunge—hasn't changed since the Fertile Crescent turned into a misnomer. All that is old is new again, and the lesson from history is that big civilizations are built on ground no firmer than the mud under their rice paddies. They, and we, are slaves to food.

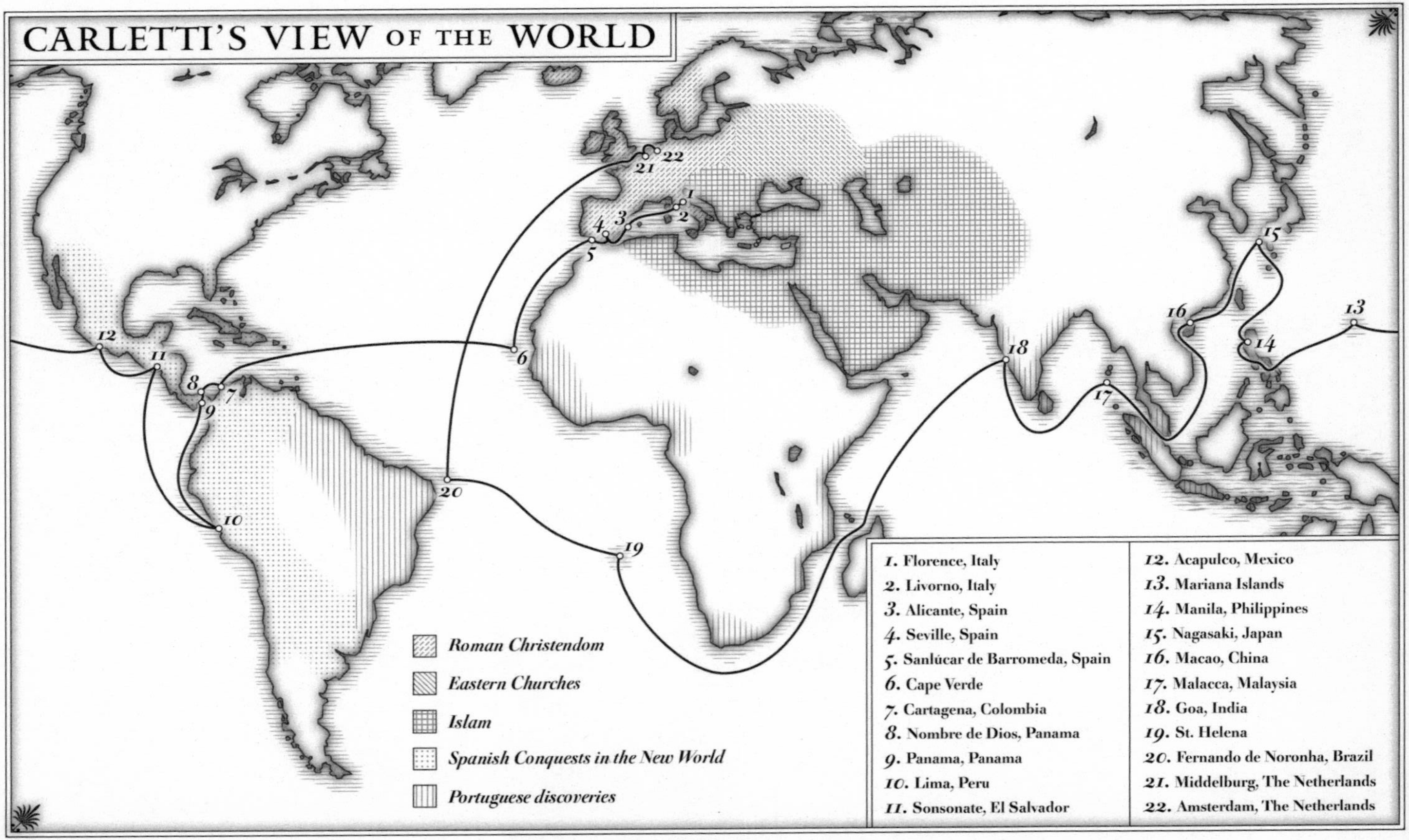
CARLETTI'S VIEW OF THE WORLD
Roman Christendom
Eastern Churches
Islam
Spanish Conquests in the New World
Portuguese discoveries
1. Florence, Italy
2. Livorno, Italy
3. Alicante, Spain
4. Seville, Spain
5. Sanlúcar de Barromeda, Spain
6. Cape Verde
7. Cartagena, Colombia
8. Nombre de Dios, Panama
9. Panama, Panama
10. Lima, Peru
11. Sonsonate, El Salvador
12. Acapulco, Mexico
13. Mariana Islands
14. Manila, Philippines
15. Nagasaki, Japan
16. Macao, China
17. Malacca, Malaysia
18. Goa, India
19. St. Helena
20. Fernando de Noronha, Brazil
21. Middelburg, The Netherlands
22. Amsterdam, The Netherlands

PART I

THE PRICE OF FOOD

The Three Gorges Dam

A brown dusk hangs above the Yangtze River as it drifts, hazy as stale tea, through the concrete warrens of middle China. A few miles upstream, the water still laps against fantastical crags and bamboo forest, but in downtown Yichang, it seeps along a molded channel, as grey and unyielding as the skyscrapers that roost on the paved edge of the stream. A few years ago, Yichang was the Chinese equivalent of a puddle-duck hamlet—a forgotten river city like dozens of others in the valley. Today, it's one of the new cities of the East, a rusting bunker of 4 million people living under a whorl of ozone and carbon dioxide.

You don't see the sun much in Yichang. But you do see traffic. Lane after lane of chrome and plastic and gusting diesel clang past the fluorescent restaurants and brothels, the silent blue television glow from the windows of the apartments, the sad potted trees.

If Yichang were an American or European city, it would rank, in terms of size, in the second tier. In China, it barely registers on the human landscape. But it does register on the economic one. The city stands six hundred miles west of Shanghai, midpoint along the river between the industrial coast and China's vast inland metropolis of Chongqing. That wouldn't matter much if it weren't for a particular trick of geography that would make Yichang the site of humanity's single greatest material act: the construction of the Three Gorges Dam.

The physical reality of the dam squashes the brain's capacity for hyperbole. Like the numerical value of pi or the distance between stars, it's a concept that can only be encapsulated by numbers. For instance:

The dam contains 986.56 million cubic feet of poured concrete.

It flooded 244 square miles of land.

It's propped up by 256,500 tons of metal supports.

Building it displaced 1.13 million people.

In short, it's a piece of civilization that can only really be thought of in terms of a spreadsheet.

Passing through the shipping locks on the upper section of the dam is like sailing through a steel gate into Brobdingnag. The five lock chambers are each big enough to float twenty large cargo vessels; their 130-foot-high doors are tall enough for cruise ships to putter through like tugboats. Once inside the chambers, the water drains away at a rate of a meter every couple of seconds, leaving passengers craning their necks to see the sky. It takes a boat three hours to pass through the dam, but doing so makes travelers feel like they're crossing a threshold into a changed world, one that's out of scale with everything downstream. A broken flow, leaving behind everything that's ever gone before.

The travelers are right. The Three Gorges Dam unveils a new world that stretches far beyond the cinder-block maze of Yichang.

On the outskirts of the city, the river swells to a width of about a mile and a half. Before the Chinese started to tinker with the river's flow,[1] the water churned with sediment from as far away as the Himalayas, rolling with it down into the flat, squelching miles of the Yangtze Delta to Shanghai. Now much of the grit settles against the concrete filter of the Three Gorges. One local hydrologist (who asked to remain anonymous) says that since the river ceased replenishing the delta's mud, Shanghai has actually begun to sink.

The Yangtze River cuts the nation in half, both physically and gastronomically. On the northern bank is the beginning of wheat country. To the south lie rice paddies. So long as the river remains navigable, merchant fleets keep the western hinterland connected to Shanghai's markets, and hence to the world. But when the river floods, as it once did with regularity, the catastrophe can be mythic. A Yangtze flood in 1931 killed more than 100,000 people, although this was a mere fraction of the 4 million deaths inflicted by China's rivers in a grisly season that still holds the world record for murderous natural disasters.[2]

China's history is the history of its rivers, and the dam is meant to change that. Official proclamations declare that the Three Gorges is a giant battery of clean, renewable energy, ridding a sorely gassed nation of 100 million tons of carbon dioxide and 2 million tons of sulfur dioxide emissions per year. It's meant to bestow dependable irrigation on millions of peasant farmers. Most importantly, it promises to lessen flooding from once per decade to once per century, shielding 1.5 million hectares and 15 million people from the deadly wash.[3] On the other hand, critics are worried that the dam's reservoir will silt up like a clogged drain, making the whole project not only wasteful but dangerous.[4] Earthquakes, too, are dangled as an apocalyptic possibility, as is terrorism. And then there's the question of obsolescence. With a brave, new climate burning down on our icecaps and glaciers, the twenty-first century is going to be awash in floodwaters. The dam, in short, may prove to be useless or even downright catastrophic, potentially unleashing a gigantic wave of muddy, rolling death on the river valley.[5] Yichang would be its first victim.

In the meantime, the Three Gorges Dam has risen to an unusual pantheon of human achievement: that of Epochal Engineering, stuff that sums up the human condition of the time. Stonehenge, for instance, reflected the relationship between Neolithic people and the cosmos. The pyramids proclaimed the divine nature of the pharaohs. Now the Three Gorges Dam declares to the world, in the most ostentatious manner possible, that China Is Modern. No longer is it a nation of bent peasants eking out a living among the rice plants. It's now a nation of six-lane highways and lab coats, of hydroelectricity powering the laptops, where something as primitive as a bursting riverbank belongs to the muddy past. And it's especially a nation where no one goes hungry, where even the poor can stalk the refrigerated aisle for a bag of frozen dumplings. In the twenty-first century, the China of the Three Gorges Dam need never fear starvation. It's part of the safe, clean, modern world. Part of the global food empire.

Or so it seems on first glance. In the late 1990s, some Western researchers worried themselves into a tizzy about the effect that a global China would have on the world's food markets. They suggested that a country so populous couldn't possibly feed itself, particularly since its land area under cultivation was shrinking. They thought that China's appetite for imported rice, in particular, would drain the international markets by the year 2030, driving up prices and making trouble for everyone from commodities brokers in Chicago to slum dwellers in Rio.[6] This hasn't happened. China remains almost entirely self-sufficient, consuming only homegrown rice and mostly homegrown wheat. This would be good news for everyone if it had any chance of lasting.

It doesn't. The Chinese Academy of Sciences recently stated that, due to climate and population change, "cereal production . . . [will] fall significantly as the century progresses."[7] This is bad news for everyone, because the Chinese food empire, with its tangle of farms, warehouses, refrigeration cars, corn exchanges, cash registers, and frying pans, is hopelessly intertwined with the rest of the world. Recall the cliché of the butterfly flapping its wings in the Amazon and causing a hurricane: today, we have a shrimp boat hauling up an empty net in the Mekong Delta and sparking a riot in Haiti.

To feed itself, China is resorting to the *deus ex machina* of genetically modified grain—"super-rice" varieties that are twice as productive as natural ones.[8] What biotechnology giveth, it also taketh away in the form of weird, genetically mutating pests. Super-rice needs super-pesticides, and super amounts of water and chemicals. When the Chinese planted their first strains of these laboratorial wonders, they bathed them in a wash of fertilizers. And these products cost oil. Lots of oil. So they yoked their agriculture, as Westerners did long ago, to the energy market. It's a devil's bargain at best. At worst, perhaps in some future, fateful year when the price of oil floats to record highs along with the annual temperatures, it's going to be hell.

Genetically modified crops may not even promise technological salvation anymore.[9] One of China's current experiments is with a strain of rice that produces its own insecticide, a poison tagged for a prowling plant killer called the stem borer. But the stem borer is already yesterday's villain. Even as this new rice is unleashed on the stem borer, a fresh pest, the brown leafhopper, is replacing the ailing vandal, proving again that ecology is impossible to squash into an engineer's blueprint.[10] Something unexpected always happens to mess up the prophets.

THE RISE AND FALL OF FOOD EMPIRES, PAST, PRESENT, AND FUTURE

The Three Gorges Dam exists because of the way China gets its food. And China, like all developed countries, is part of the global food empire.

Food empires are the subject of this book. They are what urban societies create to feed themselves. In their simplest formation, they're webs of farms and trails, rivers and vegetation, all of which function to deliver food from a piece of tilled land to a cluster of interested eaters. To do this well, more food must be created than the producers themselves wish to eat. The food must also be preserved and shipped on the winding journey from farmer to diner. And the food empire needs a mechanism for exchanging the food between these parties.

These three functions—surplus, storage/shipping, and exchange—are the pillars of every food empire from ancient Egypt to Victorian England. Just as there is no life without food, so there is no civilization without a food empire.

Driving a wagon of grain into a legionnaire camp; measuring hops into a beer keg destined for sale to a village on the other side of a forest; packing tea leaves in the hold of an Indiaman for the voyage around the Cape of Good Hope. Such is the daily bustle of food empires. The engineers who poured the concrete for China's cyclopean water projects were likewise working on behalf of our staggeringly complex modern food empire, one that feeds everyone who buys groceries from a store. Which, unless you're a subsistence farmer or some recluse with a fishing spear and a headful of Thoreau, means all of us.

Despite its seeming triumph over the technological strictures that hobbled its predecessors, today's food empire is cracked with very old fissures. We're making the same mistake our ancestors did, and the result is a system as delicate as a ripe sheaf of emmer wheat. One brusque stroke and the grains will fall away.

The mistake of the modern food empire is to accept three apparently self-evident assumptions. The first is that the Earth is fertile. For the last eighty years, human beings have been plowing, sowing, and reaping with a fury that the planet's soil has never before experienced. Past food empires farmed as frantically as they could, but modern advances put them to shame. Today's bumper crops, even more so than historical harvests, deplete the earth, drawing down what ecologists call "natural capital." By spending our geological endowment, we've been able to feed billions of human beings. But we haven't replaced the fund. When older food empires depleted their soil, they either expanded onto fresh ground or concocted new technologies to resuscitate the land. Then, when these strategies inevitably faltered, the food empires had to retreat, leaving abandoned cities and memories of wealth.

Our own food empire has yet to stall. For a hundred years, we've beefed up our soil with clever fertilizers and planted it with breeds of engineered crops. The question that bubbles under the Bunsen burners of the world's agricultural laboratories, though, is whether we can indefinitely cook up new biochemical fixes. Farming does violence to nature. Will we always have enough Band-Aids on hand?

The second undermining assumption for the stability of food empires is that the forecast calls for sunny, mild weather, with possible showers. That's the sort of weather we've enjoyed for generations, but it's a historical blip. Human-induced changes aside, our planet's climate is hardly static. During the Roman Warm Period, a string of pleasant centuries boosted Europe's wheat harvests and swelled her vineyard grapes. The seventeenth century, on the other hand, was entirely less comfortable, with a Little Ice Age stunting diets across the world and driving the irritable masses to war.[11]

Food empires, on the whole, grow bigger when the sun and rain cooperate. This was the case with our modern system, which didn't undergo any significant climatic shocks between the Dust Bowl in the 1930s and the droughts in the 1990s. All the truly horrific famines of the twentieth century (China, Bengal, Russia, Ethiopia, etc.) were political or economic evils. They had less to do with weather than with policy.[12] If past examples are any guide, though, when the storm clouds come, we ought to look not only to our umbrellas, but to our larders. Cities have a tendency to shrink with the grain yields.

Our third mistake is to assume that it's good business to do one thing well. The modern food empire is a patchwork of specialized regions producing large amounts of a very few commodities. This is sound economics but terrible ecology. A specialized agricultural region is fragile in the face of a particular insect or spore or an untimely spell of dry skies. Nature is most resilient when it's diverse. And since all our specialty patches depend on one another to constitute our food empire, none of them can exist alone. None are self-reliant. Remove one and the whole system unravels.

There's a fourth assumption that affects the first three, but since it's unique to our modern food empire, we have no historical lesson to glean. Just logical ones. Our food supply, like everything else in our civilization, takes cheap fossil fuels for granted. We use oil to power everything from water pumps to meat freezers; the factories that synthesize fertilizer in chemical vats use natural gas. Without a predictable, affordable flow, we can't grow and refrigerate the dizzying quantities of food eaten by our metropolises. Bargain-priced energy is the reason we've been free to breed and feed our population past the 6 billion tally. Remove the energy, and those billions, too, will be taken away.

Of course, these are a lot of assumptions on which to base something as important as the feeding of our species. They assume no pendulum swings in the price of energy. No global warming. They place existential faith in the scientists trying to mask chronic soil degradation by inventing new seeds and fertilizers. And they assume no political reneging on trade agreements—like, for instance, when India banned the export of non-basmati rice in 2008 in a panicked attempt to smother its domestic prices.[13] (Places that had long depended on having this rice to eat themselves, like Bangladesh and parts of Africa, quickly brokered exceptions and side deals that secured their imports. But what if India had really run out of food?)[14]

To be mistaken in one colossal assumption about our food empire may be a misfortune. To be mistaken in all four seems like something worse than carelessness. It seems like willful disregard for the truth. When we finally shed these assumptions, we'll realize the genuine price of the way we produce, distribute, and consume food.

Our food empire began to totter alarmingly in the spring of 2008. Initial stories quietly noted a drought in Australia and a swing in the value of the yuan. Then the headlines grew excited. Violence in Burkina Faso. Rice quotas at U.S. Walmarts.[15] Biofuel stealing the corn from our mouths. Violence in India. The World Bank declaring an international crisis. Violence in Mexico.[16]

Panic wasn't really an unreasonable reaction. Worldwide food prices, which were already up by 25 percent compared with the first half of the decade, spiraled out of daily affordability and into the realm of luxury. Robert B. Zoellick, president of the World Bank, proclaimed in April 2008, "Since 2005, the prices of staples have jumped 80 percent. Last month, the real price of rice hit a 19-year high; the real price of wheat rose to a 28-year high and almost twice the average price of the last 25 years."[17] That spring, another 75 million people slipped off the statistical precipice into the wretched classification of "hungry."[18]

In the hysteria, not many people noticed that 2008 was the single most bountiful year in the history of agriculture. Never before had farmers coaxed such plenty from the earth, never had harvests been so lush. The weight of the global breadbasket was 2.24 billion tons, a robust 5 percent increase over the previous year. Yet food prices utterly detached themselves from the fact that we had reaped the best harvest in the entirety of human existence. That's because our assumptions had finally started to wear thin.

History has a talent for ruining comfortable ideas. In the nineteenth century, at the height of Victorian industry and the flowering of mechanization, 45 million people died when well-reasoned, generally well-intentioned British colonial policies blended, murderously, with the weather of El Niño.[19] If a true environmental catastrophe had struck the world in 2008—a drought in the American Midwest or a bad case of European corn borer in the Ukraine—it would have been an awful lesson in history. That's the negative side of the food empire. The bonds that link our pantry shelves to the wages of tractor drivers on the North China Plain are real, for both good and bad.

So even though malnutrition and hunger are inconceivable to many of the world's inhabitants, the only difference between a bond and a shackle is perspective. The U.S. Congress passes a law on biofuel subsidies, and Bangladeshis can't buy rice. A dry summer sends an Australian cattleman into bankruptcy, and Senegalese storefronts are smashed. It's no different from the way that toxic mortgages in the United States caused economies to topple in Europe.

But while a financial crisis ruins lives, a food crisis ends them. No parents ever watched their child's teeth fall out from scurvy on account of a vanishing 401(k) plan. A collapsing food empire, on the other hand, is an existential matter.

For a hundred years, our industrial food empire has been astoundingly successful, but all empires stumble and fall, with or without a few buffering centuries of decay. The Three Gorges Dam—an edifice that's almost godlike in the liberties it takes with geography—is either a symbol of our salvation or a symptom of our coming collapse. It's the high water mark of a food system in which billions of farmers, workers, and consumers (all of them eaters) are connected, and it's a reminder that, while technological leaps and commodity profits have a global effect, so do blades of grass.

CHAPTER ONE

Fairs: The Food Trade

Among the watershed dates once taught to schoolchildren—those rosters of battles and landfalls committed by Great Men with flags—the year 1591 doesn't spring to mind. It was a perfectly decent year, perhaps, but it was clearly no 1453 (the Turks take Constantinople) or 1588 (the English Channel takes the Spanish Armada). It did, however, fall on the fizzling end of the Italian Renaissance, a period that, taken as a whole, is a more sensible historical watershed than any single gory calendar date. Europe's culture was different before and after the busy centuries when Italians started fiddling with humanism. And the center of the Renaissance was the city of Florence.

History is full of major Florentines. We're used to seeing them depicted in gold-leaf frames, alive within shaded oils. We know the cool, satisfied Medicis, Michelangelo's figures' gym room muscles, Savonarola's beak jutting from his cowl. Sometimes they look overdone, with pinched chinbones in a villain or glutted cheeks in a sot. But the pictures also look modern, very much as we do, especially when contrasted with the stark two-dimensional triptychs of previous centuries.

The hero of this book is Francesco Carletti, a minor cherub in the historical fresco. He's not a central actor, just a little face grinning down from the pale cirrus on a basilica ceiling, a twinkling smudge on the border. But he has a bird's-eye view of the entire scene.

Born a contemporary of greater men in the year 1573, Francesco Carletti was no prince or painter, no condottiere lord, black-skirted reformer, or vessel of holy outrage. He was merely a trader, a man who bought and sold things, often foodstuffs, in the hope of a profit. His thoughts were unsullied by poetry, and they never moved in currents deeper than his belly, his wallet, and his libido. In short, he floated through the turn of the seventeenth century like a dinghy borne on a swell. But he was honest, in his way.

Carletti was one of the first Europeans to record a worldwide trading journey, and his memoir, written at the beginning of "modernity," is a unique record of the origins of the food empire we enjoy today. A natural observer, Carletti was an amiable, open-minded man with a keen memory for details, particularly when they involved money, sex, and food.[1] The son of Antonio Carletti, a middling merchant with interests in Spain, the teenaged Carletti left his home on the twentieth of May of the fateful year 1591 on what would become one of history's most inept business trips. It would last fifteen years and drag him, sometimes unwillingly, across the entire circuit of the globe. During his travels he accumulated and lost a fortune, partook of fleshly pleasures from Cape Verde to India, and ate an astounding variety of dinners.

So while food production, its storage, and its exchange is the subject of this book (with occasional appearances from money and sex), Carletti is its hero. Food was Carletti's chief endeavor, as it is for all of humanity. Our stomachs, more than our hearts or genitals, force us to act.

When Carletti left Florence, he traveled in the company of a friend of his family, a merchant named Nicoló Parenti who had taken him into his care and given him an apprenticeship. They boarded a galleon at Livorno and made a pleasant cruise to the sun-kissed port of Alicante, an ancient Spanish city that would four hundred years later be rebuilt as a discount Sodom for English vacationers. From there, master and apprentice saddled up for the overland trip across the south of Spain to Seville, a journey of some three hundred miles as the crow flies.

In 1591, Spain was the center of Europe's commercial world, the heart of a global empire under the rigorously Catholic Philip II. Its kings were the emperors of Austria, Holland, generous cuts of Italy, and the weird, rich alien universe beyond the Atlantic. It was Spanish adventurers who, a mere generation earlier, had sailed into nothingness and returned, addled and raving, but with their ships creaking with bullion. It was Spanish merchants who were now weighing fist-sized ingots at Potosi and flooding the European markets with doubloons.

Seville, when Francesco Carletti arrived there, was the empire's financial nexus. It made perfect sense that a well-connected Italian trader like Parenti should set up a branch office on its waterfront, while an ambitious youngster like Carletti couldn't have chosen a better place to apprentice in the money game. His situation was like that of a favored assistant following a London stockbroker on his transfer to Wall Street, all expenses paid. The two Italians worked alongside the office governing West Indian commerce, a place where dreams of fortune took shape in a royal commission, and the men who clustered on the quays talked about markets in the Yucatán, tonnage shipped from Peru, troop deployments in faraway Pacific islands, and the price of ore. The city felt important and cosmopolitan, and spiced with adventure.

But adventures don't always end with a boatload of Inca gold. Nearly seventy years before Carletti arrived in Spain, another vessel had put into the harbor of Seville's coastal suburb of Sanlúcar de Barrameda. This was the *Victoria,* captained by the Basque adventurer Juan Sebastián Elcano. His was the last surviving ship in a convoy that had departed on a westward expedition out of the same port three years earlier under the command of Ferdinand Magellan. And while Magellan's expedition was the first to circumnavigate the globe, even seventy years later in Carletti's day, commercial travel between Spain and Asia was hardly painless. Magellan himself was famously hacked to death in the Philippines, and Elcano later died on his second attempt to cross the Pacific. Conditions hadn't changed much in the three generations since.

A European setting out for the East Indies in the 1590s could still reasonably expect to die horribly by means of shipwreck, starvation, or hostile foreigner. But the adventurers weren't fools. Land degradation and population growth had made their home countries crowded and expensive—inflation in the price of food and fuel was rampant in Europe during the sixteenth century.[2] The Reformation and Counter-Reformation had whipped up a brisk business in civil war and atrocity. European economies faced less a period of uncertainty than of dread.[3] It made sense to take one's chances with the Aztecs.

Europeans could, of course, have stayed on familiar ground, tightened their belts, and prayed for deliverance. Most did. But enough kings and ministers thought to look to the oceans in their hunger for new land and fresh resources so that, after years of stifled growth, Europe's food empire stretched outward. It wasn't an ordained choice. China, too, was undergoing an unpleasant century. But instead of succumbing to the allure of fleets and tropical shores, China's rulers drove their populations in brute labor, working the land they already possessed even more intensively. The Europeans took an opposite tack, and won their gamble.[4]

Carletti's journey was part of a broader push by Europeans toward the sea. Instead of growing their own treasures, Spain and Portugal sent traders to fetch the goods they lacked. Men like Carletti blazed the first trails for the modern food empire. As the ships raised sail in Cádiz and Lisbon, Europe's fortunes began to shift.

A very long degeneracy was at last coming to an end. It had lasted a thousand years.

THE DESERT FATHERS

Blame for ejecting the Romans and plunging Europe into the so-called Dark Ages usually falls to a ménage of Goths, willful illiteracy, and Christian impotence. While barbarian invasions did sterling work at dismantling Roman civilization, it was the problems caused by the food trade that doomed Europe to its long, unprofitable slumber. And it would be food that hauled Europe back out of its slump.

When the western half of the Roman Empire sank from decay into outright graveyard decomposition, Europe went hungry. For centuries, an imperial network of farms, warehouses, shipping lanes, paved roads, and soldiery had filled the cooking pots of millions of city dwellers, particularly in Italy. That vanished with the Roman legions. Especially on the edges of the empire, the infrastructure dissolved to the point where a farmer couldn't safely carry produce to an urban market. The roads were too broken, the journey too dangerous. With the loss of transportation, merchants had nothing to offer their customers. A complex food-trading system disappeared in favor of a cautious, tinkering trade in pocket luxuries like spices and ornaments. For the mass of Europeans, subsistence farming was the only means of survival. Cities ebbed away from the fields and orchards, merchants pried their ships apart for lumber, and the old trading routes fell into disuse. In accord with the times, Europe's population shrank by half between A.D. 200 and 600. The city of Rome itself fell from a peak of about 1 million residents in A.D. 300 to 400,000 a mere century later.[5]

Urban life fell apart in the fourth century because agriculture and trade, as much as the Roman armies, had failed.

Given widespread hunger, rapine, pillage, and pessimism, some people chose to drop out—if society had given up on them, they would give up on society. Among the earliest of these recluses were devout Egyptian Christians, later called the Desert Fathers, the foremost of whom was the fourth century ascetic Saint Anthony. In an act that bears a striking resemblance to the hippie movement of recent generations, Anthony spurned the decadence and wars of society, gave up all his worldly goods, and opened an organic farm:[6]

> *[Anthony] went over the ground about the mountain, and finding a small patch that was suitable, and with a generous supply of water available from the spring, he tilled and sowed it. This he did every year and it furnished him his bread. He was happy that he should not have to trouble anyone for this and that in all things he kept himself from being a burden.*[7]

His approach caught the imagination of a disgruntled, fearful world, and people flocked to follow his example.[8] One hundred years later, John Cassian, a rising star in the church hierarchy, joined these imitators. Cassian had embarked on a tour of the crumbling corners of the empire, keeping a sort of spiritual itinerary with stops in the Holy Land followed by a long, mortifying detour in the Egyptian desert. After a few years of contemplating the evils of the flesh, he returned to the noisy ring of church politics and doctrinal controversy before settling in the south of France. Inspired by his memories of the African desert, he founded a monastery to replicate the gang of ascetics he had joined on his tour, picking Marseille as a headquarters.[9] There, he spent much of the rest of his life writing instructional books on how to build a monastic community—how-to guides for budding abbots.[10]

By the standards of the Dark Ages, Marseille was something of a resort community. Steep hills to the north isolated it from the endless wars between the Merovingian potentates, and while geography meant that its hinterland couldn't grow much food, the inhabitants could look to the water of the city's deep harbor for sustenance. Marseille sits near the mouth of the Rhône, commanding the best waterway into the French interior. It was one of the few urban centers to prosper during the Dark Ages, and it did so by trading wine, fish, and grain between France and the wider world of the Mediterranean. Trade allowed Marseille to expand just as other towns were dissolving into goat pasture, and it grew rich enough to build suburbs when most other cities were only growing their cemeteries. Marseille even constructed a lavish baptistery, the grandest in Europe at the time, and "siege-proof" battlements.[11]

It seems ironic that Cassian, who insisted that his monks take vows of poverty, chose to plant them in the middle of one of the few vibrant economies on the map. Perhaps he wanted to test their commitment by exposing them to luxury. More likely, he was a pragmatic enough manager to understand that, while an individual monk may deny his biology, a monastery needs kitchens and markets. There was also an element of chicken and egg to Cassian's settlement. A monastery is an economic gift. In a continent where trade and agriculture were busily decomposing, Cassian's monastery gave Marseille a jolt of industry, because his monks didn't merely pray for the next world. They worked very hard to improve this one by producing food.

WORK, PRAY, EAT

Stark spirituality and communal living proved to be a popular mix.[12] A few decades after Cassian's death, another monk, Saint Benedict of Nursia, tweaked the rules that governed Marseille's monastery into something standardized and replicable—a Model T of group asceticism. These Benedictine monasteries spread, and by the end of the eighth century, chapter houses studded the landscape, each of them forming a nucleus of industry and food production within an otherwise shiftless continent.[13]

By growing and storing food surpluses, the monasteries became business, cultural, and financial centers, as well as dietary hubs. Monks were such noted businessmen that one medieval writer observed that, around one monastery, the River Seine was "a channel for vessels" that "trade in many goods."[14] Abbots signed trade agreements with other abbots. The monks at St. Denis, for example, had a long-term arrangement to buy salt, wine, and oil from their colleagues in Marseille.

Benedict had invented a successful business model. And he'd done it on the principle that it shouldn't feel horrible to be a monk. For example, instead of eating the two or three meals per week recommended by Cassian, Benedict advised his monks to keep up their strength for hard agricultural work. This meant regular dinners (two per day during the summer). Cassian's idea of a "sumptuous repast" was "parched vetches with salt and oil, three olives, two prunes, and a fig."[15] Benedict had more engaging tastes. For a typical lunch, he suggested a pound of bread and two cooked dishes—a fairly good diet for the time. Furthermore, instead of spending their nights in metaphysical combat with demons from the screaming, windy wasteland, Benedictine monks enjoyed six to eight hours of sleep, with mattresses, blankets, and pillows. Had the Benedictines followed a truly ascetic rule, they would have been too frail for useful farming, an activity that, to Benedict, was as vital as prayer.

Benedict's easing of Cassian's strictures broadened monasticism's appeal beyond a circle of zealots. People who couldn't, or wouldn't, live within their stations as nobles or serfs sought out monasteries, as did those displaced by war (a constant) or hunger (equally so). Monasteries, particularly once they codified their governance under Benedictine rule, meant security and even the hope of betterment. The lowest serf could find food and shelter among the monks. He might even learn a trade. Abbot Ælfric of Eynsham, writing a couple of generations before William conquered England, described the central position of monks in this society:

> *The throne stands on three supports: laboratores, bellatores and oratores. Laboratores are they who provide us with sustenance, ploughmen and husbandmen . . . Oratores are they who intercede for us to God . . . Bellatores are they who guard our boroughs.*[16]

It's a tidy encapsulation of feudal roles, but it doesn't do justice to the *oratores,* the monks. As well as praying for the good of the world, the monks undertook practical improvements by tearing out rocks and brambles and planting neat green fields.

Europe's medieval monasteries weren't all Benedictine; the Irish in particular had their own monastic tradition dating to the fifth century. But aside from a few itinerant wanderers, monks all tilled land and cleared forest. They all traded food. Since the monasteries (much like modern transnational corporations) outlived the monks who inhabited them, and since unlike secular landowners their property didn't disperse among generations of legatees, they accumulated amazing wealth over centuries devoted to farming, trading, and gathering inheritances from people hoping to buy a happy afterlife. They became financial hubs.[17] And they expanded outward to the frontiers, pushed by the monks' consecrated work ethic, by royal decree, and by allied merchants (often monks themselves).[18] Combining their agricultural learning with holy rigor, monks hiked into the woods of central Europe and changed the wilderness into tilled earth.[19]

This was new. Since the fall of Rome, people had developed the habit of eating only what they could grow on their immediate patch of ground, or perhaps what they could swap with a neighbor. That's no basis on which to nurse a triumphant return to civilization. To hoist itself out of poverty, Europe needed to grow more food than the farmers themselves could eat, and it needed a mechanism to trade this surplus. The monasteries supplied both the means and the mechanism.

THE AGRICULTURAL REVOLUTION OF A.D. 900

Typically, a monastery took root when its founders, often funded by a royal patron, cleared a section of forest inhabited only by wildlife or by undesirables (not unlike the way modern developers declare eminent domain on fringe neighborhoods to remake them for the common good—although the displaced communities aren't usually too happy about the wrecking crews). At first, the fledgling monastery sent for necessities like flour and meat from its brother houses, establishing trade routes into the shadowy neighborhoods of the continent. Then, after the new monastery's fields had started to flower and its herds had started to multiply, its self-sufficiency encouraged people to settle in the semi-tamed locale, making the monastery into an economic center of a rapidly "gentrifying" environment. By the tenth century, the process had brought millions of acres of fallow moorland, forest, and swamp into cultivation.[20]

In England, for example, deforestation was practically a form of penance. After the Conquest, King William, worrying about the moral stain of killing so many people during his invasion, tried to find a way to whitewash his soul. The Church had tallied a bill of 120 days of penance for every Saxon soldier killed, leaving the victorious Normans with a dire scheduling problem. How would a busy baron, or indeed a king burdened with the task of subjugating a hostile population, have time to pray? The answer, naturally, was to hire professionals to do the job.[21] Starting with a great monastery erected on the very site of the Battle of Hastings, William and his pious barons embarked on a campaign of monasticizing the English countryside, usually by planting the monks in "worthless" land, for example, "in a desert surrounded by swampy valleys and by forests out of which only a few homesteads had yet to be carved."[22] These monks didn't spend all their time sitting in chapels. Within a few hundred years, they had hacked and churned "hundreds of thousands of acres" into arable soil.[23]

The monks applied themselves to farming as zealously as they applied themselves to praying for the souls of their patrons. They became professionals. They studied crop rotation and tinkered with metallurgy, striving to make their brief time in the temporal world more productive. For example, until the age of monasteries, Europeans worked their fields with simple scratch plows, essentially a form of weighted knife that cut a shallow furrow in the surface of the ground. Since these didn't dig deep, they could be hauled by a single donkey, but they also couldn't reach the inner nutrients of the soil. Scratch plows required two perpendicular passes to properly churn a piece of ground, so fields looked like little patchworks of squares. The monks changed this by introducing the moldboard plow, a heavy instrument (possibly of Slavic origin) constructed in three parts.[24] A primary blade cut downward, deep into the earth, while a second, horizontal blade severed roots under the surface, making an incision like an upside-down T. A sloping section followed the horizontal blade and churned the newly cut soil up along the side of the machine. These improvements were, in terms of plows, astonishing. The moldboard could slice through wet northern soils, dredging up nutrients and organic matter to nourish the crops and increase yields. A single pass was now sufficient for any job, so farmers could farm longer tracts. Since they weren't limited to squares, they could follow the natural contours of the land, which prevented erosion. Also, the action of flipping up the dirt to one side of the furrow helped trap moisture, again increasing fertility.

The moldboard plow, in other words, might have been a boon to human progress on the same level as steam power and the invention of the wheel. But because the wretched contraption required an entire team of animals to pull it, pricing it out of the reach of the average peasant, it's likely that, as late as 1066, most farmers still picked at their fields with scratch plows.[25] The technology was for those who could afford it, like monks.

Monasteries were quick to adapt other technologies as well, primarily in food processing. Water mills had vanished from the European landscape with the Romans, leaving generations of people to grind their grain with querns, or hand mills. The monks rebuilt the water mills, and when a monastery was first chartered, the new abbot or prior usually made a point of securing a monopoly on milling rights from the king.[26] This freed labor from the daily toil of grinding grain and channeled it into more useful pursuits, like building cities.

FAYRE IS FAIR

Despite any residual Christian leanings toward poverty, a monastery had a commercial relationship with its tenants, one that would have looked familiar to modern farmers yoked to twenty-first-century agribusiness firms. The abbots were legal bullies with an arsenal of contracts and lawyers. They wanted nothing to encroach on their fertile turf.

Milling rights provide a good example of the monkish mentality.

Monasteries forced peasants to cart their grain to the abbey mills, representing a saving in the macroeconomic sense. But it annoyed the peasants. They resented having to pay for something they could accomplish themselves with a little sweat. The monasteries enjoyed the milling fees, of course, and there are many examples of abbots using gangs of thugs to coerce peasants into laying down their querns.[27] Sometimes, the monks even cracked a few skulls in the name of industry.[28] And an industry it was. The bishopric of Worcester garnered more revenue from milling in the year 1299 than from any other source.[29]

Medieval history is packed with goonish holy men. In Glastonbury in 1234, for example, the monks elected one Michael de Amesbury as their abbot, a gentleman who thought nothing of forcing thirty-two people described as "*quasi liberos*," but previously free of duties, to work for the monastery.[30] Warming to his executive powers, Abbot Michael called in unpaid rents and repossessed ten water mills from the hands of peasants, citing monopoly rights that hadn't been enforced in decades. The peasants, who were locked to the land and unable to shake off the demands of the monks, had no recourse but flight to the cities and destitution, or prayer.[31]

The monks also understood that growing more food than they could eat was a waste of time if all the grain did was sprout fungus. In order to trade food for something desirable, like a stack of vellum sheets or a day's work from a stonemason, they needed to store it until they could transport it. Since transport in the Middle Ages usually meant a torpid oxcart or barge, the food needed to be preserved for a long trip. So the monks brewed beer.

Although common in ancient times, beer had a tendency to spoil, which caused revenue losses, which frustrated the monks, who began to tinker with the recipe. One preservation method was to boost the alcohol content, thereby killing bacteria. This required lots of experiments with temperature, yeast strains, and, probably, hangovers. Higher alcohol requires more sugar, which comes from adding more barley, so high-alcohol beer was also costly to brew. It was cheaper to simply add an antimicrobial agent, which the monks discovered in the flower of *Humulus lupulus*, a climbing plant that grows in marshy hollows throughout Europe, commonly known as hops.[32] Simply adding a handful of hops during the fermentation process makes beer last longer. If stored properly, it will last for months—ample time for a clever abbot with good connections in other chapter houses to sell the contents of his overflowing cellar.

Hops had been picked for centuries before the monks started adding them to beer. The Romans had eaten wild hops and used them to stuff pillows and insulate walls. In the twelfth century, the nun, mystic, and musical composer Hildegard von Bingen wrote about the medicinal uses of hops oil.[33] But the first evidence for hops cultivation comes from ninth-century England, where the remains of a sunken riverboat yielded traces of pollen from a domesticated variety. The timing of hops domestication coincides with the period when it was first used as a beer preservative. In 822, Abbot Adalhard of Corvey exempted his millers from the job of collecting hops, implying that in this period they were collected wild rather than cultivated, and that they were used for brewing.[34] But, by 859, Bavaria had sprouted hops gardens, which shortly spread to Bohemia and the rest of central Europe, where their produce took the crowning spot on the national drink menu.[35] Bohemia and Bavaria are still home to the world's four noble hops, like the Saaz, which is used to give Pilsner Urquell its aromatic, bitter snap.

Breweries and monks were conjoined in the popular imagination of the Middle Ages, and rightfully so. In William the Conqueror's Domesday Book from 1086, his survey notes that the monks at St. Paul's Cathedral in London brewed nearly eighty thousand gallons of beer per annum.[36] Naturally, there were jokes, like this one from 1295:

The Abbot of Burton brewed good ale,
On Fridays when they fasted,
But the Abbot of Burton never tasted his own,
As long as his neighbor's lasted.[37]

Thanks to their innovations with hops, monks could store their surplus grain in the form of beer, squirrel away harvests, and sell them, even over distances. They had turned decay and fermentation to their advantage. With a salable (indeed, addictive) product, and with a ready-made network of business contacts in other monasteries, monks revived the European food trade, shifting it away from a trickle of luxuries like gems and silk into a steady rush of suds. Aristocrats began to take an interest in trading commodities instead of solely taking a cut on the sale of expensive trinkets.[38] Nor was beer the monks' only valuable. They sold cheese made out of surplus milk, wine from grapes, and honey. The food trade had returned to Europe, and it appeared most noticeably in market towns like St. Denis near Paris.

The modern "Renaissance faire" with its bespectacled wenches and roast turkey legs has two things in common with genuine medieval fairs: ferocious profiteering and regulation. In the modern version, fair organizers turn a dollar not only on leather corsets and henna tattoos, but on pizza and soft drinks. Medieval monks, too, understood that food retail was a serious business, and the secular government, then as now, knew that it could make a lot of money by controlling the permits to sell food. In Merovingian France, the king kept the right to grant charters for fairs, like the one that King Dagobert reputedly granted to the abbey at St. Denis in 629. In terms that modern lawyers would applaud, the charter reads:

> *In your solicitude and prudence be it known to you that we have decreed and established in honor of our glorious lord and patron, Denis, a fair for gathering together once annually at the Mass which falls on the ninth of October, all the merchants dwelling in our kingdom and those coming from beyond the seas. This gathering will be on the road which goes to the city of Paris in the place called St. Martin's Hill. And you, our officials for this market, and all the citizens of our kingdom, shall know of this market, and especially those who come from beyond the sea to the port of Rouen and to the port of Vic to buy wine, honey, and madder.*[39]

Of course, no one made money unless people showed up. Merchants had to be encouraged, or threatened, into attending. Any merchant who tried to do business outside of the fair was fined twice, once by the king and once by the abbey. The abbey also collected tolls on the roads leading to the fairgrounds, further filling the Church's coffers.

The St. Denis fair, which in Carolingian times was the largest in Europe, was more than just a place to buy sausages. It was similar to today's Walmart—a place where an aggressive business plan created abundance and selection. At the St. Denis fair, Dutch cheese could find its way into the basket of a Parisian wife, and Saxon wool sellers could drink a jug of wine from Mainz.

Fairs were so lucrative that abbeys sometimes committed the sin of bearing false witness in order to hold them—in the ninth century, the monks at St.-Germain-des-Prés forged a royal charter granting them a fair, dating the document to the seventh century. The benefits were worth a little penance.

By enforcing their monopoly on food processing, investing in new agricultural technology, and controlling the retail industry, abbots could achieve bigger economies of scale across the food system. There was now a potential for larger and more efficient plantations than had existed since the fall of Rome. The abbots also realized that specialization could be lucrative. Regions developed reputations for particular products whose sale made everyone richer.[40] And so the cycle repeated itself. Farms expanded, forests shrank, cities grew, and people found the time and resources to build cathedrals and breed more babies. And to feed them, of course.

Today, the lordly agro-industrial corporations fulfill much the same role as the monasteries, minus spiritual services. They control the inputs used by farmers, the methods of tillage, and the destination of the produce. It's an ancient idea. Like the monasteries, they've made a lot of money from food processing. They determine the way people eat, with most of the food on Western dining tables produced by a tiny number of firms. Four of them slaughter more than 80 percent of American beef. Four of them own 60 percent of American terminal grain facilities. Three export 81 percent of the nation's corn, as well as 65 percent of the soybeans. Moreover, the agribusiness companies are metastasizing. Between 1989 and 2002, the top four American pork-producing firms increased their domestic market share from 34 percent to 59 percent.[41] Seed companies usually work under the same corporate roof as the labs that brew the fertilizer. A single corporation will now feed an animal, slaughter it, and pulp its carcass into frankfurters.

Statistics such as this make modern academics liken agribusiness to an hourglass, where food grown by thousands of farmers is processed by less than a dozen companies that in turn sell it to millions of consumers. It's the same model used by the abbots who once looked out from the windows of their chapter houses and saw nothing but wheat, workers, and windmills. The monasteries used technology to create economies of scale, much as today we benefit from the bounty of industrial processes.[42] They understood how profitable it was to constrain the use of land and seeds and water, to squeeze profits out of a monopoly on mills and markets. The same holds true for modern corporations. A broad rule of the industrial food system holds that only the largest, most technologically savvy farms will thrive. By gobbling up its smaller neighbors, today's agribusiness forces less domineering farmers, as in the medieval period, to abandon the land and move to the city.

The issue of seeds and seed saving is particularly analogous to the medieval situation. In traditional agriculture, a small percentage of one year's harvest was saved for the next planting. Over time, this meant that locally adapted varieties of crops evolved, and biodiversity flourished. With the advent of modern plant breeding, and especially with the introduction of genetically modified seeds, this is no longer the case. Modern plant breeding involves crossing very specific "parents" to create high-yielding "offspring." These fruitful results are called hybrids. But they have a serious limitation: their own descendents (i.e., the seeds produced when two high-yielding hybrids pair up) are thin, low-yielding duds. There's no point in saving seeds to plant for the next season, since the happy combination of genes that made the hybrids so valuable can't be inherited. Farmers must, therefore, buy new seeds from the seed companies every year. Just like medieval peasants who had to pay to use the abbey's mill rather than grinding their flour on hand querns, farmers today pay for something they once took freely from nature.

Aren't the fatter harvests worth it? Perhaps. But while hybrids have given the world astounding bounty, they're especially tempting targets for opportunistic spores and beetles. To grow so inflated, too, they need extra nutrients and water. They can't survive a drought, and their appetite for minerals degrades the soil.

Nor do the seeds come cheap—most farmers, especially those in the developing world, construct precarious towers of debt to pay for each season's update. Farmers who plant a high-yielding seed accept a gamble. They know that their harvests will dramatically improve, but they also understand they might bet away the farm should bugs or weather wreck the crop. The risks are, of course, hidden from urban shoppers. If one farm fails, the market will supply the lost produce from another quarter, with nary a missed bushel of corn. But farmers, naturally, find the risk more personal. To offset the chance of catastrophe, farmers indebt themselves to buy not only miracle seeds, but modern fertilizers and pesticides—almost always manufactured by the same companies that sell the seeds. Many of these corporations then buy back the harvested commodities and churn them into lucrative processed foods. While this cycle delivers inexpensive food to billions of urbanites, it's also driven up input costs and consolidated farmland under fewer and fewer owners. Small-scale farmers find themselves on a treadmill, so it's not surprising that many of them want to step off.[43]

In the fourteenth century, these ex-farmers might have apprenticed as stonemasons. Today, they may find work in call centers or shopping malls. Or they may drop out of life entirely. In India, thousands of farmers have killed themselves after borrowing money to purchase miracle seeds, fertilizers, and pesticides from agricultural corporations. When harvests fail (as they periodically will) these farmers are left with no prospects to pay the loans back. Some of them have drunk the very pesticide they indebted themselves to acquire.[44]

Is a class of financially bullied, despairing farmers (either medieval or modern) an acceptable price for a food supply deep and rich enough to support a civilization? Certainly, on the condition that it works.

It didn't for the monks.

THE PENDULUM SWINGS

By the tenth century, the monks' windmills, fairs, and breweries (and dairies, beehives, bakeries, salt pans, and piggeries) had created a landscape where many Europeans no longer had to scratch out a subsistence crop. Forced or paid to abandon the land to agricultural specialists, people had moved to the cities. Commercial towns, which a few centuries earlier had disappeared from all but the old heartlands of the Roman Empire, sprouted in places like Dorestad in the Netherlands, or York in northern England.[45] There were ensuing hiccups, like the Vikings (who inhabited York for a time), but in general, society walked a steady line toward stability and wealth. Toward progress.

By then, the Dark Ages had lightened into the High Middle Ages, yielding monasteries by the hundred, universities in market towns like Oxford, Paris, Bologna, and Salerno, and splendid architecture. Christian faith and money from the food trade coalesced into their consummate jewel at the cathedral of Chartres, famous as the perfection of medieval art.

People started to have more babies. The population in Europe in the year 650, during the trough of malaise and Visigothic misbehavior, had dipped to about 5.5 million. Six hundred years later, it had risen to about 35 million.[46] These babies probably weren't the direct work of the monks (although many clergymen contributed heartily to the gene pool), but it is a measure of the prosperity they brought to the continent. Even as towns burgeoned, so did the rural population. Farmers pushed into the hills, clear-cutting unused land and turning it over to crops.

In this, geology helped. The rich soils of northern Europe had never been cultivated, even by the Romans. Scratch plows were too feeble to cut through millennia of roots, so the first generation of monastic farmers using their teams of oxen and heavy plows produced astounding harvests. Even many fields that had been cultivated by the Romans had lain fallow for centuries, soaking up organic matter and fertility. The bigger harvests from these energized plots of ground were the fuel for Europe's population boom. But it couldn't last.

A food supply that's based on a temporary bump—in this case, tapping into centuries of accumulated soil fertility—will eventually settle to more sustainable levels. For a while, innovation—crop rotation, moldboard plows, specialization—maintained the bump. But as the medieval period reached its apogee, the new farmlands started to run out of nutrients. The soil degraded in fields that had, a generation earlier, produced record crops.[47] Harvests thinned, and a population that had swelled with the cornucopia faced a very dire future.

Climate, too, took a hand in the medieval food empire. Just as in the case of the Roman food empire that had expanded during a period of meteorological goodwill (see chapter 2), the climate in Europe warmed gently throughout the Middle Ages. During this time, the Vikings colonized Greenland, and other Europeans, led by the example of monks, found that they could cultivate ground that, a generation or two earlier, had been too dry and frigid to yield crops.[48]

By the 1220s, however, there were hints of a pending fall, long before Chartres Cathedral had even been formally dedicated. The charcoal sellers who hawked their fuel at the southern end of the newly built nave began to boost their prices, as did the timber sellers. There simply wasn't as much wood as there used to be. Winemakers, who poured drinks for the idle stonemasons and laborers in the northern stretch of the building, had to ask a few more sous for a cup. Their vines were less generous than in the past.

Deforestation, and its ever-present twin, erosion, were at work in the most fertile region of France at the pinnacle of a civilization's confidence. It wasn't a catastrophe yet, but the first cracks had begun to appear in the monks' carefully wrought vision of earthly order. The blame for this falls on the most industrious monks of all: the Cistercians.

In the twelfth century, Saint Bernard of Clairvaux built a new order on a foundation of righteous outrage. Very personally, he loathed the rich, federated Benedictine monasteries that were centered on the lavish chapter house of Cluny, and he singled out their mealtimes for particular denunciation:

> *Course after course is brought in. Only meat is lacking and to compensate for this two huge servings of fish are given. You might have thought that the first was sufficient, but even the recollection of it vanishes once you have set to on the second. The cooks prepare everything with such skill and cunning that the four or five dishes already consumed are no hindrance to what is to follow and the appetite is not checked by satiety . . . The selection of dishes is so exciting that the stomach does not realize that it is being over-taxed.*[49]

Bernard, and many of his contemporaries, had no patience for gourmands. They thought the Benedictine order was corrupt, that it had forgotten its roots in the Egyptian desert. Like religious reformers before and since, they wanted to steer the Church back to a straight and narrow ideal of poverty and prayer. So in 1115, Bernard and his followers institutionalized their ideas at Clairvaux Abbey. The Cistercians, as they were called, lived like ascetics, journeying into the wilds to escape the temptations offered by towns and cities and working the land themselves instead of renting it to sharecroppers. A contemporary critic marvels at Cistercian vigor but doesn't think much of their sincerity:

> *[The Cistercians] obtain from a rich man a valueless and despised plot in the heart of a great wood, by much feigning of innocence and long importunity, putting in God at every other word. The wood is cut down, stubbed up and leveled into a plain, bushes give place to barley, willows to wheat, withies to vines; and it may be that to give them full time for these operations, their prayers have to be somewhat shortened.*[50]

Cistercians had a reputation not unlike that of the American pioneer, taming the wilderness through a steady drip of sweat. The truth is more nuanced. Cistercians were less Davy Crocketts in tonsures than savvy agricultural managers, and despite the order's professed zeal for sackcloth, they became fabulously wealthy landlords (unlike the mendicant orders such as the Franciscans, who didn't treat poverty as a business).[51]

The Cistercians practiced something called grange economy, in which they built a hub of farm buildings from which they would stretch out and claim the surrounding landscape. They accrued tremendous wealth from these land grabs, from the produce they cultivated on the new farmland, and from the fact that, as churchmen, they didn't actually have to pay any tithes to the Church.[52] Within a generation or two, their riches eclipsed those of the Benedictines, leading, in turn, to a fresh crop of reformers accusing them of corruption, worldliness, and stumbling from the narrow path of Matthew 19:21 ("If thou wilt be perfect, go and sell that thou hast, and give to the poor, and thou shalt have treasure in heaven").

More than temporal success, the most striking impact that the Cistercians had on Europe was that they chopped down all the forests.

Completing the job begun by the Benedictines, the Cistercians' deforestation created a final agricultural boost—medieval Europe's last hurrah in gobbling up the continent's virgin soil—but, again, it wasn't sustainable. The 1086 Domesday Book, for example, records that the frontier moorlands in Yorkshire were largely desolate. Manorial accounts from a few hundred years later show a massive expansion of agriculture in the Cistercian period, where "hundreds of thousands of acres" came under cultivation.[53] Gerald of Wales, writing around 1200, observes:

> *Settle the Cistercians in some barren retreat which is hidden away in an overgrown forest; a year or two later you will find splendid churches there and monastic buildings, with a great amount of property and all the wealth you can imagine.*[54]

Which is exactly what happened on the Yorkshire moors. Henry VIII would later destroy these monasteries, but they left flat, drained farmland where once had stood impassable wood and bramble. Today, in the northern city of Leeds, high school students occupy the ground that the monks of the Kirkstall Abbey long ago cleared and leveled to grow crops to be carted overland to markets in Leeds and York. It's a sports field now, ringed by squalls of traffic. On account of the Cistercian food trade, Yorkshire had ceased to be a wilderness.

THE PENDULUM SWINGS BACK

By the time the Cistercians hacked down the forests of Bohemia and Yorkshire, real estate in Europe had gotten expensive. Even marginal land, bits of scrub and hilltop, needed to come under the plow to feed the growing markets in the cities. Since chopping trees and tilling hilly ground is a sure means of exhausting and eroding soil, over time, the harvests worsened. The monks kept pushing their farms outward, even plowing uplands that once pastured sheep and cattle—animals whose digestive systems had done an effortless job of fertilizing the earth. With the loss of the livestock's manure and the added cultivation, the ground blew and washed away even quicker.

The grim consequences of deforestation and soil degradation struck just as Europe's population surpassed the Roman peaks. From the beginning of the twelfth century, the fecundity of medieval women soared, their progeny surviving on a strong, monk-driven economy and an abundant, monk-grown food supply. Their food empire was working so well that a shrinking number of rural workers could support a growing population of urbanites. Money multiplied, too. Kings and abbots bought expensive stone architecture for which they needed coin. They minted this using silver from new mines sunk in outlying territories, particularly in eastern Europe (even then, mines had a dismal effect on the landscape, stripping it of trees and poisoning the water with chemicals used for smelting). More money in circulation meant higher prices. With the additional burdens of deforestation and higher fuel costs, Europe raced into two hundred years of inflation.[55]

Food and wood, in particular, went up in price from about 1100, on account of both lower supply and greater demand from the millions of new consumers. By the end of the thirteenth century, margins between supply and demand had thinned to a razor's breadth. A decline of 10 percent in a year's harvest spelled hunger; a loss of 20 percent of the harvest meant famine.[56]

And then the financial system imploded. For centuries, bankers in Siena had loaned heavily to Europe's royal houses, financing wars and armies. They overextended themselves on architecture, cavalry, and crusades, so when harvests dropped and manors or cities defaulted on their loans, the banks collapsed. In 1298, the Gran Tavola bank of the Bonsignori, the Rothschilds of their day, failed. Rents soared as landlords struggled to pay their debts. Work on Siena's great cathedral came to a stop. Florentine banks rushed to grab business from the Sienese, but they didn't have much better luck. Defaulting had become a medieval habit.

Worse was to come. Bad weather was always a threat to peasants, and around 1300 the Medieval Warm Period ended. The cause was likely a combination of sun spots, volcanoes, and melting Arctic ice disrupting the ocean currents. Most Europeans wouldn't have noticed the creeping frigidity, or if they did, they likely shrugged it off as a divine whimsy. Iceland plunged into a freeze, and the cold swallowed

Greenland's Viking settlements.[57] For most of Europe, the crisis truly began with a midsummer storm in 1314. It rained too much and for too long, drumming flat the ripening crops and rotting them on the stalk. The grain harvest proved both late and short, and the next year was worse. Dikes collapsed, the sea engulfed fields and pasture, and an epidemic carried by Mongol raiders, possibly anthrax, managed to snuff out much of the continent's livestock.[58] In England, the price of wheat jumped eightfold.[59] In 1316, it rained again, and Europe toppled into the worst famine in its history.

The poor were the first to die, of course. When the great abbeys and castles closed their doors, chroniclers recorded gruesome accounts of cannibalism and corpses spirited from the graveyard to the table. John de Trokelowe, a British monk, described the disease that scavenging food caused:

> *A dysentery-type illness, contracted on account of spoiled food, emasculated nearly everyone, from which followed acute fever or a throat ailment. And so men, poisoned from spoiled food, succumbed, as did beasts and cattle [that] fell down dead from a poisonous rottenness.*[60]

In the town of Ypres, which had a population of about 25,000, there were 2,794 burials at public expense between May and October 1316. Banditry, lawlessness, and war followed on the heels of famine, prompting inevitable religious outbursts. To a devout society like that of medieval Europe, it was easy to see the disasters as acts of a punitive God. An English rhymer put it this way:

> *When God saw that the world was over proud,*
> *He sent a dearth on earth, and made it full hard.*
> *A bushel of wheat was at four shillings or more,*
> *Of which men might have had a quarter before . . .*
> *And then they turned pale who had laughed so loud,*
> *And they became all docile who before were so proud.*
> *A man's heart might bleed for to hear the cry*
> *Of poor men who called out "Alas! For hunger I die."*[61]

One of the more spectacular reactions to the famine happened in France. An army of furious peasants invoked the ghosts of the Pastoureaux rebels who had, seventy years earlier, ostensibly avenged King Louis IX's defeats at the hands of the Muslims by burning down a lot of French towns and churches. The second Pastoureaux rising was much more destructive, with about forty thousand rebel fighters driven by hunger as well as Christian activism. Blaming King Philip V for the famine and marching under the leadership of defrocked priests, they rampaged through the countryside, heading for Paris. On the way, they made a particular point of massacring Jews and lepers; in Verdun-sur-Garonne, five hundred Jews committed suicide to avoid capture by the insurgents.[62] Eventually, loyal men-at-arms destroyed the Pastoureaux, hanging hundreds of them on trees throughout the south of France. But the rebels were symptomatic of something bigger than a spontaneous bout of apocalyptic psychosis. They were as much an outcome of the famine as the blackened winter fields and the empty farmhouses. Their animating spirit was hunger.

It's likely that 10 percent of Europeans starved to death around the year 1316.[63] Worse carnage lay ahead. In October 1347, a mere generation after the famine, the bubonic plague hatched in Sicily. Within the year it had filtered upward along the peninsula, and from Italy it spread across the Alps and the Pyrenees, devastating France in June of 1348, England in December, and reaching as far as Scandinavia by early 1349. Famine, bad weather, and the faltering economy all blazed trails for the epidemic.[64] But it was actual roads—the very same ones that the monks used to trade foodstuffs—that funneled the disease into every doomed valley and hamlet.[65]

When the bacteria *Yersinia pestis* first appeared in fleas, which appeared on rats, which appeared in human communities, those communities no longer existed in the quiet isolation of past generations. By the fourteenth century, European towns were linked by the thrumming trade that the monks had nurtured with such devotion. Plague carriers—perhaps the very monks who trundled their beer to market—infected monasteries and villages from Sicily to Scotland. Along with beer and cheese, the food trade spread contagion. What's more, the plague's arrival in Italy and its subsequent killing of 20 to 45 percent of Europeans was really a consequence of inadequate customs controls. The infamous Genoese vessels that first carried the plague into Sicily had arrived from the Crimea, where they had been trading slaves from eastern Europe and spices from the Silk Road. The food trade, in the form of Europe's taste for eastern spices, had imported Black Death along with the peppercorns.

Weakened by years of hunger and an imploding economy, Europeans died by the million.[66] Food prices had already been exorbitant since the famine, and during the plague many fields lay fallow, which further reduced supply. But after the blight had subsided and the bodies had been cleared away, the food trade started to find an equilibrium again. So many millions of people had perished that there was no longer as much competition over the few cartloads of bread that found their way to market. Prices dropped. And since a large portion of the workforce had suddenly died, wages for laborers went up. With more money to spend, the survivors found that they could both eat and afford to buy things, so the demand for manufactured goods began to recover.

Full purses and full bellies meant that there was no longer an economic need to toil at plowing the hilltops and gullies that had been under cultivation for the past century. People's diets changed. Instead of grain, which requires hands to plow, seed, cut, thresh, and otherwise work for long hours, farmers found an appeal in less laborious foods. They returned to stock ranching, which had been on the decline since the monks' agricultural revolution had popularized a more intensive use for real estate. Cattle and sheep appeared in pastures that were now green with clover, but had once been golden with barley. There was even enough land now for frivolous uses. Rabbits had long been considered a luxury stock that only the nobility could afford to breed—the animals need lots of room to hop and nibble, and they're nutritionally ineffectual. After the Black Death subsided, it was the rare farm that didn't sport a rabbit hutch, and the steam from bubbling hasenpfeffer rose above a new Europe.[67]

It's very difficult to imagine the horror and cataclysm of the fourteenth century. The combined battery of soil degradation, plague, climate change, a ballooning population, and poverty were disastrous enough to destroy medieval civilization. Today, the only comparable nightmare might be felt in the gloomiest boneyards of North Korea, or in African wastelands stripped of wood to build pyres for the victims of AIDS. But over time, medieval Europe healed her wounds, and her ossuaries were encrusted with beautiful masonry. The packed bones are still there. In the town of Kutná Hora in what is now the Czech Republic, for example, the thirteenth century Sedlec Ossuary couldn't cope with the increased business in the fourteenth century. It had to be enlarged to accommodate thousands of extra skeletons. Today, visitors step down through arches spanned with dozens of femurs and skulls to enter a chapel lit by a fifteen-foot-wide chandelier, whimsically constructed from human bones. It hangs from a daisy chain of jawbones, while a Bohemian coat of arms, also made from the same grim materials, stares from the wall at four giant mounds of earthly remains.

At the end of the fourteenth century's parade of horrors, Europe's population had fallen by between 25 and 45 percent.[68] Simple farming and the rudimentary trade of foodstuffs had given the world a Chartres, but along with the barley, farmers had planted the seeds of that world's ruin. Europe didn't sink into the same shadows it had known after the fall of Rome, but it did stumble. In the future, there would be new ideas about God and about humanity's place on the globe, but first there was a lot of clearing up to do. The Turks were about to seize Constantinople; the Moors still held pockets of Spain. To the east, the Golden Horde was burning down half of Eurasia. It would be another hundred years before Europeans again felt the confidence they had known in the thirteenth century, before agriculture and the food trade had betrayed them.

MANURE FROM THE BONES

Rich topsoil fueled the growth of the medieval food empire, much as soil degradation dragged it backward, weighed, of course, with the effects of climate change and disease. And of overpopulation, which was a direct result of the wonderful topsoil. It's a cycle that's not exclusive to medieval Europe. If you rip native plants out of any patch of dirt on the planet and reseed it with alien ones, that soil will wear away. Crop rotation, fertilizer, and efficient plows slow down the degeneration, of course, but the very chemistry of earth means that food empires have always been built on a paradox. More food means more people, whose appetites are incentive to chop down trees and plow fresh ground—the precise recipe for soil erosion.

Plato, in his *Critias,* describes an ancient scene of deforestation and soil erosion, but he may as well have been writing about the end of the medieval food empire:

> *The consequence [of erosion] is, that in comparison of what then was, there are remaining only the bones of the wasted body . . . all the richer and softer parts of the soil having fallen away, and the mere skeleton of the land being left.*[69]

The modern world, too, is no stranger to deforestation, soil degradation, and their muddy consequences. Tractors and plows now grind up an entire quarter of the earth's land surface. In the Amazon, an average of 17,500 square kilometers is converted to agriculture each year, mostly to provide pasture for cattle and soy used for both oil and livestock feed.[70] The soy market is particularly greedy, and harvests of it doubled in Brazil between 1994 and 2004, so that the crop now accounts for 10 percent of the country's agricultural exports, most of which is shipped to China and the EU.[71]

The simple fact is, when you cut a tree, you loosen the earth beneath it. Nothing will fix that, except perhaps another tree. A study called the Millennium Ecosystem Assessment estimates that by 1950, development had cleared as much as 40 percent of the world's tropical and coniferous forest. About 70 percent is expected to be gone by 2050. Apart from the legion of other environmental ailments this arouses—from rising temperatures to expired sloths—these figures mean the soil is dying.[72]

The UN's Food and Agriculture Organization says that by the mid-1990s, 5.8 million square kilometers of forests had been cleared, 6.8 million square kilometers had been overgrazed, and 5.5 million square kilometers had been degraded by bad agricultural management. In the inimitable prose of a UN agricultural report,

> *In 1950, some 115 million km^2 of the Earth's surface were undegraded, vegetated land. Just 40 years later, almost nine million*

> *km²—an area as large as China—were classified as "moderately degraded," with greatly reduced agricultural productivity. A further three million km² were "severely degraded," having lost almost completely their original biotic functions. Almost 100,000 km² are beyond restoration.*[73]

Which is to say, we have a problem.

Michael Stocking, an emeritus professor in natural resource management from the University of East Anglia in the UK, is an expert on the links between food security, deforestation, and soil erosion. He's spent a lifetime sounding the alarm in the pages of fusty academic journals, warning of worldwide hunger unless we stop destroying the earth's topsoil. He cautions that generalizing about something as complex as soil quality is impossible, since different earth types respond to overcultivation and deforestation differently. But, he says, crop yields always plummet when the soil erodes, even if the land is smothered in fertilizer.[74] This is especially true for thin, tropical earth in places like Africa, which can least afford a stingy harvest.[75]

Even geochemically blessed nations are worried about erosion. According to the journal *Science*, 75 billion tons of topsoil wash into the sea each year. Asia and Africa are the most denuded continents, but even in the best-managed landscapes of America and Europe, soil disappears about seventeen times faster than it's replaced. In 1995, this cost the United States an estimated $44 billion.[76]

The cost is certainly high, but it's nothing compared to the misery suffered by the medieval Europeans when the ground washed away from under them. That hasn't happened in American and European grain fields yet, but two facts are indisputable: the world population is rising, and we're losing the topsoil that supports it.

Stepping aside from the language of science, Henry David Thoreau, who thought a lot about society's relationship with the natural world, summed it up best. "Alas for human culture!" he wrote. "Little is to be expected of a nation, when the vegetable mould is exhausted, and it is compelled to make manure of the bones of its fathers."[77]

CHAPTER TWO

Larders: What Do You Do with Ten Thousand Tons of Grain?

The city of Seville, in Carletti's day, had yet to achieve a romantic crumble, the feel of a wilted rose familiar to modern tourists. In 1591, it swelled with colonial gold and Baroque architecture instead of brick apartment towers and Brussels cash. But both then and now, with its mazes of bars and dancing rooms, its broad squares clopping with fine carriages, its beauties draped in Manila silk, it would have been an exciting place for a teenager to learn about money and freedom. There, with his family half a continent away, young Francesco Carletti might have developed a taste for good living.

His occupation in Seville was a social one, with dips into abacus work and bookkeeping. It's easy to envision the young Italian strolling along Seville's riverfront, stopping to count the ships mooring on the wharf by the Torre del Oro, noting the dates on the barrels of wine and olive oil in the warehouses, perhaps sniffing at the perfume of oranges and fried sardines from across the river in Triana.

Seville was where all the business of the Spanish Empire came to be (loudly) conducted. Its navigable river and comfortable port made it a natural launching point for western expeditions, and the monarchy had granted the city a monopoly on New World trade. As a result, Seville became the larder of the empire. Gold, people, and food moved through it in colossal quantities, sometimes only pausing to collect a few official stamps, sometimes lingering for much longer. Gold and people tend not to spoil in the Andalusian sun, however. Food does. So Seville became a city of warehouses.

The mid-sixteenth-century painter Alonso Sánchez Coello imagined a scene from a generation earlier, in the late 1490s. His painting shows a convoy of anchored ships streaming with sailors, behind which workmen and mounds of lumber crowd the quayside of a market town. Above them rises the skyline of Seville, still a row of unfinished splinters. But industry was changing that.

Food bound for the East Indies or Peru needed to be stored in Seville before loading onto ships like the ones in Sánchez Coello's painting. This was easier said than done, since Andalusian summers commonly simmer around the body-heat mark of 98.6 degrees Fahrenheit. Shelf lives were short, a pungent reality well known to a clan of Sevillan merchants called the de la Fuentes, who, in the generation before Carletti arrived, rose literally from rags to riches.

The de la Fuentes were rag traders. People with carts and sticks and piles of buzzing linens. But when Spain conquered the Americas, it set the commercial life of Seville alight with slaving, ranching, mining, and government graft. To a tired ragman on the Calle Sierpes, the opportunities must have beckoned like a line of white, laundered sheets. The de la Fuentes decided to stake their fortunes on the New World, specifically on olive oil and wine.

In the fall of 1548, one Gómez de la Fuente spent 7,337 ducats on a cargo of clothing, household items, tools, iron, conserves, wine, and olive oil.[1] Once bought, the goods must have waited for weeks in a family storehouse, biding time until the Atlantic ships were ready to take up their cargoes in November. After being transferred and loaded, the goods endured a two-month ocean voyage, arriving in Panama around Christmas. Gómez unpacked everything onto a train of one hundred mule-loads, which arrived in faraway Lima sometime in early 1549. There, in the ruins of the Inca Empire, on the edge of an unknown sea, the former rag trader opened a shop selling Spanish wine and oil.

His gamble worked. Enough expatriates were hungry for the flavors of home that Gómez more than doubled his investment. Profits on ventures like this commonly recouped between 200 and 250 percent of the initial outlay, even after counting for losses on the six-thousand-mile journey. The de la Fuentes' account books are filled with references to olive oil spillage, broken vinegar casks, and wine souring in the muggy thrash of a transatlantic voyage. A generation later, when Carletti embarked on a similar journey, the risks hadn't changed. Nor had the lure of profits, which were still tempting enough for a young Italian to dream of matching the grand de la Fuente score.

This sort of confidence was a new development. Carletti was one of the first Italians in centuries to look outside of Europe and think the world a playground. He lived in a time of expansion, of spending and making money, of swagger. But it had happened before, of course, when Italians had spun an empire out of legions, highways, and a mesh of farms, warehouses, merchants, and consumers. Then, all roads, especially the ones traveled by merchants with their wares, led to the warehouses of Rome.

NATIONAL SECURITY AND A WAR ON TERROR

Rome wasn't fed in a day. Even at its peak, in the brief, golden decades under the Antonines, the imperial city was perennially at risk of starvation. It simply had too many people for local farms to feed. To survive, Roman city dwellers depended on warehouses that stored the daily bread for hundreds of thousands of people, and on a precarious shipping network that hauled grain across the length of the empire. Apart from the obvious problems of logistics and weather, the long distances meant that ancient Roman bureaucrats had to contend with pirates.

High-seas robbery has a venerable tradition in the Mediterranean. Homer's heroes seemed to consider it, if not polite behavior, at least unsurprising. Bragging to his host King Alcinous, the shipwrecked, helpless Odysseus says, "The wind drove me out of Ilium on to Ismaurus, the Cicones' stronghold. There I sacked the city, killed the men."[2] Not, perhaps, the most ingratiating thing to tell his host, but to these ancient heroes, pillage was their right. Pirates once caught Julius Caesar himself and held him for ransom. In the Hellenistic period, abduction by pirates was a trope in popular plays and books, culminating in the novel *Callirhoe,* a classical sex-and-swordplay potboiler in which not one, but *two* pivotal plot twists involve chance enslavement during a sea crossing. Piracy, like bad lighting and tuberculosis, was one of the ancient world's accepted misfortunes.

The great pirate raid on Ostia in 68 B.C. changed that. Rome, though still a republic in name, was an empire in every other sense. As well as being the only military bully left in the Mediterranean basin, Rome was the sole commercial power. From the port of Ostia, fifteen miles away from the city, hundreds of thousands of tons of commodities—grain, olive oil, fish sauce—wound up the Tiber River to an expectant, and opinionated, populace. A troublesome sandbar just off the coast kept the biggest ships from mooring inside the actual harbor, so they unloaded their cargo onto little boats that scuttled back and forth from the quays like tipsy beetles.

The longshoremen had a grueling job of it. Rome's Senate understood that hungry citizens have a habit of lynching their government representatives and burning down public buildings. So, from 123 B.C. until the day the Goths grazed their horses in the Forum, each Roman citizen was entitled to a welfare payment, a daily allotment of state-funded food. This would have amounted to five thousand tons of imported wheat having to cross Ostia's sandbar every week, and that was just for the citizens. Counting the bellies of Rome's women, children, and hundreds of thousands of slaves, the actual sum of imported grain was much, much greater.

And then, one night in the first century B.C., the pirates arrived.[3] Usually when Romans were fighting civil wars against one another, their armies battled on dry ground. Pirates, encouraged by the scheming little monarchs on the fringes of the empire, took advantage of Rome's inattention to naval matters. The Greek biographer Plutarch describes the pirates' confidence, how they ran fleets of light, fast ships with strong crews and skillful pilots, fortified by signal stations and coastal battlements. Much worse, to Plutarch, was the "odious extravagance of their equipment," their "silvered" oars, gilded sails, and purple awnings, "as if they rioted in their iniquity and plumed themselves upon it."[4]

Their biggest outrage was yet to come. No contemporary accounts of the Ostia raid exist, but we can imagine the pirate cutters darting fast between the hulking grain ships anchored at the sandbar, the quick hooks and torches, the burning sails and plunging bodies. They sank an entire consular fleet moored in the harbor, then landed to loot the warehouses and shops. As the raiders subjected Ostia's citizens to the club and rope, one enterprising gang struck out along the Appian Way and grabbed two high-ranking praetors. Another group snatched a nobleman's daughter for ransom. Then they burned down the town.

Within days, the price of wheat in Rome had skyrocketed to ten times the cost in the markets of wheat-growing Sicily.[5] Panic struck the city population as people realized that, trapped in an urban net of brick and marble, they might starve. A quick-thinking tribune named Gabinius drew up a piece of emergency legislation, the *lex Gabinia*, which authorized military force for a war against "piracy"—an unusual step at a time when formal wars tended to be launched against enemy states, not against a commonplace activity. The law granted unprecedented power to the Roman military commander: complete dominion over the Mediterranean waters and of lands within four hundred furlongs of the coast. This effectively meant command of everything in the empire, as well as considerable territories outside of it. In addition, the appointed war leader would receive a free hand with the public treasury, power to levy unlimited ranks of soldiers and oarsmen, a personal staff of fifteen generals, and the command of two hundred warships.[6]

Not everyone thought that giving godlike powers to a single man was particularly wise, despite the threat to the food trade. Gabinius wanted to hand these powers to his good friend Pompey the Great, a famous soldier and politician who was angling to be the next *de facto* ruler of the Roman world. At first, the senators balked, insisting that the law went too far in undermining the republic.[7] But eventually, panicking at the thought of a recurrence of the food riots,[8] they gave Gabinius his votes, and Pompey won unlimited authority over the sea and everything within fifty miles of it.[9]

The *lex Gabinia* was probably illegal, but given the tenor of the times, national security (in this case food security) had trumped caution.[10] Pompey happily accepted his new authority and, according to Plutarch, raised 120,000 soldiers and five thousand cavalrymen, and took command of five hundred ships.[11] He divided his fleet into thirteen parts, assigning each to patrol a separate sector of the Mediterranean, thus corralling the pirates in their home ports. Shut out from their hunting routes, the pirates drew back to "their hive" (Plutarch's words) in Cilicia, in the northeast corner of the Mediterranean. There, Pompey besieged their fortresses, and after a furious three-month campaign, he exterminated them.[12]

Once again, Rome's citizens were able to dine on free, imported wheat, even though an irreversible step had been taken in dismantling their political system. But after Pompey rode down the Via Triumphalis with his pirate loot glittering in the eyes of the grateful thousands, no one questioned the legality of the *lex Gabinia*. Gabinius had understood that the biggest challenge to confront the republic wasn't civil war or Carthaginians, or even the rise of the Julian dynasty. It was grain.

BREAD ALONE

In the year that Ostia burned, Rome was a city of a million souls, comparable in size to San Jose, Texas, or to Birmingham, England. Hundreds of thousands of its residents lived in wobbly, highly flammable apartment blocks (*insulae,* meaning "islands") without refrigeration. It's surprising that the Romans didn't starve with the same frequency that they burned to death. They had no trains to deliver produce and no modern plows to farm it. Their idea of an effective fertilizer program was prayer. But Rome was an Iron Age society that somehow managed to feed a very modern crush of population. In future centuries, a medieval Europe shorn of cities would suffer far more frequent famines. How did the Romans, using no better tools than scratch plows, oxen, and sails, feed themselves?

Consider what an urban citizen ate. In the second century A.D., an expatriate Greek named Publius Aelius Aristides wrote:

> *If you want to see everything, you must either travel round the world, or else go and live at Rome. There you can see so many imports from India and Arabia, that you would think the trees in*

these countries would be for ever bare and that the inhabitants will have to come to Rome to ask the Romans to supply them with their own products.[13]

To Romans of a Lucullan bent, the real privilege of ruling the world might have been access to damson plums and potted dormice. In Petronius's oft-quoted *Satyricon,* the dinner-party scene is shorthand for ancient decadence and overeating. It begins with dormice hung on little metal frames and "sprinkled with poppy-seed and honey," and a dish of hot sausages with plums and pomegranate seeds. Next come pastries made to look like peahens' eggs, goose and mullets, hot bread, and then a great platter of "plump fowls, sows' udders, and a hare with wings fixed to his middle to look like Pegasus." The host, Trimalchio, is proud of the fact that the food for his party comes from his own land. It's all locally grown. But his sheep have been bred with rams imported from Tarentum in Greece, his honey comes from Attic bees, his mushrooms are grown from strains that he ordered specially from India.[14] It's a Roman meal, yes, but it's of international provenance.

Petronius was a jaded courtier writing for the pleasure of his clique. His descriptions are fiction, and seamy fiction at that. But even though Trimalchio's dinner never happened, similar menus were served, shocking (and calculated to shock) in their lavish excess.

In real life, the daily diet consumed by most Romans throughout the classical age was as exciting as toast—which is exactly what they ate.

When we think of Mediterranean food today, we envision fresh meat and fish cooked with herbs like parsley or rosemary, pasta, vegetables and garlic, wine and olive oil. With its damp winters and dry, hot summers, the Mediterranean climate excels at producing grain, grapes, and olives. It's not especially adept at growing green grass, so stock farming is concentrated in the hardier species, like sheep and goats. Dairy cows, in particular, don't thrive.

Of the common produce, grain is the obvious staple, particularly wheat and barley. The Romans were enthusiastic barley eaters. This plant grows well in dry conditions and in the poor, alkaline soil that coats the limestone bones of Italy. It matures faster than any other grain, needing only 60 to 70 days in the spring or 180 days in winter, which gives farmers time to sow again if a first crop fails.[15] Wheat is fussier. It needs darker, richer soils, and a few additional inches of rainfall. But both grains are naturally suited to the region.

In terms of nourishment, however, wheat is preferable to barley. It supplies 10 percent better nutrition by weight and 35 percent more nutrients by volume.[16] An adult can live (unpleasantly) on about a pound of wheat per day; for equivalent calories, a person would need to swallow about 1½ pounds of barley. Hence wheat isn't as heavy to transport as barley, and it's easier to husk, particularly the "naked" varieties. Wheat is also ideal for making into leavened bread—during fermentation, the glutens in the cereal trap the carbon dioxide and lactic fermentation released by yeast. This is what makes bread rise. At the same time, yeasts and lactic bacteria predigest some of the complex sugars in the wheat starch, making them better suited for our listless human stomachs.

So, from very early times, wheat commanded a higher price than barley and was the preferred grain for trade. At wealthier tables, the daily bread would have been pale wheat sourdough, while poorer homes would have lived on dark barley flour breads and porridge.[17] Despite its importance as a reserve crop, to be eaten in times of want, barley always had a reputation in Rome for being woefully low class. As punishment for dereliction of duty, cowardly or incompetent soldiers received rations of barley instead of wheat.[18]

Tastes in bread evolved over time, changing as the empire absorbed new grain-growing provinces and slave labor. In the first century B.C., kneaded bread was probably uncommon. *Panis clibanicius,* or flat bread, required less work and was the standard fare (the contemporary writer Cato took note of a recipe for kneaded bread, implying that it was unusual and worthy of a historian's attention). A few generations later, roles had switched and crude *panis clibanicius* was the oddity.[19] More familiar was homemade *panis artopticus*, and more common still was the commercial bakery loaf, *panis furnaceus*, a five-inch-thick wheel of bread sliced into eight wedges, exactly like a pizza. In imperial times, a domestic lunch would have likely seen the family at their table, grabbing slices topped with cheese, cooked vegetables, or sausage.

Since most urban families survived on bread, it's no exaggeration to say that the ancient city was founded on its bakeries. Baking was a very upwardly mobile profession, and a successful bakery owner could die rich and envied by his peers. One tomb from the first century B.C. contains an elaborate relief showing scenes from bakers' lives: sieving grain, checking its quality, sieving it again, and then grinding it into flour, all while being monitored by government inspectors who issued receipts at every stage. Then the bakers kneaded the dough, shaped it, and baked it in enormous dome-shaped ovens. Finally, they loaded the bread into baskets to be weighed by yet more government inspectors, who issued a final receipt. Donkeys, water mills, and slaves performed most of the actual labor.[20]

They wouldn't have enjoyed it much. In his second-century novel *The Golden Ass*, Apuleius describes working in a Roman bakery:

> *Ye gods, what a set of men I saw! Their skins were seamed all over with marks of the lash, their scarred backs were shaded rather than covered with tattered frocks. Some wore only aprons, all were so poorly clothed that their skin was visible through the rents in their rags! Their foreheads were branded with letters, their heads were half-shaved. They had irons on their legs. They were hideously sallow. Their eyes were bleared, sore and raw, from the smoke of the ovens. They were covered with flour as athletes with dust!*[21]

NOT BY BREAD ALONE: OIL AND FISH

While the urban lower classes survived on bread, they didn't thrive. An all-wheat diet lacks protein, calcium, and vitamins A, C, and D.[22] Children, in particular, develop rickets if they eat nothing more than grain.[23] So while the Romans never puzzled over the geometry of the food pyramid, they did understand that a diet consisting solely of bread and barley causes physical degeneracy, and they also understood that eating fish and olives prevented and healed it.

The Romans loved their olives. Per capita consumption of olive oil in antiquity is estimated at about five to six gallons per year (compared to the half quart that the average American consumes each year).[24] A mere 3.4 ounces will fuel a person with a thousand calories (eighteen times that of an equal dose of wine), as well as essential fats, fatty acids, and vitamins A and E. Lower-class Romans probably consumed one-third of their daily calories in olive oil.

Being indispensable, olive oil was an enormous business. By the first century B.C., most of Italy's olives grew on enormous plantations owned by wealthy senators; the smallholdings of republican lore had been largely swallowed up in buyouts and civil wars. As always, slaves performed the actual work. Balancing on ladders, they shook the tree branches with one hand and caught the crop in trays held by the other.[25] After picking out the twigs and dirt, they stored the olives in warehouses to dry. Then they pulped them, pressed them, and decanted the oil from the residual "black water" (leftover seepage and plant bits). The ornery senator Cato, writing from his viewpoint as a rich politician who liked to pose as a gentleman farmer, suggested that the job required supervision. Slaves were liable to take shortcuts:

> *The gatherers want to have as many windfalls as possible, that there may be more of them to gather; and the pressers want them to lie on the floor a long time, so that they will soften and be easier to mill. Do not believe that the oil will be of greater quantity if they lie on the floor. The more quickly you work them up the better the results will be, and you will get more and better oil from a given quantity. Olives which have been long on the ground or the floor will yield less oil and of a poorer quality. If possible, draw off the oil twice a day, for the longer it remains on the amurca and the dregs, the worse the quality will be.*[26]

Still, bread and olive oil alone make for a dismal diet. To enliven their sandwiches, the Romans liked to add fish. But while the shores of the peninsula are awash in delicious species, the daily catch in ancient times was by necessity eaten on the spot. Even more so than meat, fish rots extremely quickly after death. Enzymes in the liver and intestine break down the muscle tissue, making the proteins water-soluble. Although this doesn't actually spoil the flesh, it does set up a hatching ground for dangerous bacteria. Yet fish products flooded the markets of inland cities. Most Romans ate fish on a daily basis, but they didn't eat it fresh. They bought it as processed food.

An ancient method of preventing a fish from glomming with bacteria is to gut it, clean it, and smoke it. Even better is to salt it. After the headless, eviscerated creature is soaked in fresh water to remove the blood, the flesh can be drained and pressed in salt equal to 10 to 20 percent of its weight. A fish thus treated is edible for about three weeks. Add salt up to 30 percent of the fish's weight and it turns into a stiff, crusty object that never goes rotten.[27]

Salting was a useful trick, but the Romans preferred to dunk their fish in brine—their favorite preservative. They particularly liked to dissolve the fish in the liquid over a period of months, so that the bones and tissues melted into a gooey precipitate. The result was a clear, caramel-colored juice called *garum,* and the Romans poured it on most of their culinary repertoire. It tasted fierce and salty, but it was rich in protein, as was the nutritional paste left over from the dissolved animals. Both *garum* and its paste are still common in southern Asia, where eating them is said to be good for the teeth. Indeed, Roman skeletons from Herculaneum had surprisingly robust dentition, given their bread diet.[28]

Garum wasn't as big an industry as olive oil, which straddled much of the Roman Empire, but it was still widespread. And repellent. The fish-salting installations, called *cetariae,* ranged in size from a single terra-cotta vat stuck on a beach to industrial operations employing hundreds of workers. A typical *garum* factory was a sea-front building with a floor sloping toward the water, the better to swab out the drippings. A series of partially buried vats filled the fermentation room, a furnace helped dry the carcasses, and outdoor tanks or ponds thrashed with live fish. The smell can only be imagined, as can the mobs of squalling gulls that haunted the sites.

Rome's poorer social classes were addicted to *garum,* soaking it up by the bucket,[29] but anything made of fish guts left in the hot sun is bound to have its detractors. The philosopher Seneca rather shrilly writes, "What? Do you not think that the so-called 'Sauce from the Provinces,' the costly extract of poisonous fish, burns up the stomach with its salted putrefaction?"[30] The general population disagreed, even mixing it with lentils as a diarrhea cure.[31]

Despite Seneca's upturned nose, the poor needed *garum*. It was one of their most important sources for vitamins and micronutrients, without which they would have suffered from even more wretched health than they typically did.[32] And they were willing to pay. While hard statistics are difficult to come by, modern academics believe that *garum* was a black gold to the merchants who traded it across the Mediterranean. Pliny observes that "there is no liquid hardly, with the exception of the unguents, that has sold at higher prices of late."[33]

HANNIBAL LECTURED

So, on a diet of bread and fish sauce, Rome survived, at least during its infancy, when the city lorded over productive hinterland. The sea and all its edible inhabitants were a mere fifteen miles away, and the Tiber made it easy to deliver food into the city's maw. But a simple food system doesn't necessarily make for abundance. Whenever the crops failed in the Latin hills, as they periodically would, the Romans starved.

This happened early—there are records of Etruscan grain being shipped downriver during a famine in 490 B.C.[34] By the time of Pompey and the *lex Gabinia,* Rome had changed its habits. Its citizens practiced imperial eating. Instead of growing their own food and importing only in times of dearth, they relied on distant farmlands for their daily calories. In many ways this was a good thing—when they could draw on the whole geography of Sicily and Sardinia, Egypt and North Africa for sustenance, a harvest failure in Latium lost its edge. But they needed to conquer these places first.

Carthage was an old commercial culture that had established itself by shuttling goods—notably wine—along the western coasts of the Mediterranean. Sicily was an old Carthaginian outpost, and when Roman adventurers showed up with their eyes on its cities, fields, and vineyards, the Carthaginians tried to defend their investments. Over the course of three brutally existential wars, Rome and Carthage battled from Sicily to Spain to the heart of Italy and back to Africa. The second war, which starred Hannibal and his elephants, was a see-saw affair in which the balance swung mostly toward the Carthaginians. As well as annihilating Roman armies, Hannibal used food as a weapon, seizing the Campanian fields in southern Italy and choking Rome's wheat supplies.[35] But the Romans eventually soldiered through and destroyed their rivals. For extra insurance against a future rematch, they sowed Carthage's grain fields with salt.

The Punic Wars left Rome in possession of rich farms in the foreign provinces of Sicily, Sardinia, and Spain, as well as tens of thousands of Carthaginian slaves to work them. Roman traders now controlled the Mediterranean breadbasket in Egypt, free of competition from Carthaginian buyers and from the risk of a hostile navy sinking their convoys. While generally fertile, Italian soil couldn't compete with Egyptian mud, which soaked up fresh nutrients every year in the Nile flood. Egypt's seemingly boundless supply of wheat and barley meant it was cheaper to ferry food into Italy than to grow it at home.

By the second century B.C., Rome's population had already strained her hinterland to its limits. Harvests had been thinning for years. The hard geography of Italy meant that, unless a field sat near a river, it was cheaper to move a low-value, bulky commodity like wheat by sea. Every hundred miles of cartage by road would double the price of a load of grain, while water voyages cost a fraction of that, which is why fertile inland regions like the Po Valley suffered famine more frequently than the coasts. It was simply too expensive to deliver food when supplies ran out.[36]

So when the new provinces entered the Roman fold, it made good economic sense to exploit them for the city's daily bread.[37] Prices for grain plummeted and Italian smallholders went out of business, selling their lands to senatorial speculators who consolidated them into plantations. Stocked with fresh slaves, the new Italian seigneurs planted vineyards and olive groves—cash crops, the profits of which could be funneled into political careers or ostentatious villas.[38]

Wine, as much as oil, was a source of immense profits. It may have been the Greeks who planted the first vines in Italy, or it may have been the Etruscans, or even the Carthaginians in Sicily. Regardless, by the time of the wars against Carthage, the Romans were devoted tipplers, privately as committed to Bacchus as to Mars. As Rome unbalanced the scales of power in the Mediterranean in the third century B.C., tipping them sharply westward, Greek wine sales started to flow toward Italy. Imported wine was a luxury at first. In the second century B.C., Cicero's friend, the bon vivant Lucullus, remarked that Greek wine was so prized that his father refused to serve more than a single cup of it to his dinner guests.[39]

The Romans, ever thrifty, thought to supplant expensive Greek vintages with local ones. As the republic aged into an empire, Sicilian wines took pride of place in well-to-do mixing bowls, even though their flavors still mimicked those of Greek imports. For example, the senator Marcus Cato, a conservative thinker even by the standards of the second century B.C., wrote a recipe on how to make "Coan wine" without actually having to import it from the island of Cos. To capture the saltiness of the Greek drink, he recommended fermenting the grapes in seawater:

> *Take the above-mentioned sea-water and pour 10 quadrantals into a jar holding 50; then pick the berries of ordinary grapes from the stem into the jar until you have filled it. Press the berries with the hand so that they may soak in the sea-water. When the jar is full, cover it, leaving space for air, and three days later remove the grapes from the jar, tread out in the pressing-room, and store the wine in jars which have been washed clean and dried.*[40]

Cato lived at a time when vineyards and trellises beetled up from the Hellenized south and spread across the whole of mainland Italy. This was the mid–second century B.C., a time rife with land consolidation, with huge latifundia swallowing up family holdings as farmers left their fields to enlist for the foreign adventures that the Senate launched every spring. Government welfare and cheap international imports kept the price of grain low, so the big landlords ordered their slaves to plant olive trees and vines. Wine would always sell for a profit, particularly among the elite families who controlled Rome's imperial prizes.

The social ramifications of this land consolidation were staggering. Landless citizens flooded into the city, boosting the population to the million mark and multiplying the demand for quick, easy sources of compact, nonperishable food. Wheat, as we've seen, was the only answer. To grow enough of it, particularly in light of the ineffective agricultural technology of the time, the plantation owners needed slave labor on a massive scale. It's estimated that it took the work of nineteen country people (usually slaves at this point in history) to feed one urban citizen.[41]

Naturally, something was bound to go wrong. Imports, especially in the ancient world, could be disrupted. And if the imports failed, Rome couldn't survive by eating the cash crops that had replaced grain as Italy's bounty. Worriers began to worry; others began to see political opportunities in the city's bread.

In 133 B.C., a senator named Tiberius Gracchus proposed a series of land reforms that would, in theory, have jointly solved the problems of urban hunger and urban poverty. He found a lot of willing listeners. After two centuries of near-constant warfare against Carthaginians, Iberians, Greeks, Celts, and more or less every other group of people they had ever met, the Roman plebs had begun to wonder when they would start enjoying the profits of bloodshed.

A soldier by trade (as all Roman politicians were at the time), Gracchus was riding home from the Spanish campaigns when he noticed that all of the long stretches of conquered Iberia—the pale, sun-washed highlands, the wine-red soil of Aragon, the salty green hills of Asturias—were owned by a few fantastically wealthy men. Gracchus had served alongside the underpaid soldiers who had sweated and bled to conquer these lands for the state, for the common good. Instead, absentee landlords were filling these territories with miles of vines and olive groves, the profits of which passed directly into the purses of senators. To Gracchus, something had gone awry.

In theory, the unfair distribution of the land shouldn't have happened. The Senate had decreed that a portion of all conquered land be reserved for public use, to be rented out cheaply to the poor, many of whom were the very veterans who had fought to rid the land of its original owners. Apart from the city food dole, Rome lacked a functioning social security system, so these veterans often found that the end of their enlistment meant an end to their income, shelter, and sustenance.

Cheap rents were the only security they had. Plutarch describes how this system worked in reality:

> *But when the wealthy men began to offer larger rents, and drive the poorer people out, it was enacted by law, that no person whatever should enjoy more than five hundred acres of ground. This act for some time checked the avarice of the richer, and was of great assistance to the poorer people, who retained under it their respective proportions of ground, as they had been formerly rented by them. Afterwards the rich men of the neighborhood contrived to get these lands again into their possession, under other people's names, and at last would not stick to claim most of them publicly in their own. The poor . . . were thus deprived of their farms.*[42]

Flushed with righteous zeal, Tiberius Gracchus ran for the office of tribune on a platform of redistributing land to the poor so they could feed themselves. The idea, though riotously popular with the plebs, horrified the plantation owners and their moneyed allies. Gracchus won the election, but a savage political battle broke out between his populist supporters and the patricians. The plebeians accused the corrupt senators of growing fat on the suffering of the masses, while the patricians cried that Gracchus was exploiting those same masses to seize power and to declare himself king. In Rome, there was no accusation more stinging, nor more liable to result in a dagger in the sternum. Despite their endless flirtation with despotism, Romans hated the name of monarchy, if not the practice of it.

On the day that Gracchus's reforms were due for debate in the Curia Julia, the honorable gentlemen of the Senate arrived in a state of eagerness bordering on cannibal savagery. The shouting began at once, and within moments "persons of the greatest authority in the city . . . tumbled over one another in haste" to attack Gracchus. The rich men grabbed stools and chairs and began to beat his supporters to death. Again, Plutarch describes the scene:

> *Tiberius [Gracchus] tried to save himself by flight. As he was running, he was stopped by one who caught hold of him by the gown;*

but he threw it off, and fled in his under-garments only. And stumbling over those who before had been knocked down, as he was endeavoring to get up again, Publius Satureius, a tribune, one of his colleagues, was observed to give him the first fatal stroke, by hitting him upon the head with the foot of a stool. The second blow was claimed, as though it had been a deed to be proud of, by Lucius Rufus. And of the rest there fell above three hundred, killed by clubs and staves only, none by an iron weapon.[43]

Italian party politics were never the same again. But the slaughter was more than just a shift in civil mores. It was a symptom of a wider change spreading through the Roman world—a change in its food system.

A QUESTION OF LOGISTICS

By the time Tiberius Gracchus lay in pieces on the Forum pavement, Rome's auxiliary farmlands included more or less the whole of the Mediterranean basin. With so much land under cultivation, the main challenge wasn't in growing enough food, but in delivering and storing it. In this, Rome suffered all the pre-industrial handicaps. At best, food moved at the pace of a determined ox or a lucky wind. But *garum,* oil, and grain don't spoil easily, so preservation wasn't the dominant nuisance. A far bigger problem was logistics.

To collect African wheat, Italian ship captains sailed to the south, then east. On the outward journey to Alexandria, the thousand miles passed relatively quickly, in ten days or a couple of weeks. The return trip was less obliging. Ships sailed against the prevailing winds, having to tack their way arduously up the Mediterranean over a period of a month or two. Winter storms closed the shipping lanes between November 11 and March 10. This limited the grain fleet to a mere two round trips per sailing season.[44] Individual vessels could certainly manage quicker runs, but until the *lex Gabinia* passed (and often afterward), they risked death or enslavement at the hands of the Mediterranean's ubiquitous pirates.

The destination for Egypt's produce was Ostia, at the mouth of the Tiber, fifteen miles as the crow flies from landlocked Rome. Today, evolving coastlines have left Ostia dry, a hunkered suburb gusting with bus exhausts and traffic from Fiumicino Airport. Two thousand years ago, it was the choke point for Rome's food supply. Close Ostia, or merely tamper with the flow of grain from the port to the city, and hundreds of thousands of citizens would starve.

Getting grain from the waterside to the Roman market was a logistical puzzle that the Romans tackled with their usual vim. Ostia was a shallow port, only deep enough for fishing boats, so large ships needed to anchor offshore and be unloaded by lighters. The cavernous grain ships that made the Egyptian run didn't even bother approaching the town but unloaded at the deep-water port of Puteoli near Naples, with the grain then shuttling north in smaller vessels. From the docks, longshoremen loaded the grain onto single-masted sixty-five-ton barges (*navis cordicaria*) for the winding twenty-two-mile journey up the Tiber. To deliver a year's worth of wheat into the city took approximately 4,500 return trips, each leg of which lasted about three days, so perishables like fresh fish and vegetables went ahead by oxcart.[45] Once in the city, the barges unloaded onto designated quays studded with mooring points made from travertine blocks and ramps for the workers to haul the cargo. As a method of feeding a million city dwellers, this Ostian system was excruciatingly laborious, slow, and fragile.

As usual, the Romans tried to engineer their way out of the problem. Julius Caesar drew up plans to clear away the sandbar that prevented the heavier ships from docking, but he was murdered before he could implement it. Emperor Claudius undertook a massive improvement project in the harbor, deepening and broadening it (and spending so much time at the work site that, in his absence, his wife married her lover and attempted a coup d'état). But his plans didn't take the flow of the Tiber into account, and within a few decades the waters had silted up. Two generations later, Emperor Trajan settled the matter by ordering the excavation of a deep, hexagonal harbor inland from the Claudian one. Finally, the great grain ships could dock at the mouth of the river.

The African harvests were annual affairs, so the imports, the 390,000 tons of raw wheat that composed a third of Rome's total diet, needed to be stored for long periods.[46] Grain is heavy; if piled to a height of two meters, it exerts about 12,000 kilograms of pressure per square meter. Two-thirds of this force is lateral, so the wheat needs a stout wall upon which to lean. It spoils if exposed to humidity of more than about 10 to 15 percent, so an effective granary also has to be dry and well ventilated. And it has to be sealed against the incursions of mice, and cool (below 60 degrees Fahrenheit) so bugs don't breed. Finally, it needs to be guarded from human thieves.[47]

The Romans invented a standardized model for their storage buildings (*horreum*), exactly as they had invented standardized models of army camps, roads, and town squares. Built out of brick faced with concrete, the storage houses had small windows and raised floors to allow the free movement of air. The largest example in Ostia, called the Grandi Horrea, boasted scores of rooms around a central courtyard and corridor, with walls a meter thick.[48] The ground-floor storage rooms alone held enough wheat to feed about fifteen thousand people.[49] An even larger storehouse in Rome held an astonishing 225,000 square feet of granary space. (To put this in perspective, consider that the arena in the Colosseum measured 29,000 square feet).[50]

GROUNDS FOR EXHAUSTION

The *horrea* system allowed the Roman food empire a measure of complexity unknown to any previous civilization. These vast storehouses, integrated with Egyptian convoys and the mathematically frenzied schedules of grain barges, meant that imperial citizens ate bread from Africa and fish sauce brewed in Britain or on the shores of the Black Sea.[51] The denizens of countless urban neighborhoods throughout the imperial world, as well as Romans, enjoyed these foods. For instance, we have records of a ten-denarius tax levied on each camel bringing salted fish into inland Palmyra, in modern Syria. The historian Livy, who lived in Rome, was an enthusiast of mackerel from New Carthage. An Egyptian named Theophanes toured the Levant in the fourth century A.D. and frequently bought salted fish products, even when he traveled deep into the interior.[52]

Cosmopolitan shoppers, exotic foodstuffs—Rome's diet had taken a tremendous leap forward with the empire. But sustainability was a problem. Its soil, for instance, was in sharp decline. Land in the Mediterranean, even more than land in North America, is fragile once its natural quilt of trees has been ripped away. Rainfall in Italy comes in heavy, seasonal bursts, which washes away the topsoil on a treeless landscape. Pliny the Elder in the first century A.D. remarked, "Often indeed devastating torrents unite when from hills has been cut away the wood that used to hold the rains and absorb them."[53] Earlier, the Augustan engineer Vitruvius observed the trickle-down effects of mountain streams, noting that, while forests trapped water in the soil, when axes stripped the forests away, rain washed the soil into the rivers.[54] But even by then, most of the damage had been done. To build the great navies of the Punic Wars, the Romans clear-cut the Apennine forests nearest to the city. Within a few seasons, the clear-running Tiber turned yellow with mountain mud. Flooding made a stew of Latin farmlands, and the vital harbor in Ostia began to silt up.[55]

Under the empire, arable land suffocated. It was farmed too greedily, and the loss of nutrients turned it barren.[56] Soil exhaustion was, however, less an imperial invention than a spur to imperial expansion. Even in early republican times, the great plain of Latium had become waterlogged—a sure sign of overworked soil, excessive irrigation, and a concurrent lack of interest in building drains. The Val di Chiana in Etruria and the Campanian plain were the only parts of Italy that really remained fertile into the imperial period, but by then it didn't matter. Romans compensated for the loss of their native land's fertility by eating bread from Egyptian wheat.[57]

To stem further deforestation and soil exhaustion, the ruthless Emperor Domitian declared, in A.D. 92, that all vineyard expansions be halted in Italy and that half of existing provincial vineyards be destroyed. This desperate measure was intended to boost grain production and prevent land from being devoted to "useless" luxuries. His plan failed, however, and after a few years, plantation owners returned to their old ways. The empire's landscape continued to erode, turn muddy, or cake with salt.[58]

By the time Rome's political fortunes had corroded, her agriculture was in full collapse. In A.D. 375, a politician named Symmachus wrote, "For in our time it has become customary that the farm land that used to feed us all now must be fed."[59] Lands that had once grown rich bushels of wheat now produced a few flimsy stalks. The government offered tax incentives to farmers, but countless families abandoned their properties.

In Constantinople's eastern territories, the urban markets survived much longer, until the sixth century. They were insulated by safe trade routes and relative political stability.[60] A government postal system, for instance, helped farmers in deep Anatolia sell their food in markets on the Ionian Sea. Public treasuries continued to subsidize irrigated olive groves in Syria and Palestine, while olive groves in Europe sank into wilderness. Bolstered by tax revenues and a working marketplace, people in the eastern Mediterranean continued selling, minting coins, breeding children, feeding slaves, and building churches and bathhouses. The landscape continued to provide, and the food trade continued its civilizing work.

But even in the east, the food empire didn't last. The breadbasket for the Byzantines was, as it had been for every other empire in the region, the Nile Valley. Wanting to exploit it even more than usual, the emperors in Constantinople yoked Egyptian farmers under a ruinous tax burden.[61] These taxes streamed into the coffers of the imperial court and bureaucracy, which swallowed approximately one-third of the empire's wealth and food—more or less the sum of all the Egyptian production.[62]

By the fifth century, farmers who could no longer pay the Byzantine taxes (like Saint Anthony, the original Christian drop-out from chapter 1) started abandoning their fields to the desert. They went to the cities and joined the massed urban poor or wandered into the rocks to starve and find God.[63] Emperor Theodosius II issued a law in A.D. 438 attempting to bind the peasants to the land. This was a desperate act to stem food riots in Constantinople and was an early manifestation of medieval serfdom. Within a century, Emperors Anastasius and Justinian would embark on huge public works projects to protect Anatolian towns from flash floods—a sure sign that the mountains had been stripped of trees and the lowland fields were swamped.

Overworking the land for the sake of the food trade had, again, wreaked its inevitable damage.

HOW TO FEED AN EMPIRE, CHEAP

Problems with the soil were not the only factors that undermined the Roman food empire. In its historical summer, Roman civilization had enjoyed a warm and productive climate, not unlike that of the twentieth century, or the years when the medieval monasteries grew and prospered. Warm weather kept grain yields high and pushed vineyards and olive groves north into lands that had only known woods and pasture. Then, at about the same time as the empire's decline turned into a screeching plunge, this Roman Warm Period ended. We know this from analyzing sediment and pollen extracted from lake bottoms, as well as from picking at the cores of ancient trees and lumber and from slicing into stalagmites. By measuring the changes in growth rings from the wood, or testing lake sludge for different species of pollen at different depths, or by boiling down stone into its chemical parts, scientists can construct a sort of weather "recast" for, say, A.D. 300. Apparently, it got a lot colder.[64]

Colder weather not only shortened the growing season, it reduced rainfall and shrank the boundaries of arable soil back from the edges of civilization, yielding ground to wilderness.[65] The effects of climate alone probably didn't cause a massive loss in productivity, but when combined with exhausted soil, economic and political problems, and the Roman dependence on transportation networks, they created a disaster.

The death of the Roman food empire, like the death of its political body, was a case of a million pinpricks, of slow attrition, one farm or *garum* factory at a time. The story of the Spanish *garum* industry is the story of the Roman food trade writ small, and on broken pottery. In Gades (modern Cádiz), the Romans spent centuries working a large-scale fish-salting operation, probably inheriting the tradition from the Carthaginians. Evidence from salt-fish amphorae shows that, starting around A.D. 100, tremendous quantities of Spanish sauce poured from

Spain into Ostia. Then the supply vanished. For a while, modest shipments of African *garum* filled the gap, but then that, too, declined.

The food trade, like rioting barbarians, is partly guilty for the collapse of the Roman Empire. Inflation in the third century led to lowered wages, debased currency, and a failed stab at price controls. Food supplies in the cities stretched thin, and families drifted back to the countryside. Imperial edicts tried to stop the exodus, but no one paid attention. When Diocletian broke the empire into two halves in the late third century, Constantinople hoarded the Egyptian grain shipments, and Rome went hungry.[66] In 364, Emperors Valentinian I and Valens further undermined confidence in the ruling institutions by demanding that taxes be paid in grain. Money, in the West, had become obsolete.

By the fourth century A.D., Ostia had degenerated into a near ruin. Pontus, a town four kilometers to the north, had sucked away much of its shipping, but Ostia's decline mirrored the problems that struck the empire's food trade as a whole. For example, by the fourth century A.D., Ostia's grain storehouses and Rome's apartment buildings—the *horrea* and the *insulae*—had all physically shrunk. They dwindled along with the population.[67] Ostia's great milling plant and bakery burned down and were never rebuilt, garbage piled up against the walls, old marbles were smashed to shore up the decaying houses.[68] Visiting the town in 387, Saint Augustine mulled his faith as a friend lay dying of a fever. Standing at her deathbed, he held back his tears and tried to argue himself into joyfulness—his friend was, after all, with God now.[69] But he couldn't really convince himself, and he felt doubly wretched for feeling wretched. He may have been touched by his environs. Ostia—like much of Europe at this time—was a depressing place. After the burial service, Augustine withdrew to the bath, but "the bitterness of my grief was not sweated from my mind." It finally took tears to do that.

As the Western Empire slowly deflated, like a moldy pumpkin collapsing into itself and humming with invading flies, the tax system was one of the first pieces to rot. Without taxes, the army disappeared. Without the army repairing the roads and crucifying robbers and pirates, the food trade stopped.

No taxes meant no one to protect surplus foodstuffs, much less guard the farmers who carted them to town or the merchants who bought them in bulk. With the failure of trade, the markets disappeared, so there was no food to sustain engineers, lawyers, and artists. No food to sustain city folk. Some trade continued, of course, but it was a matter of pockets and sacks, rather than ships' holds and wagon caravans. Instead of wheat and oil, the food trade devolved into pinches of spice. It became a minuscule affair, of interest only to the rich.

Bereft of African produce, a true famine struck the city of Rome in 383. The authorities tried to stem the panic by expelling "strangers," meaning useless characters like Greek scholars and artists (they did, however, make an exception for actors and for three thousand dancing girls). Still, the xenophobia didn't do much good, and when Alaric the Visigoth arrived a few years later, he found the Romans still hovering on the cusp of starvation. A quick siege pushed them over. The city magistrates halved the wheat ration, then reduced it to a third. It took only a few weeks for the Romans to open their gates.[70] Bread, or the lack of it, had finally destroyed the Western Empire.

THE LARDER IS EMPTY

Although they were the ancient world's managerial poster boys, the Romans forgot that the first rule of a successful food empire is to keep the larder stocked. Without a secure food supply, even the stoutest ring of fortifications won't protect a society from being overrun by Huns. When faced with the combined threats of war, soil degradation, climate change, and threatening economics, the Romans found themselves at the mercy of a single grain ship or a lucky harvest on thin soil. Their grain warehouses made the system function in good years, but a day arrived when they couldn't be refilled.

The Romans weren't proficient meteorologists (they never got past watching birds to prophesy the weather), so they can't be blamed for not noticing another rule that governs food empires: climate change happens. In good times, it's natural to expand and come to rely on food supplies from distant, marginal areas, but that doesn't mean they'll last.

That's a lesson worth remembering today. Obviously, the massive urbanization of the twentieth century is inseparable from a massive growth in the global food network. What's less obvious, perhaps, is that the twentieth-century expansion happened during a long, warm stretch of climatic goodwill. Very few droughts occurred between the Dust Bowl and the 1990s. Average temperatures during most of the last century were similar to those during the peaks of the medieval and Roman food empires, and both these civilizations declined as the weather turned foul. The monks and the Romans faced a cooling while we face a warming, but either end of the thermometer makes grim reading for farmers.

Today, many scientists think that if climate change causes global temperatures to rise about two degrees Celsius, crops in temperate zones will actually benefit from a longer growing season and from the fertilizing effect of the blanket of carbon dioxide that's causing so much trouble. (Other scientists dispute this, citing the stifling effects of heat waves.)[71] Even in this optimistic scenario, harvests in tropical and semi-arid regions will thin. Worse, if the world heats up by more than two degrees (an outcome that many scientists now think likely), the entire world's agricultural yield, and hence its food security, will fall.[72]

The lessons of the Roman *horrea* are also pertinent to today's food empire. At their peak, the Romans invested a tremendous amount of money in their system of convoys, warehouses, and shipping lanes to maintain food security—the importance of which wasn't lost on other ancient societies. In biblical Egypt, for example, Pharaoh dreamed of seven fat cows eaten up by seven skinny ones. His advisor Joseph interpreted the dream as an allegory of famine, and he added some practical advice:

> *Let Pharaoh appoint commissioners over the land to take a fifth of the harvest of Egypt during the seven years of abundance. They should collect all the food of these good years . . . This food should be held in reserve . . . to be used during the seven years of famine . . . so that the country may not be ruined by the famine.*[73]

Modern bulk food storage dates to the early 1970s, when food prices rose so aggressively that even coddled Western consumers found themselves squeezed. Playing the role of Pharaoh's commissioners, and goaded by the OPEC oil shock, the United Nations' Food and Agriculture Organization drew up plans for a strategic grain reserve that would ostensibly shield the world from famine. The crux of the idea was for the UN's World Food Programme to stump up funds to maintain a giant mountain of grain that would be released into the market at strategic times, thereby tamping down prices. It wasn't much different from Joseph's plan, except that Joseph never dealt with modern bureaucrats.

Silos around the world, and in Africa in particular, filled up with UN grain. The seemingly limitless hoard was too tempting for local officials to ignore, and the program was plagued by politicking, mismanagement, and corruption. By the end of the 1980s, all that was left was the ink on a ledger sheet. As the UN itself dryly admits, "For many countries the strategic grain reserve . . . tended to exist in theory rather than in practice."[74]

Corruption killed the strategic grain reserve, and after the Soviet Union collapsed, such top-heavy, state-funded interventions fell from political grace. The Washington Consensus came into fashion. Organizations like the International Monetary Fund and the World Bank waved the banner of open economies as a surer means to achieve food security. But the dogma of the marketplace is the opposite of Joseph's advice to Pharaoh. Food storage, the free marketers insist, is wasteful and ineffective. They argue that the cost of storing foodstuffs in imperial bulk is too expensive (although that didn't put off the bureaucrats who built Rome's *horrea*). Since stored food doesn't earn any interest, it's considered an "opportunity cost." The prevailing economic logic claims that it's wiser to sell your food and invest in a T-bill, knowing that the market will let you exchange your T-bill for bread if you really need it.

Since the 1990s were years of record harvests, everyone assumed that world food supplies would continue to expand forever. Regional shortfalls could be most efficiently met by the market. The idea of saving—even on the household scale of pickling, drying, and preserving the fruits from a home garden—lost its allure since the hungry years of the 1940s. In the place of a well-stocked larder, the modern food empire's motto became "Just enough, just in time."

A "just enough, just in time" production and supply chain makes sense to a company selling plastic widgets, but it's a terrible way to run a food system. Consider the case of Malawi. In 2001, this southern African nation was an impoverished, slowly democratizing country. It was shockingly poor, but it hadn't suffered a famine in generations. When the rains came late that year, though, the maize didn't grow with its usual vigor. Fields flooded, and unripened grain rotted on the stalk.[75] The government turned to the strategic grain reserve, housed in a series of giant silos studding the fields between the capital city of Lilongwe and its international airport. But when the guards hauled open the silo doors, it came as a shock (to some people) to see that the strategic grain reserve held no grain. Corrupt Malawian officials probably hid the food and then sold it on the market once prices were at record levels. But blame also falls on the Washington Consensus. The IMF had encouraged Malawi to reduce its food reserves and rely on the market to solve any emergencies. And so the Malawians starved.

It's easy to write off the experience of a small African country as an aberration, but food security isn't Malawi's problem alone. Their misfortune was a microcosmic reflection of the global food system.

Agricultural economists are fond of the term "supply-to-use ratio," meaning how much supply exists compared to consumption. In the mid-1980s, for example, the world's food carryover stocks were about 35 percent of a year's usage. But by 2008 this had fallen to 15 percent. In the United States, soybean reserves dropped to a twenty-day supply—not the end of the world, perhaps, but certainly a crisis for food processors as soy oil dried up, while the lack of soy meal left poultry farmers scratching for alternatives.

In February 2008, an agricultural economist from Purdue University named Chris Hurt observed that "with global demand for grain and oilseeds at record levels and a weak U.S. dollar, foreign buyers are outbidding domestic buyers for American grain." Hunt predicted an imminent food crisis, with a strong euro unbalancing grocery bills and leaving Americans overcharged for their native crops.[76] He was right. Food prices soared, and global reserves evaporated.

Despite record harvests between 2000 and 2007, the world ate more food than it produced. Back in 1998, human beings grew 1.9 billion tons of cereals and ate 1.8 billion tons of them. Since then yields have risen, but so have our appetites, and there's a disjoint between the two. In five of the last ten years, the world consumed more food than farms have grown, while in a sixth year we merely broke even.[77] Reserves are bottoming out. Even without a climate trigger, the ledger shows some unpleasant mathematics.

Food prices fluctuate at the best of times, but now they're steadily ripping into American pocketbooks. Prices have risen at twice the rate of baseline inflation, and they're unlikely to settle in the coming years. China and India will soon be rich enough to heave their weight onto the merchant's scale. Luckily for us in the West, that hasn't happened yet. The Chinese are still self-sufficient in major grain crops, but they're likely to want to go shopping in the near future. Nor is supply growing at the speeds we knew during the postwar farming boom. During the flush 1990s, few countries bothered to invest in agriculture, and scientists don't think we'll soon see any magical breakthroughs to make Eden sprout in a desert.[78]

It's not a reassuring picture, but it's a familiar one. The fourth-century Romans might have looked at our *horrea* today and shaken their heads.

CHAPTER THREE

FARMS: GROWING FOOD FOR PROFIT AND ENVIRONMENTAL RAPINE

In 1593, Francesco Carletti's teenage idyll in Seville ended when his father, Antonio, showed up, announcing that he, too, was going to make his fortune among the imperial Spaniards. In all the adventures, deals, and outright disasters that followed, the younger Carletti never uttered a word against his father, but from his journal we infer that Antonio was a conniving soul. Hearing that his son was thriving among the powerbrokers of Seville, Antonio closed shop in Florence and set out to capitalize on his family connections. He was no sooner reunited with his son than he ordered him to risk his life on a questionable—especially morally questionable—business venture.

Antonio's plan was to send Francesco south to Cape Verde, off the coast of Africa, to buy slaves. Francesco would then accompany the human chattel across the Atlantic to the West Indies, where the mines and latifundia of the New World paid well for African labor. Of course, the Carlettis could easily lose everything. The Atlantic crossing was dangerous, and the slaves might sicken and die. A chance storm cloud might sink both ships and investors' fortunes, and take the banks down in the whirlpool.

Much like twenty-first-century financial institutions, sixteenth-century Spanish banks had little regulation, and they overextended themselves to death. Since no one stopped them, they didn't hesitate to fund half-cocked expeditions to India, bankroll adventurers who had more bravery than navigational sense, and bet on convoys bound for the ocean bottom. Royalty, too, used the money deposited in Seville's safes and strongboxes as a means of funding private get-rich-quick schemes. When these investments soured, the bank's depositors lost the money. The bank would then fold, spreading the ruin even further.[1]

Ominously, Carletti's scheme didn't work from the start. In his journal, Francesco doesn't specify the details, but so many "difficulties" arose in making arrangements for the trip that it's likely the green apprentice botched it. Whatever the cause, Antonio lost faith in his son before he ever boarded ship, so he decided to go along on the journey to supervise. Too much money was at stake to trust to the wisdom of a two-year business trainee.

Spanish law expressly prohibited foreigners from trading in the colonies, which ought to have been a cruel setback to Antonio's business plans. But the Italian pair overcame this obstacle through the time-honored tradition of fraud. After drawing up legal papers placing their whole endeavor under the name of a Spanish woman married to one Cesare Baroncini, a friend from Pisa now living in Seville, they laid out the true state of their arrangements in a second, secret document, which they concealed. Thus shielded by the name of Señora de Baroncini, they filed their paperwork in the office regulating West Indian commerce and sailed down the Guadalquivir River to the estuary port of Sanlúcar de Barrameda.

Today, Sanlúcar is a swampy resort town with an overbuilt beach and tour buses full of staggering sherry tasters. Four hundred years ago, it was one of the launching points for an empire. There, the Carlettis had no trouble in renting a small ship of about four hundred tons with which to make their slave run (many oceangoing carracks of the time displaced more than a thousand tons). Francesco had bought a license granting him permission to cross the Atlantic, but his father had avoided the expense and crept aboard the ship at night, undocumented. After a final inspection from the king's officials during which Antonio must have hunched silently belowdecks, the ship weighed anchor, alone and "without any convoy," on January 8, 1594.

Even in the sixteenth century, slaving struck most people as, at best, an un-Christian business. Between 1526 and 1614, Spain's University of Salamanca was home to a school of business ethics that published works exhorting merchants to think about their souls as well as their profits. The members of the Salamanca school damned the slave trade, in particular, and also argued that the newly "discovered" peoples of Spain's American colonies should have been left unmolested by the guns and ropes of the conquistadores.[2]

One of the chief thinkers among the Salamancans was Tomás de Mercado, a Dominican friar and native of Seville who studied the economic links binding his city to the New World.[3] His book detailing the sins of the merchants—*Suma de tratos y contratos*—found favor among the new cosmopolitan class (and their confessors), becoming a best-seller in 1569, with second and third editions appearing in quick succession.[4] Its ostensible point was to give spiritual guidance to Spain's busy exiles. In Mercado's own words, his goal was "to show what intention the merchant ought to have in his business dealings, what means he should choose so that he may earn his living in such a way that he does not lose his future life."[5]

One of Mercado's pet subjects was banking. Christianity had never been entirely comfortably with money, much less with usury, and theologians tended to regard banking with the same queasiness with which they discussed witchcraft. Mercado, however, was less bothered by the morality of interest than with the temptation for bankers to act irresponsibly with other people's cash. To this end, he advocated the notion that banks ought to be regulated so that they didn't risk more than a percentage of their funds. A stricter adherence to this sixteenth-century idea might have been helpful to twenty-first-century economists, but it's Mercado's thoughts on food trading, not banking, that are in hindsight the most prescient.

Grain, argued the friar, isn't like spices or bolts of silk, because people require grain to live. Due to the nature of markets, however, grain merchants have an incentive to hoard during times of want, keeping food in reserve as prices rise and then selling it at the moment of greatest profit. "Knowing that the neighbors cannot stop themselves from purchasing [wheat] . . . no matter how modest one's life might be," writes Mercado, "the salesman, with pain, increases the cost." This opportunism in the face of hunger would unquestionably tar the merchants' souls, but the true sinner was the system that rewarded the sin: the unregulated food empire.[6]

Although Mercado feared for the afterlives of businessmen, his worries took a worldly bent on the topics of grain supply, enslavement, and loss of investment. As a sixteenth-century clergyman, he can be forgiven for failing to notice the greatest (temporal) danger caused by the sixteenth-century Spanish food empire: the physical destruction of the land. Mercado never knew the first rule of ecology, which is that diversity equals strength. The plantations and latifundia spread by the Spanish adventurers were, by the exclusive nature of their flora, both specialized and fragile. These ecosystems were weak, easily pushed into waste by a dry spell or a plague of nibbling insects.

Although the Salamanca school didn't realize it, the true legacy of unfettered trade wasn't merely hunger and damnation, but a system of producing and distributing food that was bound to collapse.

THE GRAPES OF WRATH

As they walked away from Eden, Adam and Eve looked back westward, over their shoulders toward paradise. A western isle is where the dying sun finds its rest, where the Irish looked for Tír na nÓg, where the Greeks sought the Hesperides. In one of the most romantic passages in romantic English poetry, Tennyson's Ulysses rouses his old comrades with their "free hearts and free foreheads" to sail on a last, desperate voyage to the west, hunting for Elysium before the dusk of old age.

Poetry aside, a lot of people took these directions literally. Roman-era adventurers sailed to the Islands of the Blessed, their name for any of the green strings of land including Madeira and the Canaries, the Azores, and Cape Verde. Plutarch quotes a pair of sailors who survived a reckless voyage in the Atlantic and describe landfall at islands, which, they say,

> *enjoy moderate rains at long intervals, and winds which for the most part are soft and precipitate dews, so that the islands not only have a rich soil which is excellent for plowing and planting, but also*

produce a natural fruit that is plentiful and wholesome enough to feed, without toil or trouble, a leisured folk. Moreover, an air that is salubrious, owing to the climate and the moderate changes in the seasons, prevails on the islands . . . Therefore a firm belief has made its way, even to the Barbarians, that here is the Elysian Field and the abode of the blessed, of which Homer sang.[7]

When the Roman Empire passed, so did memory of the Fortunate Islands. A thousand years went by before the Renaissance Portuguese, speaking a very different form of Latin, once again made landfall on the shores of the ancient paradise. Charmed by the rich soil, salubrious air, and the wholesome fruit, the Portuguese turned the islands into a big slaving fortress. By the time Francesco and Antonio Carletti arrived in the sixteenth century, Cape Verde was a rowdy naval station where European ships collected supplies and human chattel before nosing into the windward isles of the archipelago—a final glimpse of earth before the weeks of unbroken blue that led to the great plantations of the West Indies. It was a launching point for Europe's colonial expansion, and for the countless Africans being kidnapped and forcibly funneled into the New World.[8]

Francesco Carletti and his father hoped to join this stream of grim caravels, but rather than noting the verdant, lush environment, Carletti noticed something else when he arrived in Cape Verde: the smell of goat, which the locals hung and salted in the tropical air. In return for cargoes of semolina wheat, vegetables, and dried fruit, European ships took on tons of the island's salted goat meat, to be eaten by the sailors of the colonial fleets. The animals thrived on the steep deforested and eroded heights of the islands, and their meat was a good source of protein (and jaw muscle exercise) for the crews.

The transformation from the lush islands of Roman times to the eroded rocks of Carletti's is the fault of Europe's expanding food empire. That and planetary mechanics.

In 1291, a pair of Genoese explorers named the Vivaldi brothers discovered that the winds in the Atlantic Ocean operate like giant pinwheels, rotating clockwise north of the equator and counterclockwise to the south. These trade winds sweep down from the North Atlantic before veering west off the coast of Africa. So when the Vivaldi brothers sailed from Europe into unknown waters, they were most likely swept first southward past Senegal, then thrust out to sea.[9]

It's a good bet that the Vivaldi brothers arrived at the Fortunate Islands, where they might have admired the scenery, bartered with the natives for fruit and fish, and taken on fresh water. Then they would have waited for a favorable wind. And waited.

Eventually, they would have noticed that the wind never changed direction. It always blew west, in the opposite direction of home. The Vivaldis had failed to grasp that, to return to Europe from the Fortunate Islands, a sailor needs to take a mad, illogical leap and sail into the terrifying infinity of the Atlantic. He needs to point the prow of his vessel west and trust to planetary mechanics. If the sailors were still alive when they neared the Americas, they would have had to steer north along the coast to about 40 degrees latitude where, if the season were right and the vessel still seaworthy, they would catch the Westerlies and a pure, fast blow back to home and glory. The Vivaldis couldn't pull it off. They were never heard from again.

A little more than a hundred years after the Vivaldi fiasco, a second, altogether more impressive phase of European exploration began when sailors from Portugal, Spain, and Genoa ventured south from their customary ports around the northern nub of Morocco. These sailors broke centuries of European complacency about the sea routes to the south of the Pillars of Hercules. To the north, traders had long plied the routes between Iceland, Greenland, the Newfoundland fisheries, Britain, and the Iberian Peninsula—a triangle trade developed selling English wool for Icelandic fish for Portuguese fruit, oil, salt, sugar, and wine.[10] But the southern routes didn't draw much traffic until the 1400s, when the Portuguese, hungry for new agricultural land, set about clearing the forests from these Fortunate Islands. The people who actually chopped the wood were, for the most part, slaves.

African slavery on the industrial scale known by Carletti was a relatively late development, emerging well after the Portuguese colonists arrived in the 1440s. The first slaves on Madeira were either European—most likely "new Christians," Jewish or Moorish converts whose faith had come under suspicion—or Guanches, the native Canary Islanders.

The Guanches had, at first, fought guerilla battles to keep the Portuguese from establishing a foothold on their territory, but firearms and disease snuffed out the resistance. Soon Ferdinand and Isabella of Spain, following the Portuguese lead, subjugated the main island of Gran Canaria by landing hundreds of soldiers equipped with horses and modern cannon. The campaign took five years to exterminate the natives; wiping clean the island of Tenerife took another three. With the possible exception of the West Indian Arawaks, the Guanches were the first people to be driven to extinction by European colonialism.[11]

At first, the new slaves worked mostly in clear-cutting the very forests that had given them shelter from the invaders during their guerilla war. As well as timber, the trees yielded resin. After sawing up pine logs, the slaves shoveled them into three-chambered ovens, which, over a slow, twenty-four-hour burn, reduced them to the gleaming black pitch used to caulk European ships and seal wooden aqueducts.[12] But it was a more lucrative treasure that drew the attentions of the islands' new masters.

One of humanity's shared characteristics—a biological whip, if you will—is the sweet tooth. We love sugar. The received evolutionary wisdom holds that this is because of its rush of calories and its jolt to the bloodstream. Eons of scarcity drove us to favor the most efficient means of delivering energy into our bodies; nothing is quite as useful as sugar for getting through the rougher parts of an Ice Age.

Until the medieval period, Europeans, like bears, ate most of their sugar in the form of honey or fruit. When the Arabs smashed across the Mediterranean in the eighth century, they brought with them sweet-smelling, fibrous sugarcane, which they had learned to grow and process from the Indians, who also exported the crop to China. For many centuries the Middle East was awash in sugarcane juice. So when Europeans wondered what to do with their new conquests in the Fortunate Islands, they decided on sugarcane plantations. Sweets were a cash crop for which there was always a market.

By 1452, the first mill on the islands had opened, and soon dozens of sugar-processing houses were smoking day and night, burning up the woods. The islands were transformed. "Madeira" means "wooded," and sources described Cape Verde before its colonization as a dry, "well-wooded" land that also possessed "streamlets of water" and a "great quantity of grass."[13] No longer. As the immigrants and their slaves sharpened their axes and invested heavily in goats, the forests vanished. The settlers also lit fires to clear farmland, some of which burned continually for as long as seven years. A Venetian named Alvise de Cadamosto, writing in the latter half of the fifteenth century, observed of one fire that a group of settlers "was forced, with all the men, women, and children, to flee its fury and to take refuge in the sea, where they remained up to their necks in the water, and without food or drink for two days and two nights."[14]

To compound the damage, one Bartolomeu Perestrello (father-in-law to Christopher Columbus) had the idea of releasing a family of rabbits on the island of Porto Santo. In short order, the bunnies had "overspread the land, so that our men could sow nothing that was not destroyed by them."[15] The attentions of the rabbits were so terrible that this first European colony on the Madeira archipelago had to be abandoned, unable to feed itself. Subsequent colonists tried to exterminate the pests, but as late as 1455, the island was a lapin stronghold. By gobbling up most of the native vegetation, the rabbits caused a massive ecological collapse from which the Porto Santo never recovered.

By the 1560s—a mere century after the first colonists arrived—an English traveler noted the striking absence of trees on the islands, stating, "Wood is the thing that is most wanted."[16] With the forests gone, wind and rain took their toll on the island soil. Streams baked dry in their beds. Native species vanished, replaced by opportunistic migrants like Perestrello's rabbits. There were less obvious plagues, too. Miles above the dust, rainfall patterns shifted. Forests had previously drawn clouds in what's called a fog drip, an unusual form of precipitation that kept water trapped in a perpetual, moistening fog around the islands. On one of the Canary Islands, for example, a particular "rain tree" attracted enough condensation to form two permanent pools of water that flowed from its base.[17] Sir Richard Hawkins, writing in the sixteenth century, describes the effect of such trees:

Out of this Valley ordinarily rise every day, great vapours and exhalations, which by reason that the Sunne is hindered to worke his operation, with the height of the Mountaine towards the South-east, convert themselves into moisture, and so bedew all the trees of the Valley, and from those which over-top this Tree, drops downe the dew upon his leaves, and so from his leaves into a round Well of stone, which the Naturals of the Land have made to receive the water.[18]

Clear-cutting made the land hotter, so the clouds sniffed back their raindrops and withdrew. Even if no one chopped them down, the rain trees died from the lack of moisture, and the islands began to heat and crack.

Despite the sinister turn in their environment, the islanders continued to produce sugar. They were making money, and they would continue to do so until climate change and economic globalization forced their hand. This happened soon enough. In Carletti's day, people across the globe had noticed something amiss in the weather. From the mid-sixteenth century to the early nineteenth century, Europe experienced some of its coldest weather of the second millennium, and this string of bad weather made a mess of crops and people's immune systems. Dubbed the Little Ice Age, the shift in the sixteenth century was itself likely caused by changes in ocean currents, volcanic activity, and less solar energy reaching the planet—astronomers from the time observed an unusual scarcity of sun spots. This contributed to a single-degree drop in average temperatures across Europe. While such aberrations may seem piffling, if spring temperatures drop by just a half degree, the growing season can shrink by ten days. Just as bad, the shift caused the added hardships of harsh winters and unpredictable rainfall.[19]

Plantations suffered the most from the freeze. Any plant grown on a large scale, so as to yield the most productive harvest, needs a rich draft of nutrients and water for it to flourish. The monocultures on plantations drain the soil not only of water, but also of organic material. Clumps of organic matter trap moisture and keep fields resilient, able to withstand droughts and floods.[20] Within a few years of planting sugar plantations on the islands, however, the organic matter had worn away, exposing the soil to a meteorological pummeling.

The final blow came from the market. In the sixteenth century, new colonies in the Caribbean began to compete for the European sugar market, offering a larger, cheaper supply of cane. The prevailing winds meant that any ship leaving the Fortunate Islands for northern Europe had to pass by the Caribbean, so the new colonies were actually better placed to reach European customers than were the Fortunate Islands. Isolation also prevented Caribbean slaves from escaping; long coastlines made transport easy; and the local winds kept the mill blades spinning.[21] So by the late sixteenth century, sugar production shifted entirely to New World spots like Jamaica and Barbados, which had all the blessings of geography and none of the Fortunate Islands' environmental devastation (yet).

As the native green vanished and sugarcane rotted unsold, the name "Fortunate Islands" became another agricultural misnomer. The islanders needed a new product to sell. Some of them had to wait four hundred years for the arrival of charter planes and beach holiday packages. Others, like the residents of Cape Verde, found a niche in slaving and in goats. Madeira found its salvation in wine.

The unique flavor of Madeira wine is supposedly due to an act of obnoxious customs inspection. A Portuguese ship with a hold full of island wine met with an ornery official at the entrance of the bay of Hong Kong. Ordered to dump the wine overboard, one of the sailors, overcome with the tragedy of the waste, started drinking. He discovered that, shaken for months at sea and heated by the equatorial sun, the flavor had actually improved. This sauna bath treatment is what gave exported Madeira wine its unusual tang. By 1794, a man named Pantaleão Fernandes concocted a more controllable means of delivering consistency. He added alcohol to red wine, then poured the spiked mixture into huge vats and slowly heated it by about five degrees Celsius per day until it reached 55 degrees. After simmering at this temperature for three months, the wine could be slowly cooled and sealed in oak casks for aging.[22] The resulting drink—sweet, long-lived, and practically impervious to extremes of temperature—proved so popular that, in the more nautical stretches of Europe, "Madeira" came to simply mean "wine." Americans in particular liked it since it didn't require cellaring and could survive the long, humid summers on the Eastern Seaboard.[23]

The first colonists on Madeira had brought vine cuttings, but wine only came to the fore as an industry after Jamaica had stolen the sugar business away. It happened in a vindictive twist of royal politics. Charles II of England had married the daughter of the Portuguese king. In a bid to ingratiate himself with his in-laws, and to thumb his nose at the hated Spaniards, he exempted Madeira wine from the English prohibition on continental vintages. Having no other wine to buy, the English came to prefer it in all their outposts, particularly in American ports.

To meet this demand, Madeira's farmers needed a reliable variety of grape, one that was suited to the tropical climate, the dry, exhausted volcanic soil, and the winds. Naturally, they looked for it in the same place that people in the Renaissance always looked for answers: to the ancient Greeks and Romans. The classical world held all the wisdom of science, art, and philosophy. Why not viniculture? So the colonists bought seeds and stock cuttings from Crete.

The farmers on Madeira didn't realize, however, that the ancient Greeks and Romans had made a hash of their wine industry. The environmental wreckage that spoiled the Fortunate Islands had also bedeviled the ancients, and for the same reasons. They, too, had known a wave of exploitation and prosperity, followed by collapse. They, too, had learned the price of the gift of Bacchus.

GOD IN THE CUP

When the god Dionysus left his native India and arrived in Greece, he brought a present to give to his new worshippers. It was a wondrous fruit, capable of magic. Euripides describes Dionysus's gift in his tragedy *The Bacchae*:

Then streams the earth with milk, yea, streams
With wine and nectar of the bee,
And through the air dim perfume steams
Of Syrian frankincense.

The immigrant literally creates a land of wine, milk, and honey (and psychotic insanity; *The Bacchae* ends in a famous scene of intrafamilial dismemberment). Dionysus, who was able to make vines sprout from the planks of a ship or to drown it in liquor, was very much a god with a theme.

In truth, the Greeks drank wine long before they worshipped Dionysus. As history's most devoted oenophiles, they explicitly equated wine with civilization and carried it to their colonies in France, Italy, and the Black Sea region. Wine drinking is so rooted in Greek culture that it's impossible to differentiate the two. But the Greeks always remembered that the vine was a transplant. A foreign gift. And it came from across the sea.

The oldest evidence for wine consumption is from a storage vessel found in Georgia, dating to 6000 B.C. There's evidence of grape consumption from much earlier, but the Georgian find is the earliest instance of wine residue. On a large scale, viticulture, like every other form of farming, took shape in Mesopotamia and from there spread to Egypt and the Levant, and north to the Black Sea. Greece was wine's European gateway, and Crete was the gateway to Greece.

One of the earliest European wine bowls dates from 2000 B.C. in the Minoan palace of Phaistos on Crete. It's a remarkable utensil, with a painted stem and ornate motifs of lilies and trumpets that give it an almost rococo flair.[24] It wouldn't look out of place on a shelf in eighteenth-century Vienna. The Minoans who made it were probably the first Europeans to practice the wine trade.

Along with bull jumping, an apparent matriarchy, and a taste for expressive frescoes, the Minoans are remembered as a seafaring people who built a trading empire around the Aegean. They imported vines from Anatolia or Palestine and then paid back the favor by selling wine to the coastal cities of the Levant and Egypt. Archaeologists have found Cretan wine vases in Lebanon. While other islanders from Lemnos and the Cyclades "tramped" goods around the region without ever building trading posts, the Minoans kept a permanent base in the Levantine city of Ugarit. They also sold drinks to the pharaoh. One Minoan palace, Zakros, grew as a hub solely to serve this Egyptian trade.[25]

Even the myths paint the Cretans as natural vintners. After Theseus killed the Minotaur and eloped with the Minoan princess Ariadne, he jilted her on the island of Naxos, preferring to return to Athens as a bachelor. At once, the girl rebounded into the arms of Dionysus himself, who swept her into the company of immortal spouses. Wine and Crete, in the bluntest terms, were bedfellows.

The product that the Minoan ships shuttled around the eastern Mediterranean can still be drunk today. On the southern Cretan site of Myrtos-Pyrgos, not far from the hotels and snack bars of present-day Ierapetra, archaeologists unearthed a warehouse that would have stored as much as four thousand liters of Minoan wine (450 cases). Laboratory analysis showed that the drink contained traces of tree resin, which was presumably used by the ancients to line their amphorae and keep them airtight, thus reducing the chance of spoilage during long, sweltering trading missions. So Minoan wine must have tasted something like modern retsina, the dry, slightly bitter drink familiar to diners in Greek restaurants. Today, retsina takes its distinctive flavor from pine resin added in the last stages of fermentation. (Like Champagne or sherry, retsina is unique to its region, and EU regulation prevents other places from trading wine under its name.)

The quantity of wine in the Myrtos warehouse was far too great to be consumed by the inhabitants of a small Bronze Age farming town, even one made up of prodigious alcoholics. It was marked for trade. Additional finds on site—a funnel, vats for treading grapes, impressions of grape leaves on pottery—prove that the town hosted a thriving wine industry. Other Minoan sites yield evidence of pressing floors and collecting basins.[26] Wine was big business in the early Bronze Age.

By the nineteenth century B.C., the Minoans had pieced together a very profitable trade network, a mercantile empire of sorts. This trade required organization. To function, trade needs reliable roads, safe sea lanes, and warehouses.[27] So Crete built palaces.

The Knossos archaeological site's palace is still impressive, even though it's been reduced by three thousand years of weather, earthquakes, and the tinkerings of foreign adventurers such as Sir Arthur Evans. Knossos had a thousand rooms. All of the Minoan palaces had broad, paved yards ringed with ochre columns, tiers of airy houses and sweeping stairwells, bull motifs, and buoyant pictures of dolphins. The Minoans lorded over fleets and roads, controlling the movement of wine and other goods around their trading routes. They owned storehouses, creameries, and breweries. They engaged in big business, and likely big government too. While a single Minoan entrepreneur could conceivably have hammered together a warehouse and hired a guard, no private individual could have floated enough square-rigged galleys to police the Cyclades. For the goods that benefited Cretans as a whole—roads, clear mountain passes, a navy—they needed the authority of the group.[28]

But in creating authority and developing trade, Crete's society changed. In the early Bronze Age, about 3000 B.C., Minoans lived on small farms, growing what grain they needed to feed themselves. There's no evidence for any social strata steeper than that between a farmer and his donkey. But with the Minoan Empire came a Minoan aristocracy who inhabited the palaces and drank the wine, often in ceremonial rites.[29] We have records from mainland Greece of daily diets from this period, and wine wasn't poured at the dining tables of peasants but reserved for the pleasure of the rich, and for honoring the gods. Mostly, though, it was used to trade.

From this trade came money, which allowed the Minoan elites to set their hands to painting, to architecture, and to building a civilization.[30] The less fortunate spent their lives picking grapes. As social inequity deepened, the landscape also changed: forests were cut down, and the soil eroded. It's the familiar story of both Madeira and Rome, but it happened in Crete first.[31] The Minoans, however, didn't last long enough to suffer the slow decay brought about by environmental degradation. Around 1500 B.C. the entire culture disappeared into a cloudy mix of natural disasters, including a spectacular volcanic blast and tidal wave. Tottering and wounded, the Minoans received the final helpful push into the grave from their Mycenaean neighbors on the Greek mainland.

The Mycenaeans are a murky bunch. They flourished from about 1800 B.C. to 1100 B.C., fought the Trojan War long before Homer spun their legends into the foundation of Western literature, and built the brawny architecture that survives in magnificent blocks of stone at Tiryns and Mycenae near the Argolid coast. And then they vanished. No one really knows why. Unlike the Minoans, who collapsed at the peak of their strength and vibrancy, the Mycenaeans came to a more complex, altogether less exciting end. This is odd. The Minoans were, as far as we can tell, a quiet, peaceable culture. They liked to paint pictures of pretty undressed youths with wavy hair; they had no interest in warrior tombs. By contrast, the Mycenaeans were a flexing, macho civilization, fond of heraldic lions, chariots, and funerary arts. They loved to bury gold and weaponry with their valiant dead. If any culture should have gone out with a bang, it was the Mycenaeans, but they simply disappeared.

Among the possible culprits are the Dorians—invaders or migrants from the north who broke a lot of pottery near the Mycenaean palaces around the time they were abandoned (and who then likely settled down in the shadows of the old palaces and engendered the future Spartans and Corinthians). Other suspects are pirates, the so-called Sea Peoples, an anonymous group of miscreants who vandalized the Levantine and Cypriot trading towns around this time and then vanished from the already blotchy historical record.[32] Equally likely is that Mycenaean agriculture declined when a shift in climate ushered in a long stretch of bad weather.[33]

All these factors almost certainly played a role in undermining a society where problems had been planted centuries earlier. When the ancient Greeks were still subsistence farmers, long before the days of palaces, ornamental wine bowls, or trade routes, they worked small, diversified farms. Every family tried to grow its own wheat for bread and barley for beer, and it kept a few goats or sheep for milk. Farms clustered near sources of fresh water, while the rest of the landscape stood thick with native forest. Bronze Age Greece was a patchwork of grain surrounded by dark forests of Mediterranean pines.

Over the centuries, the weather in Greece softened, and tweaks in the smithies led to better tools. The Greeks grew more food and raised more babies. As society evolved, so did agriculture. People spotted an opportunity in the grapevine. They diversified. They started breeding sheep in large numbers for cloth and meat, and oxen that could be yoked to the new plows. Generations would pass without a famine, and people learned to turn an extra bushel of barley or an extra bucket of grapes into a tradable commodity, like booze. Along with cheese, alcohol had a long shelf life and could survive an uncomfortable sea journey to a faraway market. It began to make good economic sense to stop growing foodstuffs for the family table and put them on the merchant's scale.[34]

When a Greek farming family's only ambition was to feed itself, farmers would grow a mixed parcel of food, perhaps enlivened by the odd pig. But over time, as the entire culture grew wealthier, some farmers would have discovered that their land had an exceptional terroir for grapes. Their neighbors would have wanted to buy their wines, and the region would earn a reputation for good vineyards. Another valley, not so blessed in grapes, might have boasted rich grass and tender mutton. The farmers in this region, logically, would have given up on wines and devoted their land to pasture. Both regions would have traded and, with the profits, some of their descendents would have built towns and created a new economic class. The farmers were using what's called comparative advantage, and it happens when people realize that they can barter wine for greater quantities of bread, mutton, and vegetables than they could grow for themselves. So farms specialize. The story of agricultural development in Greece (and Rome, and Madeira) is a story of comparative advantage. Surplus food and drink generated by trade then become the fuel of urban life.

Over the centuries, as the islands and peninsula started to become crowded, farmers ventured up into hills that had once been dismissed as too thorny a prospect for the axe and plow. Innovations in metallurgy and the breeding of draft animals helped them open the forests, break new ground, and fertilize the soil. Water, of course, is scarce in hilly country, and by clear-cutting the primeval woodlands, these pioneers inadvertently damaged the ecosystem, weakening it in the event of drought or thunderstorm. The aristocrats pressed hilly common land into vine cultivation for the sake of the wine trade (reaping a bonanza of timber and charcoal as a bonus from clear-cutting), and the soil never recovered.[35] Toward the end, the Mycenaeans tried building terraces to stop the erosion, but this cost an awful amount of effort, and it didn't work. The Mycenaean giant didn't have feet of rich, fertile clay, but of bare stone.[36]

When the climate dried up, successive droughts wracked the delicate earth, making each cloudless summer cumulatively worse than the last.[37] Aristotle, who lived centuries later, leaves us an account of what it might have been like:

> *Places that formerly enjoyed a good climate deteriorate and grow dry. This has happened in Greece to the land about Argos and Mycenae. In the time of the Trojan War Argos was marshy and able to support few inhabitants only, while Mycenae was good land and therefore the more famous. Now the opposite is the case . . . for Mycenae has become unproductive and completely dry . . . What has happened in this small district may therefore be supposed to happen to large districts and whole countries.*[38]

Although Aristotle was from a different age, he understood that food empires are only as robust as their weakest link. When connected by a mutually dependent network of imports and exports, a farm's failure becomes a city's riots. An early frost in the provinces can unseat a king just as it will damn a peasant to hunger. The environment and the social world are part of the same brittle system.

While the details of the Mycenaean fall are lost, the pattern is consistent with collapses in Carletti's Europe, the Roman Empire, and the medieval monastery economy. Each of these societies initially accomplished the three tasks necessary for urban dwellers to put bread on their tables—they grew surpluses, they built larders and breweries and roads, and they established fairs, markets, and a merchant class. In doing so, however, these societies expanded past a sustainable size.

There are three reasons for their overreach. First, in each case, premodern cities grew on the food surplus grown by tilling virgin soil. Second, these cities depended on climatic good luck, on long bouts of mild weather that helped crops flourish. Third, they relied on specialist farmers. But none of these factors were sustainable in the long term. Virgin land loses its potency, climates change, and specialized farms are, by nature, vulnerable to misfortune.

When yields started to decline, each society tried to expand farther or farm more intensively. They developed new technologies and brought marginal land under cultivation. These strategies worked for a time, but they ultimately meant that cities continued to grow. Eventually, the solutions only exacerbated the root problems. So when a crisis arrived, the trading routes that had helped to liberate people from the land, or created the incentive for extra production and regional specialization, became chains. There was nothing for many urbanites to do but look backward.

THE WEAK HEART OF TODAY'S FOOD EMPIRE

In the Yorkshire Dales National Park in northern England, you can glimpse a landscape at the precise moment of a food empire's collapse. The land around the upland lake of Malham Tarn is a place of deep hues and hard lines—inky water and clouds flush with temperament. Cobbled villages on the hillsides meld into limestone crags, and pastures are streaked with crowberry and dark willow. The sweep of the land is almost too dramatic, too flawless in its tourist board aesthetic. Here is England at its windblown height, the rough country of the Brontës' woolly swordsmen and midnight-eyed heroines, a counterpoint to the thatch and rosebushes of the south. It's where England is closest to the wild.

But in the thirteenth century, Malham shimmered with pale, civilizing wheat. You can still imagine how it once looked if you walk, just before dusk, along the edge of the tarn's curving cliff, once the lip of a giant Ice Age waterfall. From the top, if you squint into the lowering gloom, you can see a very different shadow of history laid out in the grass and stones: small rectangles, faded outlines of tiny medieval farm plots. Their owners had worked them increasingly hard until the fourteenth century, when they suddenly stopped. Today, government subsidies pay for sheep and rough cattle to crop the moorland grass.

The medieval farmers who worked around the Malham Tarn sold their grain in the grey market squares of towns like Skipton, nine miles away. The urbanites who bought it practiced stonemasonry, or choir singing, or any of the other trades that built the medieval world. So when the farms disappeared, leaving only traces on the hillsides, so did the civilization. The countryside in the north of England has never regained the crowds it knew seven hundred years ago.

Modern ecologists, the scientists who try to understand why forests burn down or why pests gobble up particular crops, would have had stern words for the medieval Malhamites. Deforested uplands, intensive grain cultivation, soil exhaustion, lengthy trading routes, and a dependent urban population are the sorts of things that keep ecologists awake at night. Malham Tarn, Mycenae, the Fortunate Islands, and ancient Rome are ideal case studies in landscape vulnerability, poster children for the type of ecosystem that "flips" at the first misfortune.[39] Ecologists could point to a host of analogous systems in the natural world (like the boreal forest, for example, that grows undisturbed for a hundred years before suddenly collapsing when a lightning strike sparks a fire). They could use graphs and scatter plots to show that these food empires were dependent on landscapes just so productive of food, and just so homogenous in species, and just so bound into corridors of trade that they were accidents waiting to happen.[40] And then they'd coolly note that when the climate chilled, and the rains became unpredictable, and the land withheld its generosity, millions of people died.

Our own food empire has a lot in common with these historic examples.[41] Urbanites around the world rely on just a handful of crops—wheat, corn, rice, and soy—to provide the majority of our nutrition. These crops are usually grown as a continuous monoculture, or as a part of a relatively simple crop rotation, in just a few primary areas like the Ukraine, the Great Plains, and China's river valleys. From the perspective of the ecologists, we depend on a highly vulnerable system—"an accident waiting to happen."[42]

Another similarity: medieval Europe, ancient Greece, and Rome all went through a massive bout of human population increase, buoyed by improved agriculture. So have we. Despite the best efforts of war, pestilence, famine, and death, modern human beings are multiplying at a dizzying rate. At the International Institute for Applied Systems Analysis (IIASA) near the Austrian Alps outside of Vienna, statisticians and computer modelers concoct extraordinarily sophisticated predictions of population trends. Housed in a retired Hapsburg palace, the wonks eat their lunchtime sandwiches in mirrored ballrooms glazed with frescoes. These rooms and flowered courtyards were once the ornaments of an aristocracy that's long dead; perhaps the shades of history help the wonks look forward. Regardless, the scientists here estimate that we'll add another 2 or 3 billion members to our species before the numbers level out.

Considering that we added 2 billion in the past twenty years alone, the limit may not be far away. "Sometime before 2100," say demographers Wolfgang Lutz, Warren Sanderson, and Sergei Scherbov, "the great centuries-long expansion of the world's population will come to an end."[43] Whether these numbers level out in an apocalypse or a condom campaign is uncertain. Whichever way it goes, there are going to be a lot more mouths to feed before the reversal.

The ancient and medieval farmers also cut down most of their trees. So have we. In places that lend themselves to farming, forests have become a historical figment. Over the past one hundred years, much of the world has evolved from a wild quilt of prairies, savanna, forest, and mixed farms into a monochrome sea of wheat, corn, and soybeans. Cutting wood to grow soybeans or graze cattle kills the topsoil. As the UN's kindling-dry Millennium Ecosystem Assessment puts it:

> *In the last three centuries, global forest area has been reduced by approximately 40%, with three quarters of this loss occurring during the last two centuries. Forests have completely disappeared in 25 countries, and another 29 countries have lost more than 90% of their forest cover.*[44]

Climate change, too, is a catastrophe we hold in common with our forebears, except instead of blaming sunspots and volcanoes, we have to blame our fossil fuel habit.[45] Even if we shut the spigot on all the carbon dioxide emissions in the world and plug up all the methane-belching ruminants, we'd still have to live with a half century of wrenching temperature hikes.

All these analogies don't even account for what economists call the "negative externality" of environmental degradation. This means that while big monoculture plantations create endless tons of "affordable" soy, it's only "affordable" if the cost is tallied without regard to tomorrow's crop, or to the hidden costs in water supplies, or to oil prices. Or to the whole Gordian knot of twenty-first-century life. "Affordable" is relative.

Despite all the gloom, sustainable agriculture is not a fantasy. Not quite. There are a few societies—historical and current, both—that have grown abundant food without degrading their natural environments, marching their armies onto foreign ground, or flooding their horizons with monoculture crops. For instance, on the South Sea island of Bali, a system of carefully managed rice terraces fed a dense press of human beings, lasting centuries before it degraded with the arrival of new industrial inputs and farming practices.[46] Perhaps a more useful example, though, is close to one of the authors' own experiences.

A fifteen-minute drive west of Niagara Falls, tucked within the fruit belt of southern Ontario, sits the Fraser family farm. The landscape is an idyll of soft hills, woodlots, and licks of blue water, while the occasional little barn or vineyard adds contours to the gentle green. The soil is sandy and well drained; a line of irrigation pipes runs from a pump in the pond to the mixed fields. In the evenings, deer and raccoons amble out of the woodlots to make mischief in the orchards.

The proprietor of the farm was Frank Rutherford Fraser, the author's grandfather. A graduate of the local agricultural college in the days before chemical fertilizers had swamped the curriculum, he was an ardent believer that the most reliable input is human sweat, and although he used pesticides and fertilizer, he generally preferred to nurture his crops with labor. If "organic" would have struck him as a childish, left-wing catchword, he generally farmed in a manner that would have struck both his nineteenth-century forebears and today's upscale food markets as natural.

The lesson of the Fraser farm, of sustainable farming everywhere, is that farms should mimic nature. Too many nutrients in the soil cause water pollution, and too few mean degradation, so the sustainable farmer balances them by rotating crops, planting diverse flora, and slicing up the land with hedgerows and studding it with trees. Such a farmer plants perennials that keep roots in the soil throughout the year, and he pastures livestock on fallow ground.

Second, sustainable farms largely use muscle instead of machines. Virtually all of the energy on the planet comes from solar heat stored in vegetation (fossil fuels are just ancient sun rays locked into decomposing plants). For a farm to be truly sustainable, it can't depend on the finite generosity of oil wells, so it must remove combustion engines as a major input. Hence a step back to muscle power.

To follow both of these two rules, farmers have to accept the third: sell local. By cutting their reliance on engines, sustainable farmers cut access to faraway buyers. A sustainable food empire would be one wherein most farms support their local populations, rather than selling their wares on the global commodities markets. Not for all products, of course, but we would need to reduce the percentage of globe-trotting produce in our shopping baskets.

Our needs are no different from those of our ancestors, but we depend on the bounty of intensive, specialized farms, and we're reliant on trucks, ships, and planes to keep us from going hungry. Our technology lets us gather food from the breadth of the globe. We've drawn water from deeper and deeper wells (see chapters 4 and 6). Chemical fertilizers fight soil exhaustion (chapter 5). We gas the pests that swarm across our vast monocultures with ingenious poisons (chapter 8). Jet travel and modern coolants deliver New Zealand lamb to New York dinner plates (chapter 6).

Of course, if we obeyed the lessons of history, we'd shuffle our crops, clip the lengths of our trade routes, store more food, and politely ask people to move away from our metropolises in the name of sustainability. A historical reading of our food empire would mean a social revolution. While such a revolution might seem impossible, we may want to ask, is it avoidable? Will our technological brilliance save our food empire, or is it like the medieval agricultural boom? Is it a temporary fix, a boost for a few generations, before an inevitable reckoning?

PART II

THE PRICE RISES

An Experiment in Survival

It's hard to be lyrical about autumn light when it's poured out of a factory. In the Yangtze Valley, the November air filters through a cottony wrap of carbon dioxide. Low-grade petroleum dribbles out of pipes, pools in black rainbows on the tarmac, and catches in the sharp edges of coughs, which are everywhere. Human coughing, as much as truck gears and scooter farts, is the soundtrack of today's China.[1]

Downstream from the Three Gorges Dam, the valley unspools in knots of rust and bleached greens. Every few hundred meters, a plot of furled bok choy tapers into an apartment complex, which abuts a clanging gasworks, which rattles and whooshes alongside the beached hulk of a red container ship long since hauled out of the river and dumped. And in between them all jut little fingers of ripening rice. There's no distinction between town and industry, countryside and junkyard. China has embraced the concrete mixer school of planning.

Chinese smog isn't the woolly, grey blanket that smothered Western cities when they awoke, hungover, from decades of too much coal and diesel. Nor is it the greasy haze that sticks to summer asphalt. Rather, it sinks, grey toothed, into crannies of leaf and human skin, dusting people's lungs and hanging on the backs of buildings like mold. It's smog not as a choking cocoon, but as a totality of air and land and water, as muddy sky and gassy earth. Less than a half mile from the road, between the weeds and cinder blocks, a carnival ground drips with neglect, but even from this little distance the top of the Ferris wheel is lost in an inky swaddle.

Buried in the smog is one of the most important scientific laboratories on Earth. Even though this is a premier research facility, it's no sterile bunker sealed with airlocks and bathed in disinfectant, and while it's engaged in one of the most vital biological experiments of the twenty-first century, there are no high-voltage fences. In fact, it looks like a plain clump of rice paddies surrounded by miles of identical rice paddies. The lone hint that it's something more is a flaking metal tank draped with scaffolds and painted with the Roman letters FACE: "Free-Air Concentration Enrichment."

The scientists here are growing rice, and they're careful to mimic the precise methods and tools used by millions of other Chinese rice farmers. The difference is what's locked inside the giant tank. Through a tangle of pipes and dials, the scientists are slowly choking their crop with a steady ooze of carbon dioxide and ozone. Their intention is to simulate the exact atmospheric conditions that computer models predict will smother the earth within the next fifty years, and they want to know if food can grow in it. They're going to see whether our future skies will ruin our daily bread.

Other researchers have conducted similar tests in laboratories, blasting single plants with poisons and ticking off their degrees of wilt. But isolated samples are little use for predicting the future of a whole planet. Crops don't grow under hermetic lock and germ-free bubble. They're shaken by rain and chewed by larvae, burned by heat waves and shadowed by untimely clouds. So the petri dishes are largely irrelevant, leaving the FACE experiment as the world's most educated guess at how our food will grow in coming generations.[2]

The FACE conclusions aren't necessarily self-evident. Carbon dioxide, while galling for animals and a major cause of climate change, has a bracing effect on plant growth. Plants like it, and they grow bigger when they're gassed. So while heat and drought will hurt the green things of the earth, the clogged, muggy air of the twenty-first century will actually help them bloom in a process called carbon dioxide fertilization. What the results will be of the interaction between climate change (probably a bad thing) and carbon dioxide fertilization (probably a good thing) is one of the great unanswered questions of the twenty-first century.[3]

Less encouraging for rice farmers is the ground-level ozone resulting from motor vehicles, a gas that stunts and smothers vegetation. Since there aren't yet any major projections of global food production that estimate the damage inflicted by ozone pollution—this despite ozone's threat to about a quarter of the earth's land surface—we can't calculate the planet's future bounty with any real confidence. But we've already felt a small measure of what's to come. In 2008, the Royal Society calculated that ozone pollution destroys between $2 billion and $4 billion of arable crops each year in the United States alone.[4]

The Chinese FACE experiment will take years of tallying poisons and jotting up comparative growth models before its scientists utter any conclusive words of doom. But the Yangtze Valley rice station is only one of many FACE stations throughout the world, some of which have already published dour reports. "Current projections of global food security are overoptimistic," is a typical conclusion.[5] They also say that ozone is more dangerous than was once thought. And vegetable life is more precarious.

The farms of the lower Yangtze Valley, in the delta that ultimately broadens out to encompass Shanghai, look nothing like the tilled infinity of the American Midwest, let alone the clipped softness of England or the green geometry of the Île-de-France. Though cultivated by human hands for longer than any other place on earth, they're a rumpled carpet of green and tan, of tufted rice sprouting on every conceivable stretch of soil between the dirt tracks and the freeways.

Rice is everywhere. November is the late harvest, and the paddies have been drained, leaving the plants to brown in the grey autumn air. Knives in hand, villagers lope into the fields to cut the stalks and pile them in handfuls, which they flog against the tops of wooden tubs or on the rungs of ladders. This shakes loose the seeds, which the farmers pour into handcarts and wheel to the nearest road. Mindful of traffic, the farmers rake the rice across the pavement, spreading it to dry as cars and buses slowly crunch through the kernels, casting them up in mounds and spinning wheels in ruts jammed with long grains. It's not just the roads that are used to dry rice. A UN report says that "sports game and open-air courts" are also commonly used for this sort of impromptu food processing.[6] In the world's most populated country, no flat surface can go to waste. Besides, the tires loosen the seeds from the bran.

After the road rice dries, the villagers rake it into bags to be carted to an unlit dirt-floored barn where, under rafters simmering with spiders, they thresh it with a diesel engine attached to a drum. This job takes time and a tolerance for gas fumes as the machine puffs rice dust into the cobwebs, which drape low with chaff. Dogs nose at the door, not daring to venture near the din. Compared to the industrial farms of America with their satellite imaging and robotic tractors, Chinese rice farms are ineffective, even quaint. The effect is compounded by demographics. Nearly everyone young enough to hold a factory position moves away from the villages, so the farmers are uniformly old—troops of elderly women and men on bicycles, armed with sickles.

Despite its inefficiencies, this system's accomplishments are remarkable. The 2007 rice harvest yielded 187 million tons—significantly ahead of China's needs.[7] Obesity is rising in the cities and diabetes wards are becoming more crowded. In particular, the Chinese are eating more meat. In 1989, an average city-dwelling Chinese person swallowed 21 percent of his daily dietary energy in fat and 66 percent in carbohydrates. By 1997, that percentage had floated up to 33 percent fats, with most of this change due to higher meat consumption.

A hearty meal today—say, a business lunch with the suits from a company that sells hothouse orchids to Shanghai—is a festival of protein. Ten meat dishes are the norm: duck's tongues wrapped around slender forked toothpicks; whitefish simmered at the tableside in a sauce of Szechuan peppercorns (natural anesthetics that go down like little nips of novocaine); bulging, slick dumplings, sizzled in lard; a ground pork turnover quick-fried in a nest of garlic shoots; slices of top round thickly sauced; shrimp, pork, chicken, beef. Only after the meat courses do noodles and rice appear, settling like mortar into the remaining nanometers of the stomach cavity. It's a banquet worthy of an allosaurus.

Compare this, then, with the Chinese wedding feast that appears in Pearl S. Buck's 1931 novel *The Good Earth*. In that different age, a cook stretches the capabilities of two pounds of pork, bought with the savings from months of labor. She combines "sugar and vinegar and a little wine and soy sauce" to bring forth "all the force of the meat itself."[8] Aggressive saucing remains a hallmark of Chinese cuisine, but today, affluent Chinese no longer follow the old rule of eating a mouthful of rice with every bite of meat. It's hard to imagine a Chinese mother today making her daughter clean her plate by threatening the curse in Maxine Hong Kingston's *The Woman Warrior:* each leftover grain would be a pockmark on the face of her future husband.

In China, as in the West, gluttony is no longer a source for shame.

CHICKEN LITTLE OR A LOT OF CHICKEN?

The Chinese own some impressive technology, namely the same miraculous seeds that farmers from Maine to Mumbai have adopted in recent years, seeds specially bred by agro-industrial firms. These high-yielding incarnations of wheat, rice, and maize, while wonderfully bountiful, don't work unless they're smothered in fertilizer, water, and pesticides. The same goes for the next generation of seeds, the infamous genetically modified crops that are starting to appear on farms worldwide. In its frenzy to grow, China embraced these seeds and doused its earth in enough chemical nitrogen to eclipse every other country for the title of Most-Fertilized Nation.[9]

Engineering, too, has worked marvels in concrete. Almost as astonishing as the Three Gorges Dam is the South-North Water Transfer Project, a public works initiative of pharaonic proportions. Scheduled to take fifty years to complete, it pledges nothing less grandiose than a wholesale shift of water from China's damp southern regions to the relatively arid north. As with the Three Gorges, the project is so enormous that it's an abstraction: thousands of miles of canals funneling 44.8 billion cubic meters of water per year, linking the Yangtze, Yellow, Huaihe, and Haihe rivers.[10]

The bulging contents of Chinese refrigerators are a testament not only to the prowess of modern seeds and chemicals, but also to state agricultural edicts. The government has been giving cash incentives to farmers to adopt the new technologies, and the bribes have paid off. A few decades ago, the idea of Chinese abundance seemed laughable, if not heartless in light of the misery of the Great Leap Forward. China's people were malnourished, importing food to survive. In the 1970s, however, the Communist government started to experiment with free enterprise in the form of the Household Responsibility System, in which farmers were allowed to grow surplus food and sell it for profit. Free trade and food trade were like rainfall on parched ground. While the West took the better part of two centuries to ratchet up food production to the abundance where we can kill ourselves with corn syrup, the Chinese did it in a few decades.

In the wake of all this development, productivity, and the biggest water-transfer project since the Great Flood, China's agricultural future may finally be secure. Perhaps only Cassandras see apocalypse in an Asian drought. Yet grim prophecies persist, as crop yields, on a per capita basis, are declining just as demand rises.[11] The increased harvests brought about by new seeds have come and gone in China and the West, and short of a yet-to-be-realized genetically modified miracle, there's not much foreseeable room for improvement. Climate change looms. In the face of heat, crowding, and the dwindling efficacy of our magic seeds, the world has no answers on how to keep the buffet open indefinitely.

This isn't China's problem alone. It's everyone's. The loudest Cassandras are the neo-Malthusians, echoing the gloom of the nineteenth-century Reverend Thomas Malthus, who observed the Irish and noted that overpopulation among people, as among all animals, leads to calamity.[12] Stanford biologist Paul Ehrlich, a butterfly specialist, is prominent among these voices,[13] arguing that "continuing to expand harvests is likely to prove difficult because the inherent constraints of a finite world will increasingly come into play."[14] To put it simply, the Malthusians figure that we can't grow more food than we do now because the planet can't support it.

The Malthusians are opposed by a cheerier camp called the techno-optimists, who echo the ideas of the late University of Maryland economist Julian Simon, arguing that the world's booming population represents humanity's triumph over death. There is an irony, he remarked, in seeing Armageddon at a time when the earth is more fruitful than in all of its history.[15] With the enormous exception of Africa, the twentieth century proved Simon (and his fellow optimists) right. Simon and Ehrlich even made a friendly wager in the 1980s on whether commodity prices would rise due to scarcity. Simon bet they would go down, and he won.

So long as the chemist, the hydraulic engineer, and the crop scientist keep ahead of the troubles of nature, Simon may have the final word. China certainly thinks so, and it is investing in sprawling fertilizer factories, plant genetics labs, and the South-North Water Transfer Project, betting that technology can win the race against population and climate change so long as it's coupled to the food trade. In 2008, the Communists reversed decades of policy and allowed farmers to lease land to one another, laying the legal foundations for a familiar pattern of consolidation. One of the costs of this is a swelling urban population, as landless peasants look for jobs in town and spend their wages to buy rice—rice that's grown on land their fathers had once tilled.[16]

But this is a small price to pay for the benefits brought by full modernization. Modernization means no more drying rice on the open face of a busy public thoroughfare, no 7 percent annual loss of crops to scavenging insects and rats, no infinite man-hours wasted on Iron Age farm technology. Instead, China will go shopping. When it does, the world is going to need to breed better plants and build more irrigation, boil up more potent fertilizers, and create more efficient shipping routes and storage depots. It's going to need all this to meet the demand.

But even if that's technically possible, is it sustainable?

CHAPTER FOUR

Water: Irrigation's Questionable Cure

The moral price of slavery wasn't lost on a sixteenth-century soul like Francesco Carletti, even though he was a businessman. When the time came to mark his seventy-five "Moors" with a silver brand heated in the flame of a tallow candle, he quailed at the thought of putting fire to baptized flesh. He could hardly avoid the conclusion that burning, chaining, and selling people was a sin, and his fears were reinforced when, during the Atlantic crossing, he had to dump seven bodies into the sea after a rash of "a flux of the blood." But Carletti kept his mind on profits, taking comfort in the certainty that God knew he really felt awful about the whole business.[1]

Sailing west from Cape Verde, it took the Carlettis, *père et fils,* thirty days to make landfall at Cartagena. Antonio, lacking colonial travel documents, sneaked ashore while his son greeted the Spanish customs inspectors, who immediately threw him into prison for slaving without a license. This was a trumped-up charge, concocted to extort money, and within a few days, a ship arrived in port carrying the correct paperwork. The Italians were off to a grim start. Worse was to come. Both fell sick with a tropical fever, and the price of slaves bottomed out of the market. The Carlettis lost 40 percent of their capital, and, even though the fever soon passed, their finances would take much longer to recover.

Instead of returning to Spain empty-handed, they decided to chance the rest of their money on a cargo of manufactured goods bound for Nombre de Dios, the gateway to Panama and the Pacific, 230 miles to the west. In Cartagena, Carletti wrote of the excellent local pork and spiderfish. Nombre de Dios offered nothing better than tasteless bread from maize ("Turkish grain"), giant toads, bats, and mosquitoes. The Italians didn't linger but loaded their goods into riverboats and set out across the isthmus in search of better prices and trading opportunities in Panama. It was a hard journey, spoiled by rockslides and a diet of roast bananas. They took a mule train across the jungle, often wading in mud up to their bellies, "with such weariness and misery that we thought never to reach the desired city of Panama." But in September of 1594, they did.

In the late sixteenth century, Panama was a town of cattle barons. The local supply of rich, inexpensive veal deeply impressed Carletti, who wrote that the colonists' diet was so opulent that they ate beef on Sabbath and during Sundays, Tuesdays, and Thursdays in Lent. "This is permitted because of the lack in that place of fish," he noted, even though Panama is a coastal city. The Spaniards ate steak on holy days, it seems, because they could.

After a few months of heavy dinners, the Carlettis had fortified themselves enough to undertake the most harrowing stretch of their journey: a twelve-hundred-mile ride in an open boat down the coast of South America to Peru. A steady, contrary wind blew up from the south, so the trip took two and a half months of patient sailing and tacking. The wretched passengers marinated in salt, froze in storms, and poached under the equatorial sun. Antonio nearly died of exposure, but after about eighty days of torment, father, son, and cargo arrived at Lima, the chief city of a "kingdom of infinite provinces."

There, Carletti ordered a salad. Astounded by the complexity of the pre-Columbian ditch systems, he gaped at the Peruvian lettuces, "with leaves incomparably longer than ours."[2] Rightfully, he attributed this to the quality of Incan waterworks:

> *[The wonderful horticulture results], I think, from its never raining in that region and from the strength of the sun, which nonetheless is tempered by the water that they bring from the rivers, irrigating with it the fields and whatever land they want to use for the sowing and other cultivation. The crops, again, become fattened by those waters, which come from the mountains, most often turbulently*

because up there it rains a lot. And in that way they bring all their crops to perfection, and in such abundance that in many places they reap wheat twice each year.[3]

Carletti was equally impressed by another example of New World irrigation. After selling their goods in Lima, they returned north and stopped in Mexico, where they marveled at the Aztec floating gardens, fields that had been constructed on the surfaces of shallow canals:

There are many canals of water which flow by diverse routes . . . above these canals they make fields on branches woven together . . . they move these fields from one place to another, now into the shade, now into the sun, as they please or have need to do. And there they cultivate diverse things with much artfulness.[4]

What Carletti describes is almost certainly a form of agriculture known today as *chinampa* farming, a hydrological feat that provided the material basis for Aztec civilization. In the early years of the Aztec Empire, before the spread of the technique, cities like Tenochtitlán drew their food from the hinterlands and sold it in daily markets that drew thousands of shoppers.[5] Mexico is naturally blessed with a bewildering variety of produce, but toward the late pre-Columbian period, the region's huge urban populations needed to eat more than the hinterlands could grow. Although the empire's rulers sometimes used human porters to truck grain from faraway fields into the urban centers, the city's throngs required a more efficient way to put maize on the table. *Chinampa* farming was the answer.[6]

A sixteenth-century source describes the process:

Using canoes, workers ferried squares of sod into the middle of shallow, swampy lakes. For seed beds, they laid the sod onto floating reed mats, forming blocks of arable ground separated by narrow canals. These islands could be moved around to capture the sun and allowing for early germination. Larger, more permanent islands were built in a similar way and supported everything from groves of fruit trees to fields of maize.[7]

Evidence of beans, squash, chili peppers, Mexican cherries, hawthorn, and prickly pear have all turned up in the remains of these lake farms, which might have covered some nine thousand hectares. Irrigation, more than armies or temples, was the foundation of Aztec society, art, law, and science.[8]

Earlier Mesoamericans hadn't fared so well at producing food. In the eighth century, classical Mayan cities like Tikal and Palenque replaced their neighboring jungles with maize fields, but clear-cutting and intensive farming trapped them in a broken hydrological cycle. So when the rains stopped falling on the Yucatán around the year 800, the fields dried up. Drought may not have been the only reason the Mayans abandoned their monumental stone cities, but it wouldn't have encouraged anyone to stay. Over time, the populations filtered into the wetter highlands, where they remained.[9]

Today, quiet pyramids still lord over the archaeology in these classical Mayan ruins, and if the security guards permit, a tourist can risk a broken ankle and climb the steps to look out across an unending haze of green. The jungle washes up against the parking lots and souvenir stalls at places like Tikal, where howler monkeys perch above the tourist buses. But the land here was once cut with farms and furrows. It was once a tame country, until the rains failed and the maize vanished with it. And then so did the cities, the people likely flowing back into the countryside to rummage for a less urbane diet.

Drought has been an existential problem for agricultural societies ever since they first appeared. Rain clouds, even today, are a fickle basis for a civilization, and so it's fitting that one of history's earliest civilizations defined itself by how it adapted to the whims of atmospheric pressure.

MESOPOTAMIA'S FIX

One of the more familiar images on television nowadays is that of an American soldier, shellacked in battle dress and sand dust, his eight-thousand-pound Humvee growling under a bleached Iraqi sun. Behind him stand ancient walls, knocked to pieces by mortars and riven by high explosives.

It's such a common picture that it's slipped into cliché, a shorthand for everything from the dollar tag at the gas nozzle to Yankee hubris. Even as army helicopters set down in Babylon, their rotor blades shaking the old bricks into powder, the story of those old bricks is forgotten among the headlines of bombs and body counts.

Six thousand years ago, Iraq was the superpower sending expeditionary forces to seize natural resources and coerce other countries into lopsided trading pacts. Its power was agricultural, and this depended on control of a vital strategic asset: the water in the Tigris and Euphrates rivers. Around 3500 B.C., the Sumerians carved through the muddy flats around these rivers, constructing a dense mesh of dikes and ditches that converted swamps into arable fields and gave the Sumerians one of the world's first stable agricultural surpluses (China had the other).

Barley, and the web of roads, shipping lanes, and trading relationships that turned it into wealth, built the walls of Uruk and composed the *Epic of Gilgamesh*. The Sumerians eventually ruined their environment, alienated their workers, overheated their economy, and spread their army too thin for it to prop up the flailing body of the state, but they started well, making the Fertile Crescent fertile.

From about 7000 B.C., human beings lived in the uplands of the Tigris and the Euphrates (the name "Mesopotamia" is from the Greek for "between rivers"). Agriculture slowly took root, starting as a rain-fed system that likely emerged when the climate in the region dried out and made foraging more arduous.[10] The farmers spread southward, into the nutrient-rich alluvial flood plain between the two rivers, where, perhaps inspired by the runnels spreading outward from the riverbanks, they concocted the novel idea of digging irrigation canals. Over the centuries, the landscape changed into a patchwork of emerald wheat, turning gold as it ripened in the scalding sun.

One of the first cities to arise in the floodplain (one of the first cities to arise anywhere) was Uruk. By 3000 B.C., it stood as a testament to the political weight of a grain surplus, its colossal stone walls guarding huge ziggurats, temples, and palaces that flaunted the might of their priest kings. Uruk was a place of stunning wealth by the standards of the Neolithic period, although most of the benefits were hoarded by a sliver of the population. That wealth began with a food surplus, but by the third millennium B.C., its owners had locked it into a very profitable system of roads, caravans, sailboats, and middlemen. Uruk and its neighbors were rich on account of the food trade.

To sell their food, the Sumerians used three main trading routes. The Euphrates led to Syria and Anatolia in the north and northwest. To the east, land routes linked Mesopotamia to the Iranian plateau. Southern roads led to the Persian Gulf and the regions of Dilmun, Magan, and Meluhha. Each route was a conduit for all the material pleasures known to the Bronze Age: metals, textiles, semiprecious stones, ivory, woods and reeds, cereals, alliaceous vegetables like garlic and onions, condiments, oils, unguents, resins, shells, and probably pearls, as well as a small array of finished products made of wood, metal, or stone. Of the three trading routes that the Mesopotamian aristocracy used to feed their appetite for luxuries, the most important was the southern, which led to the Persian Gulf and its Indian ports. Oxcarts loaded with grain rumbled down the trading road, to be loaded onto boats and delivered to eastern tribes and villages.

In exchange the Mesopotamians got copper. Around the dawn of the second millennium B.C., once the city of Akkad had squashed its competitors for dominance of the region, the Akkadians replaced their old stone sickles and tools with copper and paid for their copper with food.

The scale of the grain trade at this time is astonishing. Records from about 2100 B.C. document a 21,000-liter grain shipment; 714,000 liters are mentioned in another. Considering that the daily barley ration in Uruk at this time was 1 to 2 liters per person, such a cargo could have fed the largest known Bronze Age community on the Persian Gulf (Qala'at al-Bahrain) for nearly half a year. So we can guess that the coastal people lived on a diet of Mesopotamian cereals, paying for their daily bread with copper ore that they shunted out of inland mines. The coastal towns grew larger and the inland ones grew richer, with kings roosting over the burgeoning temple treasuries.[11]

To keep this system working, the Mesopotamians had to be attentive to their fields. The earliest irrigation works in the Fertile Crescent were simple ditches, but later generations showed a mania for brickwork. They lined the canals with fired yellow bricks, laying down a grid that, by the year 1800 B.C., covered ten thousand square miles.[12] These canals were the basis of Sumerian power and food security, which became the basis for the Sumerian food empire, the greatest in the world at the time. With one exception.

IN PRAISE OF GRAIN

A long time ago in China, a woman named Jiang-Yuan went for a walk in the countryside. As she strolled under the pines and through green, quiet hollows, she came upon a curious indentation in the ground. It was shaped like a man's foot, but it was far too big to have been made by one of the peasants from her village. It looked like the mark of a giant. Not knowing that it had been made by the foot of the Jade Emperor himself, Jiang-Yuan stepped into the impression and, to her understandable surprise, conceived a child.

When she gave birth to the boy, her neighbors suggested that she leave the infant to die in the forest as he was bound to be unlucky. Jiang-Yuan sorrowfully agreed. She took her son out into the woods and left him there, hoping at least that his end would be quick.

It wasn't. Wild creatures protected the child, who was called Qi, "the Castaway." A flock of birds fluttered above him, sheltering him from the elements with their wings, then lifted him in their talons to fly him back to his mother. Seeing her son borne home in such an unorthodox fashion, Jiang-Yuan realized that she had made a terrible mistake, embraced the boy, and raised him as a mother should.

His early exposure to nature created a lifelong bond, and from a tender age, Qi was always picking at the ground, tugging at leaves and roots and sniffing the juices from herbs. He had a particular knack with wild grains, which he coaxed to grow tall and full. People called him Hou Ji, the Prince of Millet.

This story comes from a volume called the *Shi Jing* (*The Book of*

Odes), parts of which date to about 1000 B.C. (although some of the poems were likely inspired by much earlier stories). One of these poems describes Hou Ji's flair with beanstalks, hemp, rice, and wheat and how he taught the Chinese the secret of agriculture:

> *Having cleared away the thick grass,*
> *He sowed the ground with the yellow cereals.*
> *He managed the living grain, till it was ready to burst;*
> *Then he used it as seed, and it sprang up;*
> *It grew and came into ear;*
> *It became strong and good;*
> *It hung down, every grain complete—*
> *And thus he was appointed lord of Tai.*
> *He gave his people the beautiful grains—*
> *The black millet, and the double-kernelled:*
> *The tall red, and the white.*
> *They planted extensively the black and the double-kernelled,*
> *Which were reaped and stacked on the ground.*
> *They planted extensively the tall red and the white,*
> *Which were carried on their shoulders and backs.*[13]

The legends say that Hou Ji became the ancestor of the Zhou dynasty, which ruled China for nearly a thousand years. As an agricultural deity, he lacks the dramatics of Persephone or the weirdness of Cybele; he's more of a Promethean instructor without gigantism or thunderbolts. Mythical Chinese agricultural heroes generally come across less like celestial powers than technicians. Stories connected with the Yellow Emperor, for instance, tell of the floods on the Yellow River being controlled not by divine command, but by the digging of canals. Another hero called Shennong, the "Emperor of the Five Grains," undertook the gargantuan task of tasting every plant in the world, cataloging which were good to eat, which were useful for planting, and which were poisonous. Like Hou Ji, Shennong is credited with teaching farming to the Chinese, along with the art of tea drinking.

Myth isn't history, but the legends do reflect what a godlike job it was to learn to recognize the edible parts of the natural world. Invariably, the societies that took the first, doddering steps toward civilization discovered Hou Ji's "beautiful grains," all of them grass seeds. High in vital carbohydrates, grass seeds contain lots of proteins, fats, and vitamins, but to flourish, these cereals must be planted and harvested during precise seasons. Conversely, root crops like potatoes can be planted several times a season, so long as there's a mild climate. To cultivate cereals well, a farmer has to be stable and disciplined, realizing that profit is proportionate to sweat. Excepting the vagaries of weather and insects, the most meticulous farmer—or the one who invents the cleverest plow—collects the biggest pile of grain.

Hou Ji's disciples learned that millet seeds, when buried in wet earth, sprouted into green shoots, yielding healthful kernels of grain that were easy to separate from the chaff. Other grasses—wheat, barley, rice—proved to be just as convenient in other places. With the exception of some of South America's Andean cultures,[14] every agricultural civilization in the world formed around the cousins of the grass family. South America was alone in its adherence to tubers, but while potatoes are more nourishing than grain and grow in a denser mass per hectare, they spoil quicker.[15] Grain sits well in clay pots and is durable enough to survive a long river journey or winter storage—transforming it into standing wealth and property. Potatoes in the same situation transform into slime.

The real proof that grain is civilization's miracle food is in its ubiquity. By 5000 B.C., farmers had turned the region around the middle parts of the Yellow River into a giant millet patch. At the same time, a few hundred miles to the south, a different cluster of river people were planting rice paddies along the Yangtze. Within a thousand years, hunting had declined in importance, farmers had invented increasingly elaborate tools, and brewers had begun to ply their craft. Most significantly, the Chinese no longer buried their dead in drab, boring holes. Tombs—an indicator of settled life—had come into vogue.[16]

As sedentary farming communities coalesced around fertile valleys and river fords, people took up the habit of trading things to eat—namely grain. Sometimes they carried seeds over long, even shocking distances. As early as 2500 B.C., Chinese farmers living near the northwest town of Xishanping were growing wheat—a foodstuff as alien to

China as the Twinkie. Wild emmer wheat (*Triticum dicoccoides*) is a Middle Eastern native, not an Asian one, and was the principal food of the Neolithic and Bronze Age peoples in Mesopotamia and Turkey.[17] Wheat stalks would have found it difficult to migrate across thousands of miles of hard, often mountainous, country, especially before the Silk Road opened. The seeds must have been carried to Xishanping by a person with an interest in food. There's no evidence of warfare between China and the Near East, so the wheat was probably traded peacefully across the entire length of Asia, which goes to show that imports, even 4,500 years ago, had a habit of spreading out across an ecosystem like an invasive species.[18]

Far from upsetting the balance of nature, however, these crops were a boon to early civilizations. The idea of a "native" crop is as meaningless in most cases as a "native" people. Our food, like ourselves, is the sum of very ancient migrations.

ORIENTAL DESPOTISM

Despite their admirable carbohydrates and easy growth, the actual grain plants cultivated by the early farmers had a severe design flaw. Domesticated grains are the wimps of botany. In the wild, only the toughest plants survive the assaults of insects, droughts, and natural competition. But the farmers who domesticated edible grass picked their specimens for seed size and ease of threshing, not for natural defenses. Without thorns or toxins, grasses are helpless in the face of a sparrow or a puff of mold spores. So farmers had to work hard at driving away antelope, frightening birds, yanking up weeds, and watering the roots of their delicate, overweight crops. Especially at watering. To survive, domesticated grains need a veritable deluge.

Water, more than a capable scarecrow or an active hand with the weeding, makes the difference between a reliable food supply and a field of barren straw. Water determines whether a surplus of grain will spur a farm to grow into a village, a village into a city. Plows and draft animals would have helped, too, but early farmers were utterly dependent on rain. Praying for lucky weather isn't a solid foundation for a civilization, of course, so the first food empires learned to irrigate.

A single shovel might dig a ditch, but an irrigation network across hundreds of hectares requires a society of shovels. Of workers, and hence of bosses. The Sumerians knew that agriculture breeds aristocrats (along with the marsh flies that flit above the canals.) Of course, Hou Ji wasn't called the Digger of Millet or even the Expert on Millet. He was the Prince of Millet.

As China emerged from its misty prehistory, the mythical Xia dynasty and the early Shangs gave way to the Zhou, who wrote China's first historical record. They left written letters, not simply shards and bones. The Zhou homeland was between the Yellow and Yangtze rivers, directly in the center of the agricultural revolution, and they tilled the sodden ground for nearly a thousand years (between 1122 and 256 B.C.).[19] As well as rich soil, useful plants, and navigable waterways, the Zhou possessed an abundance of buffalo, which they domesticated. They yoked plows on the shoulders of these animals and hauled earth from the irrigation ditches they laid across the floodplains. Controlling the water supply to a field allowed the Zhou to grow more grain, which they traded by loading it onto riverboats that threaded up a chain of toll stations to countless settlements along the banks.[20]

The revenues padded the pockets of an urban elite who fought wars against one another but who also wrote and painted and thought about the meaning of the blossoming human world around them—a world that could not have flourished without the twin pillars of trade and irrigation. There's an unsavory fact, however, at the heart of the Zhou flowering, which echoes what was taking place in the Fertile Crescent. Irrigation canals are horribly difficult to dig and maintain, particularly when they extend for hundreds of miles in a coordinated network. As in Mesopotamia, they required a legion of diggers and an authority to give the project cohesion. But the diggers didn't share in the profits made possible by their incessant shoveling. The aristocrats had to force them to do their jobs. After all, human beings are not badgers. We aren't molded to stoop.

The misery of digging is a theme in the *Atrahasis,* the longest of the Mesopotamian flood poems (naturally, the world's great irrigators had a whole genre of poetry about water). The poem begins with a scene of the gods digging the original irrigation ditches, the Tigris and the Euphrates:

The gods had to dig out the canals
Had to clear channels, the lifelines of the land,
The gods dug out the Tigris river bed
And then they dug out the Euphrates.[21]

Even for divine beings, digging is a grueling business. So the lesser gods, sick of sweating over their shovels, decided to go on strike, and only resolved their labor dispute by subcontracting the job. The gods created human beings, the poem tells us, for the sole purpose of doing their dirty work for them.[22]

This myth makes an important point about the nature of agriculture. It's no fun. The invention of farming and urban civilization didn't improve the daily lives of most human beings—actually, it shortened lifespans, inflicted chronic malnutrition, caused disease to fester, and condemned nearly the entire population to Adam's infamous curse. Farming a light subsistence crop in the highlands, picking mushrooms, and hunting the odd gazelle would have surely been more attractive.

Archaeologists have proven that nearly every early agricultural center suffered a plunge in the quality of diet as the farmers switched from fresh meat and vegetables to gruel made from the seeds from grass plants. Apart from the loss of pleasure, the new menu caused tooth decay—no small misery in the predentistry era. Also, most grain crops are deficient in some micronutrient or other. Maize, for instance, lacks essential amino acids, while milled grains like millet and wheat lack iron. Rice is useless as a source for protein, and since a lack of protein inhibits the body's ability to use vitamin A, Asian farmers lost their eyesight.

Furthermore, the agricultural revolution stunted children's growth rates. An analysis of juvenile long bones from Neolithic sites shows declines in length and density over the periods when farming took root. Hunter-gatherer skeletons are far more strapping than those of settled laborers, and it's only since the Industrial Revolution that we've regained the stature of our ancestors from ten thousand years ago.

The litany of farmhouse pains goes on.[23] Diseases like tuberculosis and bone inflammations were part of the new lifestyle, incubating in cramped rooms that lacked fresh air and spread by the agriculturalists' habit of mingling with livestock. Worse, the actual farmwork ground away the laborers' joints and contorted their backs. Worst of all, while hunter-gatherers had to work an average of twenty hours per week, farmers toiled for an inhumane forty to sixty hours. To rest, and indeed to survive, they needed feast days and religious excuses for slacking. Agriculture is what gave the world an immovable division between work and play.

Another of agriculture's curses was warfare.[24] Our earliest acts of organized violence might well have been undertaken in the name of feeding hungry families, perhaps in a village where the crops had failed but the scythes remained sharp. Farmers are far more willing to join gangs and commit organized murder than are hunter-gatherers. This may be partly because grain surpluses are an incentive for war as well as a resource for waging it—soldiers need feeding, and they can't fight when they're running after bison. Advanced agriculturalists, too, are organized, accustomed to discipline, and have "sunk costs" in their land. They can never turn the other cheek if a neighbor provokes them, since they've invested their whole existence in their farms. Faced with the threat of homicide, hunter-gatherers have the option of walking to a distant, more peaceable place to scrounge for berries. Agriculturalists must fight to the death. The elite of the ancient world, therefore, protected their magnificent jade statuary and bronze axes by hiring standing armies and keeping their treasures under lock, key, and savage legal edict.[25]

Finally, while agriculturalists may not have invented sexism, they did institutionalize it.[26] Historian Elise Boulding claims that in most hunter-gatherer societies, food was gathered rather than hunted, meaning that it was collected by the womenfolk. Women's role as breadwinners (fruitwinners?) gave them status, and since no one owned much more than a few strips of leather or flint, strong-armed men weren't needed much to fight over property. Not that there was anyone to fight, since hunter-gatherer groups likely kept their numbers down through infanticide and long years of breast-feeding. Academics debate details, but pre-agriculturalists probably lived in small egalitarian groups that had little temptation to kill and oppress one another.[27]

Around 10,000 B.C., the big, edible animals began to disappear from the human menu, and women's work became even more important for survival. Boulding suggests that when early "agro-villages" grew to contain more than a few hundred people, they became trading centers where the men—now underemployed due to a lack of mammoth—learned to trade commodities rather than produce them. Women farmed, men traded, which gave men an avenue to make their economic mark in society, while women remained entrenched in their ancient role. Agriculture may well have been an early step in the millennial tradition of male chauvinism.[28]

So why did our ancestors commit themselves to eons of drudgery, just for the sake of cereals? They probably had no choice. The Neolithic tribes that learned a knack for gardening were able to feed more babies. Over a few generations, their offspring outnumbered the children of their neighbors who were still chasing antelope. As the gardeners plucked weeds and killed or domesticated the local wildlife, the ecosystem changed. It became softer, more receptive to farming. This Neolithic revolution altered both the "nature" of humanity and of the Earth.

Another reason people took up farming is because the weather made them do it. Until 8000 B.C., the Fertile Crescent was too cold to yield much green, but then a few centuries of clammy rainfall made the land sprout. Populations grew. But when the clouds moved away again and the land turned brown, the wandering tribes all converged on the same damp patches, looking to stake a claim. Since the easy resources weren't enough to feed all the rovers, some of them must have adapted by hunkering down on riverbanks and settling there—they became sedentary. Others adapted by killing the people in their way. Whatever happened, the foundations for law, aristocracy, and government had been set. Human beings had learned to sit still.

There was no going back. If a wistful youth in a farming clan had looked at the open prairie and thrown down his spade to wander the hills like his ancestors, he would have starved. Agriculture changed the ecosystem through co-evolutionary adaptation, which means that domesticated plants, which lacked thorns and toxins to defend themselves, had replaced the wild species.[29] Without the help of human hands, the edible plants couldn't survive. Bad diets and painful farmwork were better than no food and death on the range.

Once the farms bloomed into cities, a bruising social inequity was created. In China and Sumer, a permanent majority underclass tilled the fields and repaired canals and dikes, supporting a tiny group of oligarchs. It wasn't so different from the sweatshop economies of today's developing world. Whereas hunter-gatherers had strolled under the Paleolithic stars in a state of rough egalitarianism, the sedentary farmers had kings.

Oppression didn't happen immediately. The earliest known city in the world was Çatal Hüyük in Anatolia, whose people lived in a cluster of homes that were more or less identical in size and austerity. If they had political leaders, they didn't have social betters. The same is true for the earliest Sumerian towns. But that changed with agricultural surpluses. Mesopotamia at its height was a land of palaces and slums, where some people were born as living gods, but most were slaves.[30] The same thing happened in China, Egypt, India, and the Americas. Like worms hatching in an apple, agricultural surpluses—stable wealth—invariably had the effect of breeding absolute monarchs.

Historian Karl Wittfogel uses these examples to argue that the Chinese and Sumerian ditches are history's first example of a coercive government, and that coercion is one of the pillars of civilization. Dictatorships are needed, like a well-placed coffee table, for civilization to lean on as it takes its baby steps. Wittfogel called this "oriental despotism," and while his theory today is sloughed off as too simplistic (after all, other civilizations emerged that were neither oriental nor despotic), the Zhou dynasty and Mesopotamian Empire were both undeniably strong, successful governments.[31]

RETREAT OF THE ELEPHANTS

As agriculture debased the human body and drove wedges into society, it took a similar toll on the planet. The most obvious environmental casualty of these unfurling tracts of grain was wildlife. In China, for example, elephants had roamed freely until the rise of the Zhou when, in the flurry of tillage, the animals became an antisocial pest. Farmers viewed them as enormous, leaden-footed thieves, nosing at their crops, so they speared them. The trespassing elephants died in such numbers that trunk meat entered the Zhou menu, and gourmets learned to prize it for its similarity in taste to piglet. A later writer noted that villagers "competed to eat their trunks, the taste of which is said to be fatty and crisp, and to be particularly well suited to being roasted."[32]

But the worst damage was to forests. Deforestation bedeviled the ancients even before the Greeks and Romans. The Zhou, for instance, swept away woodlands in massive bouts of logging, clearing space for fields, piling the cut wood to build ships and towns and to burn it in the cook fires of the swelling Chinese populace.

In Mesopotamia, upstream woodcutting loosened the hilly topsoil (as did the grazing of goats), and rain washed the dirt into the Sumerians' beloved canals. Work gangs spent incalculable hours damming the clogged waterways, digging out the silt, hauling it away, and then releasing the waters again. A myth about the incessant Mesopotamian battle against water tells of a primordial sea goddess named Tiamat, who, furious at the death of her freshwater lover Apsu, engendered a brood of monsters to take revenge on the gods. When the gods eventually defeated her, they split her body in two to form the heavens and the earth. The Sumerians, being preoccupied with harnessing rivers, viewed water as both an ancient enemy and the basis of human life.[33]

While slave labor can build a pyramid or dredge a nation of canals, Mesopotamia's problem of soil chemistry had no obvious fix. When water moves through soil, it collects sodium. Irrigation water left in 120-degree Middle Eastern sunshine evaporates, leaving this sodium as a white residue clinging to the surface clay of the grain fields. Salt starves the earth by blocking vital minerals, like nitrogen, from latching on to soil particles, leaving them to wash out to sea with the next rainfall. When the Romans wanted to truly obliterate Carthage, they sowed salt on its grain fields. To an acre of wheat, salt is murder.

Over the centuries, this annual salting destroyed Sumerian agriculture.[34] Between 3000 B.C. and 2350 B.C., fields had yielded about

2,000 liters per hectare, but by 2000 B.C. this had dropped to 1,134 liters. Within another three hundred years, the yields fell to a dismal 370 liters.[35] The withering was gradual, but Sumer's urban population hadn't shrunk along with the grain stores. Instead of selling their barley abroad, the city folk ate it. Exports suffered, as did the food trade as a whole. Desperate to make up the loss, farmers worked the fields harder, skipping the fallow years and planting more seeds, which in turn needed more water. So the salination cycle accelerated and Mesopotamia sank further into sterility.

Even the climate seemed complicit in ruining the land. The years 3100 B.C. to 1200 B.C. were particularly hot and dry in the Middle East, and farmers met the problem with heavier irrigation.[36] By 1700 B.C., the name "Fertile Crescent" had started to sound ironic as the area withered into the familiar dusty landscape of today. A contemporaneous poet wrote:

> *[The god] let milled foods be insufficient for the people*
> *vegetable food grew scant in their bellies . . .*
> *The field decreased its yield,*
> *repulsed the grain.*
> *[From being] black the tilth turned white*
> *the broad plain gave birth to wet-salt*
> *the womb of the Earth revolted*
> *no plants came up . . .* [37]

The Sumerian aristocracy was still ardent about its privileges, and as exports vanished, so did their supply of treats. Wheat was the first crop to disappear, unable to withstand the salinity. Barley, friendlier to salt, lasted longer; it's a favorite winter feed of sheep, herds of which the Sumerians bred for the wool exports that preserved (for a while) the influx of foreign baubles.

But the landscape, particularly in the south, couldn't be repaired. The exhausted, saline soil was dead. Another dry spell in the eleventh century B.C. pummeled the current masters of the Fertile Crescent, the Babylonians and Assyrians. Driven by famine, nomads from the north invaded and, after centuries of growth and expansion, the Fertile

Crescent was "plunged into a state of weakness from which it was not to recover until a century and a half later."[38]

THE YELLOWING RIVER

The Chinese, too, had troubles with water. After the Zhou came the Qin dynasty (bureaucratic, violent, known for its astounding terra-cotta armies), then the Han (brainy, commercial, known for its inventions of paper and hydraulics). Instead of mere spots of territory around the great rivers, the Qin and the Han ruled a solid mass of Asia that, thousands of years later, still constitutes the bulk of China. By the birth of Christ, the population of China had reached perhaps 55 million.[39] Around the same time, Rome and its territories were home to about 45 million.

To have gotten so crowded, the earth had to be fruitful. And for the most part, it was. Millet fields and rice paddies had spread across the breadth of China, taming a landscape that thrummed with preindustrial business. The Han dynasty in particular made a vigorous trade in foodstuffs. A quote from a 200 B.C. manuscript reads, "Rich traders and great merchants roved around the empire. No commodity was not in circulation." Another, from the same time, tells us:

> *Now the region west of the mountain is rich in timber, bamboo . . . The region east . . . has plenty of fish, salt . . . and cosmetics . . . The region south of the Yangtse River produces cinnabar, ginger . . . These are the things the Chinese like.*[40]

But something happened to change this vibrant market culture. We don't know what spurred the reversal—famine, the greed of kings—but the state decided to choke the free movement of goods. New policies restricted the peasantry from travel and forbade them from hunting in the mountains or fishing in the marshes. They also raised taxes to keep the peasants yoked to their plows. The official intent was nothing less than the imposition of serfdom, of binding laborers to the land and forcing them to grow grain. Farmers began to flee to the swamps and highlands, which filled with common people, who, in the words of one contemporary observer, "detest farming, are lazy."[41]

The Han emperors didn't impose serfdom out of malice, but to maintain the status quo and keep themselves rich and empowered.[42] In the twentieth century, academics named this sort of agricultural policy "command and control," but regardless of the moniker, it caused dreadful hardship. As the peasants chafed in semi-slavery, philosophers puzzled over how to explain, and in some cases assuage, their misery. One of them was Mencius, who pined for a more equitable past in which people could profit from their own labor.[43] Westerners might be surprised to learn that this ancient Confucian argued, too, for the natural right of subjects to overthrow a tyrant, no matter how blessed his lineage. Tom Paine had antecedents in Beijing.

But even then, the hand of government wasn't always heavy. In 119 B.C., a terrible flood on the Yellow River caused widespread famine and, for the next several years, the imperial authorities supplied 725,000 people with food and clothing until they could be relocated to drier ground. Admittedly, the government ended up using the refugees as a human bulwark against the nomadic hordes of northern barbarians, but it was still an impressive social relief program for the second century B.C.

One result of the Han repression of trade was the emergence of a casual, illicit market in foodstuffs. For hundreds of years, the authorities had seized merchants' assets, imposing monopolies on products like salt and policing everything from grain warehouses to the stalls that ladled rice into the shopping baskets of housewives. But despite the harsh strictures, they couldn't stop farmers from turning a personal profit. In the second century A.D., an educated gentleman farmer named Ts'ui Shih wrote a book called *Ordinances for the Four Peoples.* A sort of ancient Mandarin farmer's almanac, it recounts the agricultural cycle and annual rituals ("The sons, their wives, the grandchildren, and the great-grandchildren each present pepper [blossom] wine to the head of the household, to toast health and longevity").[44] Along with tips on when to harvest grass growing in sandy soil ("when the apricot blossoms are in full bloom"), it tells the reader how to get a good price for soybeans and the best strategies for negotiating a wheat purchase. The Han authorities, it seems, either turned a blind eye to the market, or simply had no means to shut it down.

The *Ordinances* also lists suggestions on what to do with these traded foodstuffs. A recipe to make pickling sauce, for example, states:

> *In the first ten days of the month, the soybean is fried; in the second ten days, the soybean is boiled. The chopped soybean is made for the mo-tu paste, which . . . is used for preserving melons, as well as for making fish sauces, meat sauce, and basic soy sauce.*[45]

The author put his cleverness and industry to better use, perhaps, in theory than in practice. Ts'ui Shih died too poor to afford a coffin, and his admirers footed the bill for his funeral. But his writings prove that the government's codes were observed in the breach, and they paint a picture of a vibrant agricultural market that lurked on the edges of state control. Under its formal edicts and the insistence of its rulers, there were free trade rumblings at the foundations of Han China.

During this time, the Yellow River earned its name. Between 200 B.C. and A.D. 200 it became clogged with the gradual runoff from the denuded grasslands and hillsides of the river valley, tinting the water a shade that a fashion catalog might dub ecru. Over the centuries, trees that had anchored the topsoil fell under the farmer's axe, and the grain stalks planted in their place couldn't keep the mud tamped down under heavy rains. So much soil washed into the river that its bed filled until the bottom was practically level with the once-dry banks. A complicated system of levees kept the Yellow River in its course, more or less, but flooding was a constant worry. According to historian Mark Elvin, catastrophic breaks occurred, on average, once every sixteen years between 186 B.C. and A.D. 153 and once every nine years during the wet decades between 66 B.C. and A.D. 34. Each time, thousands of people died.[46]

Eventually, the Han sputtered out through a combination of the usual culprits—civil war, inept emperors, calcified social divisions, barbarians. Food production slowed as the land wore out under generations of harvests. Reflecting the fall in food supplies, people had fewer babies, or their children died young. They began to rebel, and war disrupted the crop cycle. At the same time, a climatic cooling shriveled yields even further. Farms sank back into the grass. As barbarians wrested the northerly territories from the Han, they let the earth revert to a natural state, not bothering to set plows to soil. Forests grew in places that had been tilled for generations. China's food trade, and the country itself, entered one of those historical depressions called a dark age. Civilization had tired itself out for a time.

WATER, WATER EVERYWHERE?

Comparative history is a risky business because of the danger of inference, of pulling a false rabbit out of an anachronistic hat. Yet, it's possible to draw lessons out of details. For instance, we can read the victualing reports of La Grande Armée in 1812 and conclude "Never invade Russia with inadequate supply lines." In that spirit, here are a few quick generalizations about the ancient world's experience with agriculture and the food trade.

When hunter-gatherers settled on the ground above the Tigris, Euphrates, and Yellow rivers, they made a social pact that most people would spend their lives working, while a few lucky or strong ones would live as artists, priests, and kings. This agricultural pact only functioned as long as the farmers had good seeds and could water them. Water—either too much or too little—is the obsession of every food empire. Over time, none of the strategies farmers have used to control water have worked. Stability has been a glimmering illusion. It pours through our fingers.

We, in the twenty-first century, are not the ancient Chinese or Mesopotamians. Our food empire is founded on technological grounds far beyond the horizons of Uruk or Akkad, with their trowels and mud bricks. But our water supply today is also uncertain. The United Nations' Millennium Development Goals (a grand wonk's checklist of universal progress) says that water use is growing twice as rapidly as the planet's population and that about half of humanity is holding a glass that's half empty.[47] Other studies are more optimistic, insisting that "current global withdrawals [of fresh water] are well below the upper limit [of what's physically possible]," but even these concede that 2 billion people are struggling to find enough water.[48] Liquid wealth is unevenly spread. The "Water Poverty Index" measures not only the availability of water to populations in different parts of the world, but how much it costs to get it, whether it's piped out of treatment stations or dug out of slime holes, and whether it's spiked with cholera. Dry but developed countries like Israel, for example, score well on the index because good infrastructure means their citizens enjoy a dependable supply. Nearby Jordan, which has the same resources but worse infrastructure, is much thirstier.[49]

Human use isn't entirely responsible for the shortage. Worldwide, intensive agriculture leaves wider and wider swathes of soil degradation (the eternal villain), which create drought conditions.[50] With the loss of the organic matter that binds and buffers the topsoil, water seeps through the ground as if through a coffee filter, draining the nutrients past the plant roots.[51] In the vital wheat-farming region of northern China, for instance, harvests are increasingly dependent on lucky weather.[52] Since soil depleted of its sponge-like organic matter can no longer store up reserves of rainfall, China has resorted to massive, and dubious, irrigation projects.[53] Every shock to the ecological health of a region—whether it's overfarming or myopic agricultural policies—makes the land more vulnerable to a killing drought.[54] This was true in Ethiopia in the 1980s, and in John Steinbeck's Dust Bowl in the Depression-era Midwest.[55]

A final word from Cassandra: in the near future, eastern China, the Middle East, and southern Africa will dry up (while the bits that are already dry are going to get hotter). A 2007 report from the Intergovernmental Panel on Climate Change provides the sort of story that scientists read when they want a good scare. It's a rollicking yarn about snowmelt, river speed, soil type, and other hydrological variables, and its climax is a series of future projections in which the victims run out of water.[56] As we describe in chapter 2, the effects of climate change on the world's food supply may be devastating. For a while, places like Canada will benefit from a longer growing season, while areas closer to the equator (like the southern United States) will not.[57] Meanwhile, eastern North America, Europe, South Asia, and the rest of Africa all have to fix their dripping faucets or go thirsty.[58] And that's the optimistic forecast based on only a two-degree rise in mean annual global temperature. If it gets hotter, the whole world will lose productivity.[59]

Too much water will be just as great a threat as too little. The Three Gorges Dam's *raison d'être* isn't irrigation but flood control. Global warming is brewing up what meteorologists call "extreme weather events" that will increase in frequency as the earth bakes. Add melting glaciers[60] and receding coastlines, and between 2.7 and 6.9 billion people may live in water-stressed regions by 2050.[61] That's a conservative picture. Shriller voices predict that the thirsty billions will go to war over the remaining fresh water sources.[62]

Water has proved more valuable than gold before now. The Sumerians were the first people in history to come to blows over irrigation infrastructure, which they rightfully regarded with civic pride. A series of tablets from about 2500 B.C. tells the story of how the cities of Umma and Lagash clashed over a canal that marked the boundary between their respective fields. Urlumma, the strongman ruler of Umma, "drained the boundary canal of Ningirsu" and destroyed all the nearby temples and shrines before crossing the dry canal bed into Lagash's territory. "He was as puffed up as the mountains," observes the writer.

Urlumma's opponent, Enannatum of Lagash, met him at Ugigga, "the irrigated field." They had a great battle, leaving sixty Ummans dead "on the bank of the canal." Enannatum's son chased the vanquished Urlumma back into his own territory and slaughtered him.[63] In revenge, the Ummans vandalized Lagash's canals again, in return for which Lagash "wickedly flooded the diked and irrigated field."[64] And so on.

Apart from this Sumerian feud, however, history doesn't yield too many examples of war for water. Modern Israel and its neighbors provide practically the only other instance. Sandra Postel, director of the Global Water Policy Project, analyzed 1,831 water-related events from the last half of the twentieth century and determined that most of them were friendly. Water treaties are far more common than water coercion or water blackmail.[65] Perhaps it's the fluid nature of the subject, but water has a tendency to make us compromise. Even the Sumerians, ferociously as they behaved when sacking their neighbors' sacred buildings and draining their canals, were on the whole accustomed to sharing the flow of the Tigris and Euphrates. Without peace to cultivate their barley and trade it to India for copper, they would never have amounted to a historical success.

Likewise, the food trade—including water trade—is one of the best hopes that the world has for avoiding a grim future.[66] Apart from the blunt method of piping fresh water from suppliers to buyers, there's a subtler, but no less vital, trade in "virtual water." To produce a single kilogram of grain, a farmer needs to expend approximately one thousand to two thousand kilograms of water (industrially produced livestock are even more hydrologically expensive).[67] By looking at this virtual water embodied in every product sold within the global food trade, it's clear that countries like the United States and Canada export tremendous amounts of water (in the form of grain) to parched areas of North Africa and Asia.[68] Countries like Eritrea can't afford to waste precious local water supplies on growing plants as thirsty as wheat, so the food trade fills the gap, leaving local farmers free to grow labor-intensive (but water stingy) exports for cash. The dry countries receive food and conserve water, while the wetter ones receive fruits and luxury foods they don't produce themselves. Everyone revels in the glow of happy trade arrangements.[69]

Or so goes the theory. In reality, global dryness might simply raise the value of virtual water so that the muscular economic powers of the world will trade it among themselves, leaving the weakling markets out of the game. In this scenario, China hoards the world's imports, and Africa, again, disintegrates in suffering as it leaks millions of environmental refugees who destabilize the planet. The British military forecasts a future where "nearly two-thirds of the world's population will live in areas of water stress."[70] Even a group of high-ranking former American military officers—not exactly champions of environmental activism—published a report called *National Security and the Threat of Climate Change*. In its "factors for economic and security stability," it lists water second only to energy. The report also observes that two-thirds of the Arab world depends on water sources that are "external to their national borders."[71]

Water, as much as oil, is shaping the future of our global food empire.

CHAPTER FIVE

Dirt: The Chemistry of Life

It's unusual to remember your first potato. Frogs' legs, yes. Caviar, maybe. But the potato is a staple, a boring vehicle for salt. In the sixteenth century, however, potatoes were exotic enough to the European palate that Francesco Carletti took particular note of them. On his way to Lima, he found "roots called *patatas,* white in color. These, when boiled or roasted under embers, have a better, more delicate and agreeable flavor than our chestnuts, and can be served in place of bread."[1]

In 2005, the average human being ate 31.3 kilograms of potatoes per year. Carletti's descendents in Europe were the most indulgent, deep-frying, baking, roasting, and scalloping 87.8 kilograms of potatoes per capita (the hearty Belarusians outdid even the Ukrainians, the British, and the Poles, consuming a lumpen mass of 181 kilograms per head). In contrast, the descendents of the original Latin American potato farmers ate a mere 20.7 kilograms, perhaps having shifted their cultural tastes to maize, rice, and wheat under the influence of five hundred years of Spanish cooking.[2]

As with most twenty-first-century foodstuffs, China is the runaway leader in spud production. It accounted for 72 million tons of tubers in 2007, double the quantity plucked from the soil of Russia, the runner-up. The concept of potatoes sharing the same plate as Peking duck seems jarring, but China and India together produce one in three potatoes on Earth.[3] The spud is, in all senses, an international dish.

In sixteenth-century Peru, Carletti witnessed the potato at the start of its global career. It would take centuries for it to conquer the lunchboxes of humanity, to ascend from the fryer as a golden mate to cheeseburgers, or to be topped by a slice of battered scrod.

The pre-Columbian Peruvians did not eat fried fish with their potatoes, as far as we know, even though their coastal waters were brimming with anchovies. One of the world's most important fishing grounds lies fifteen miles from Lima—well within reach of the native paddle rafts—but even though early Peruvians loved fresh fish (they did, after all, invent seviche), most of the local seafood entered the food chain at a different link. Swarms of anchovies fed the birds that produced the guano that fertilized the fields that yielded such excellent potatoes. It was dung that made Peruvian crops so impressive.

Guano is one of the world's most useful natural resources. It's a superb fertilizer and, while not directly part of the food trade, for most of history it's been bound to food supplies. As late as the nineteenth century, industrial democracies were willing to go to war to control it. In the precarious balance that farmers try to hold between crop yields and soil exhaustion, fertilizer resets the scale.

As expanding societies drive their arable earth to death—agriculture leads to population growth, which leads to more demand, logging, soil erosion, and worsening harvests—they need fertilizer. It trumps all the bad stuff, revitalizing the dust. Dung, and guano in particular, does this with nitrogen.

THE STORY OF N

To grow green and healthy (and in sufficient abundance to make up a civilization's agricultural surplus), plants need a diet of seventeen different elements. When combined with sunlight, carbon dioxide, and water, these seventeen elements form sugars, proteins, and plant tissues.[4] Of these elements, nitrogen is the most crucial. It's one of the biochemical building blocks for every living thing, from babies to jellyfish to bacteria. It's also one of the main components of the DNA molecule, the foundation for the existence of all life. Nitrogen is the basis of amino acids, which are the basis for proteins, which, as anyone with a cursory knowledge of grocery labels knows, are required for animals like us to live and grow.

The problem with nitrogen is that there isn't much to go around. Certainly, there's plenty in the atmosphere—78 percent of the gassy broth around our planet's crust is nitrogen. But this comes in the unfortunately shaped N_2 molecule, consisting of two nitrogen atoms bound tightly together in what's called a triple bond. Plants can't react with this molecule, and so they can't absorb the gas and produce protein from it. It's inert. Nor can animals use nitrogen by breathing it. To get it into our bodies, we need to eat it, which is historically rather difficult, since only a limited amount is trapped in the earth's soil. Nitrogen, more than any other factor except for water, puts a cap on how much food a place can grow.[5] One of the founders of chemistry, Justus von Liebig, phrased it in a dry but pithy statement: "Agriculture['s] principal object consists in the production of nitrogen under any form capable of assimilation."[6]

Of course, our bodies need to eat other elements, too, like carbon in the form of carbohydrates. A field of sugarcane can produce a massive load of carbohydrate calories, but since those crops don't put much of a dent in our hunger for protein, they can't sustain healthy life. It's the nitrogen levels in a patch of ground, and hence in its crops, that determine its carrying capacity—how many people can survive in the region.[7] Nitrogen creates a bottleneck for food surpluses, trade, and population growth. Societies like ancient Rome tried to overcome nitrogen caps by expanding and continually opening more land to the plow. But the expansion was always wide instead of deep, stretching tillage instead of replenishing it, and it resulted in the eventual collapse of Roman agriculture. In 1920, a German named Fritz Haber noted this while accepting the Nobel Prize for chemistry: "It has become known that a supply of nitrogen is a basic necessity for the development of food crops; it was also recognized, however, that plants cannot absorb the elementary nitrogen that is the main constituent of the atmosphere."[8]

To achieve their potential and feed the world, the two atoms in the N_2 molecule need to divorce each other and bond with something else. Oxygen is their usual rebound partner, forming nitrogen oxides. Another potential mate is hydrogen, which creates ammonium or ammonia. Nitrate ions have the advantage of being easily absorbed by plant roots, which would make them excellent fertilizer except that they're negatively charged and wash away quickly from soil particles, which are usually negatively charged, too, particularly in sandy ground. Ammonium ions, on the other hand, are appealingly positive. They're actually attracted to the soil, and, while this means it takes longer for them to filter down to the roots of a hungry plant, they also take a longer time to disappear.[9] Ammonia is a farmer's nitrogen compound of choice.[10]

Until about one hundred years ago, there were only two ways to transform useless atmospheric nitrogen into valuable, plant-friendly compounds. The first was to pray for lightning to strike. A blast of lightning is powerful enough to smash the N_2 molecule apart, forcing the isolated halves to glom on to nearby oxygen atoms and form nitrogen oxide. Or onto oxygen and hydrogen atoms, forming nitric acid. These substances get absorbed by water vapor and enter plants as falling droplets. Rain really is good for the crops.

A less chancy means of fixing nitrogen comes from under the earth instead of above it. A group of bacteria, the rhizobia, eke out a living on the nodules of the roots of beans and other legumes. Rhizobia contain an enzyme (nitrogenase) that catalyzes a rupture in the N_2 molecule, the halves of which then bond with neighborly hydrogen atoms to form ammonia. Nitrogenase is unique in being able to do this, and rhizobia are one of the very few types of organisms that concoct it. The practical result is that legumes have an effortless talent for fixing nitrogen into the soil. Peas, alfalfa, and clover are a tonic for tired earth.[11]

Historically, though, the most important method for getting nitrogen into crops is to spread it on the ground, usually as a layer of manure. Human waste doesn't contain much nitrogen, but it has enough to be useful, as do urine, hair, and fingernail clippings. Farmyard waste is more potent, but even the most generous dung heap can't quite solve the problem of soil exhaustion. Most crops are simply too greedy.

For example, staple grains (rice, wheat, maize, etc.) are composed of between 7 and 14 percent protein, equaling 1.1 to 2.2 percent nitrogen. Even assuming that, after being eaten, all the eliminated waste from these grains were to be plowed back into the fields from which they sprouted (a proposition that ignores the existence of modern plumbing), a hectare planted with, say, eight tons of winter wheat would still cost the earth about 130 kilograms of nitrogen each year. Or take the case of rice. Although rice is low in protein, most rice paddies are harvested twice per year. So the soil's annual net loss of nitrogen is about the same as if it were planted with wheat.[12]

Losing nitrogen in these measures isn't devastating to the soil when the food is produced and eaten on a small, local scale. Farmers can toss manure into their fields and leave them fallow with a cover crop of clover to restore the lost nutrients. If a farm is carefully managed, there's no reason for it to ruin its soil. The problems start to occur with scale. A food empire, like the ones in Rome, Greece, and medieval Europe, grows food for the purpose of transport and trade. It shifts crops away from the place where they're grown and ferries them across continents, removing nitrogen from the land and not replacing it. This happened to the Romans and it's happening to us in the twenty-first century.

Food empires unbalance the scale and bleed nitrogen from their farmlands, which kills the food supply. And then the empires starve.

IN PRAISE OF PHYTOPLANKTON

Carletti didn't know much about nitrogen, but he understood that Peruvian potatoes were nourishing and that Peruvian anchovies cost a lot of money at the fish stand. Anchovies are flush with protein and nitrogen. On account of a slew of geographical quirks, the waters off the coast of Peru are one of the world's richest sources for edible nitrogen, mainly in the form of millions of silvery, snub-faced fishes, which themselves exist on account of little aquatic organisms called phytoplankton. Phytoplankton are responsible for carrying out the world's single most important job: maintaining the chemical balance of the oceans.

The surfaces of the world's oceans are a delicate broth of phytoplankton, nitrogen, and phosphates washed up from the underwater bedrock. If the measure of phosphates increases (by, say, human beings dumping detergents and sewage into the sea), the phytoplankton fix nitrogen from the air, adding it to the water to maintain the chemical balance. If nitrogen levels swell up, so do the phytoplankton, gobbling up the excess element. It's a perfectly calibrated system, without which life in the oceans would be a very different kettle of fish.

When phytoplankton die, their bodies float down through the water, a moving buffet feeding the fishes underneath, which in turn feed bigger fishes. But as the uneaten dregs descend past the last vestiges of sunlight, they pile up, frozen in the deepest, coldest recesses, far beyond the reach of living things. There they lie in the darkness forever unless some force, like an ocean current, stirs them back up.

Off Peru, a freezing rush of Antarctic water called the Humboldt Current hits a continental shelf and blasts all the nourishing phytoplankton back to the surface of the Pacific—directly off the coast at Lima. This gush of protein attracts Peru's clouds of thrashing anchovies. Once the current delivers up the phytoplankton, prevailing winds drive the flow westward toward Asia, where it also carries the monsoon and regulates the world's weather patterns.

The Peruvian upswell is an eternal, renewable food source, more or less. Every so often, though, during the El Niño years, the prevailing winds stop blowing and the current gets stuck in place, letting its nutrients settle in the deep. The fish go without food, and the Peruvians go without fish. But, by the following year, the cycle resumes with the flow of phytoplankton and swarming anchovies returning to their natural place.

Where there are anchovies, there are birds. Lots of birds. Flocks of gulls, cormorants, and boobies dive and make a ruckus of the sky. Huge colonies of them camp on a necklace of rocks that string along the coast of Peru, twenty miles offshore. Among the dozens of these rocks are two lines of islands, the Chincha and Lobos islands, little more than parched crags above the noisy swell. There, the birds nest, breed, eat, and defecate with deafening activity. Over thousands of years, their feces, feathers, and corpses have compacted in the region's dry air, forming a thick crust of brittle detritus—guano.

An observer from the 1830s noted that guano has an "ammoniacal odor which [contains] uric phosphoric and oxalic acids and potash, its color more or less reddish according to its exposure to the atmosphere." The writer can't quite bring himself to believe that the substance is actually dung. "It seems incredible that these guanos could be deposited by the assemblage of birds that rest together during the night."[13] Not the most glamorous of earthly treasures, perhaps, but it's one of the most useful. It's packed with compressed, plant-nourishing nitrogen.

The natural history of guano follows a veritable nail-horseshoe-rider-kingdom sequence of consequence (fixed by phytoplankton, eaten by fish, sunk, blasted back, eaten by fish again, eaten by birds, and shat onto rocks). It's also the story of how food empires try to feed their terminal hunger for nitrogen.

FECAL POLITICS

In 1852, an American entrepreneur named James Jewett, master of the merchantman *Philomela,* wrote a letter to Secretary of State Daniel Webster. In it, he asked if American citizens could legally harvest guano on the Lobos Islands, to be sold as fertilizer to the opening farmlands of the Midwest. Webster, ever the guardian of American commercial interests, wrote back, "It may be considered the duty of this Government to protect citizens of the United States who may visit the Lobos Islands for the purpose of obtaining guano."[14] Jewett went on to ask the secretary of the navy to send a warship to Peru, just to make sure that no foreigners got in the way.

At the same time, a similar discussion was under way on the other side of the Atlantic. Starting in June, British newspapers began running a series of stories about the Lobos Islands, claiming that they had, in fact, been discovered by an Englishman named Edward Lawson in 1808, and formally annexed by Britain in 1813. Appalled, the Peruvians responded by declaring the islands off-limits to foreign guano miners. Meanwhile, American and British warships weighed anchor and sailed toward the equator.

The reason for their militaristic posturing was that the world needed fertilizer, and guano was the finest to be had. The pre-Columbian Incas knew this very well. Long before the Spaniards arrived, the Incas mined guano from the islands and rowed the pungent cargo back to till into their terraced fields, which is how Inca farms supported grandiose mountaintop cities like Cuzco and Tiwanaku. So vital was guano to the Inca economy that imperial inspectors were assigned to manage the Guano Islands and forbade anyone from killing the birds on pain of death.[15]

Even should the temptation arise, killing one of the birds would be a challenge. The islands are ringed with steep cliffs and crashing spray. From miles away, sailors would have been able to both smell and see the dull, off-white substance that sheeted the rocks. A traveler from the 1850s compared one of the Chincha Islands to a table bearing a giant loaf of old-fashioned brown bread, utterly covering its surface.[16]

When the Spanish conquered Peru, they inherited these offshore guano troves. At the time, Europe desperately needed new sources of food to supplement what it could produce on its exhausted landscapes. By the fifteenth century, the population had rebounded from its harrowing under the Black Death, and multitudes of young, hungry farmhands had driven rural wages down and sent food prices up. When Carletti arrived on the wave of European expansion, markets back in the motherland were clamoring for imports. Potatoes began to sail across the sea.

In the colonies, forests fell to the newcomers' axes, virgin landscapes went under the plow, and nitrogen passed from the earth into foods and onto the colonists' dinner tables.[17] In North America, each generation of colonial farmers had to work harder to match the yields their parents had enjoyed. Within a few generations, all the nutrients that had been stored away for millennia under the old-growth trees and dense prairie roots had vanished.[18] Faced with declining yields and hungry babies, the colonists realized they needed to either replenish the ground or put more land under cultivation. In the United States, they did both.

Nineteenth-century American and European travelers to Peru observed, first with incredulity, then with greed, the magical effects of guano:

> *Without the guano the volcanic and sandy soil of the province of Arequipa is almost unproductive but when used it yields in potatoes forty-five for one and in maize thirty-five for one. It is so active that unless watered soon after it is applied round the roots of the plants it dries them or as the country people say burns them up.*[19]

By the 1840s, Peruvian merchants working under government contracts had begun an industrial mining operation on the Chinchas. The shrewdest of these merchants was Domingo Elías, who by the end of the decade had forced all competition out of the market. Since the government set a standard price per ton of guano but didn't worry about labor methods, Elías harvested his prize by working slaves to death while lining the pockets of his political cronies.[20] He subcontracted all the actual mining to other businessmen, who originally assigned the work to gangs of convicts and army deserters. Peru's plantation owners (of whom Elías was a prominent example) had long been complaining of a labor shortage, particularly since African slaving was nearing its end. Elías turned to the Pacific and, by 1849, began importing indentured Chinese to mine guano. Not long after he set up this system, Elías petitioned the government to be allowed to hike his fees by 25 percent, citing bogus labor costs. His friends happily signed the check.

By 1852, two-thirds of the guano miners were Chinese who had signed an eight-year contract in exchange for the cost of their passage to the New World. Many of them had been kidnapped or tricked, believing that they were going to mine gold in California.[21] The voyage from China was something out of the dark, wet hell of the African slave trade (one group of miners committed suicide en masse before even arriving), and conditions only worsened once they landed on the Chinchas.[22] Each worker had a quota of five tons of guano per day. George Washington Peck, a future American congressman, visited the islands and wrote:

> *I seem to see them at their work their slender figures quivering under the weight of loads too heavy for them to wheel for every one who went ashore remarked that they took loads altogether disproportioned to their apparent strength . . . I observed Coolies shovelling and wheeling as if for dear life and yet their backs were covered with great welts . . . It is easy to distinguish Coolies who have been at the islands a short time from the new comers. They soon become emaciated and their faces have a wild despairing expression. That they are worked to death is as apparent as that the hack horses in our cities are used up in the same manner.*[23]

Since Peruvian guano had appeared on the American market in the 1840s, it had won the reputation of a miracle product. Newspapers published frothy accounts of its efficacy on the soft hills of Virginia, swearing that it boosted wheat and tobacco yields by five times or more.[24] Advertisers hawked its properties on cornfields and flower beds.[25] By 1854, it had become so prized that American merchant ships filled the port of Lima with cargoes bound for the Mississippi.[26] In Baltimore, imports between 1844 and 1854 ballooned from 445 to 175,849 tons.[27] Investors saw it as a means to get rich but were stymied by the fact that a single company held the monopoly on British and American guano imports. A firm called Antony Gibbs and Sons of London had negotiated a deal with Peru granting it exclusive control of the guano trade to the eager American and British markets. Infuriated, the Royal Agricultural Society offered £1,000 reward for the invention of a guano substitute. The Americans took a more muscular approach.

In his 1850 State of the Union address, President Millard Fillmore declared that Peruvian guano had become so "desirable an article to the agricultural interests of the United States" that it was the government's solemn duty to "employ all means properly in its power" to bring it into the country, cheap.[28] Fillmore's words escalated the diplomatic volleys between the United States and Peru. That year, the Americans had tried to negotiate a lower price for guano, but the Peruvian government refused to deal. Shortly afterward, James Jewett "discovered" new mounds of guano on the Lobos Islands, a few miles west of the Chinchas, even though Peruvians had been harvesting the rocks for centuries. Blind to history, Jewett wrote his fateful letter to the secretary of state, and when Daniel Webster wrote back encouraging Jewett to steam ahead with his guano claim, he was sending a direct provocation not only to the Peruvians, but to the British. Broadsides in the press erupted on both sides of the Atlantic. Naval ones seemed sure to follow, but ultimately the whole business fizzled, partly due to frantic diplomatic maneuvering between the embassies in Lima.[29] Congress backed down. So did Webster—a rare defeat for the man whose indomitable rhetoric inspired the popular twentieth-century story *The Devil and Daniel Webster,* a Faustian tale in which the secretary of state out-debates Lucifer himself.

The idea that America could exert its might to safeguard strategic resources like guano led to the Guano Islands Act, which Congress passed in 1856, explicitly granting itself the right to use military force to secure bird droppings. Over the next decades, American entrepreneurs cited the act as justification to lay claim to roughly one hundred different Pacific and Caribbean islands.[30] Imperialism won the day. But by the end of the nineteenth century, guano would start to slip from prominence in the food trade.

The existence of guano was a weird trick of climate and topography. Because it was exclusive to a handful of ocean crags, there would never be enough of it to fulfill the demands of huge food empires like Britain and the United States. The very nature of the mining operations ensured that the industry had no future. On the Chinchas, for instance, miners killed the birds and trampled their nests, so the mined guano could never be replaced. Even if they hadn't slaughtered the gulls that laid the golden eggs, the original deposits were the sum of thousands of years of heat and digestion. There was no putting back the dung.

The world needed a more dependable fertilizer to help feed the growing populations of the industrial nations. Of a number of obvious solutions, none were ideal. Natural saltpeter—potassium nitrate and sodium nitrate—encrusted stretches of the Atacama Desert in northern Chile, and by the late 1800s, millions of tons of it had been cut and shipped to the industrial markets. But by the turn of the twentieth century, that too had been depleted to near exhaustion. Crop rotation and clover, the time-honored methods of fertilization, were always an option, but the mill workers of Birmingham and New Bedford needed lots of food quickly, and leaving precious arable land unsown meant that demand always exceeded supply.

Headlines of the time screamed about the nitrogen crisis, the end of wheat, and the imminent collapse of the Civilized Way of Life. A chemist named Sir William Crookes, in his presidential address to the British Association for the Advancement of Science, said that "England and the civilized nations stand in deadly peril of not having enough to eat."[31] Politicians latched on to the crusade and issued a worldwide call for the discovery of a renewable source of nitrogen. The rallying call took on apocalyptic tones. Crookes didn't shy from hysteria when he cried that the nitrogen crisis would mean that "the great Caucasian race will cease to be the foremost in the world and will be squeezed out of existence by races to whom wheaten bread is not the stuff of life."[32]

Crookes was right in that even "the great Caucasian race" are slaves to their bellies, but he was wrong in implying that a taste for rice was an existential advantage for non-Europeans. The entire world, rice and wheat eaters alike, faced a chronic food shortage. In fact, Asia was much worse off than Europe, and millions were wracked with hunger and malnutrition at the dawn of the twentieth century. Unless the riddle of how to fix atmospheric nitrogen into the earth was solved, it seemed likely that Europe might well suffer the same hunger as Asia. The quest to split the N_2 molecule had begun in earnest.

Its fulfillment took an odd form, even a sinister one, paralleling in many ways the later, more explosive splitting of the atom. Both scientific advances were made by German Jews. Both were justified in the name of ending wars. Both produced atrocious suffering and environmental wreckage along with their blessings. And both ushered in a break with the preindustrial world, pushing civilization through a door and locking it behind.

WAR EMPIRES

Napoleon said that an army marches on its stomach, but he might have added that an army marches *for* its stomach as well. Organized warfare, as opposed to sporadic tribal murder, originally had nothing to do with true gods or map boundaries or Helen of Troy. People invented war for the sake of capturing food surpluses like livestock, especially cattle, but also grain.[33] As noted above (in chapter 4), the earliest butchery committed on the Neolithic flats might well have been undertaken for the sake of feeding hungry children, perhaps in a place where the harvest had failed but the tools were still sharp.[34] Food and war have always had a very close relationship.

Fritz Haber, the Nobel-winning chemist who spoke so authoritatively about nitrogen, was born in 1868, during Germany's adolescent growth spurt. His mother died shortly after childbirth, leaving him to be raised by his large Jewish family and by his father, an alderman and pigment seller. This was at the time of the *Kaiserreich*, the semi-constitutional monarchy under Wilhelm I, when all of Germany was uniting under the Prussian banner. New factories steamed for the glory of the fatherland. New railroads whistled for the good of the people. It was a time of bombast and recooked myth, of stirring words like "*Volk*" and "*Sonderweg*." It was a very exciting time to be a German.

The young Haber studied in Heidelberg, where Professor Robert Bunsen lit a flame in him for the joys of chemistry (yes, that Bunsen). Although he didn't share the natural, incandescent brilliance of his future colleagues Niels Bohr and Max Planck, Haber possessed a remarkable single-mindedness, an ability to work doggedly through a mental challenge.[35] This eventually drove him to mental breakdown. In fairness, nervous disorders were extremely fashionable in Germany at the time, possibly as a result of the country violently launching itself from a rural, even sylvan culture into one of radical modernity in the space of fifty years (Germany boasted five hundred mental sanatoriums by 1900.)[36]

Haber converted to Protestantism in 1892, trading "his Judaism for a professor's chair" in the words of his more cynical observers. Regardless of his spiritual sincerity, Haber obviously felt himself to be more German than Jewish.[37] He was nimble in climbing the academic ladder—in one year he published seventeen research papers in a half-dozen scholarly journals.[38] His perseverance even won him the directorship of the prestigious Kaiser Wilhelm Institute for Physical Chemistry and Electrochemistry. But his life's great undertaking truly began in 1903 when a company called the Austrian Chemical Works offered Haber money to research a method to create ammonia, the simplest form of fixed nitrogen. His experiments didn't work, but a few years later he returned to the laboratory when another chemist wrote him a series of rude letters, mocking him over his failure. This time, his industrial paymaster was Badische Anilin- & Soda-Fabrik, BASF, which today is sufficiently alive and well to post sales of €58 billion in 2007, according to its corporate website. Even a hundred years ago, BASF was Germany's biggest chemical producer. Armed with money, research assistants, and a state-of-the-art gas compressor, Haber determined to finally solve the riddle of the nitrogen molecule. By 1909, he had made a breakthrough.

Using his compressor, Haber discovered that the N_2 molecule would split when heated to 400 degrees Celsius and squeezed to two hundred times the normal atmospheric pressure at sea level. The unattached atoms could then bond with hydrogen to form ammonia.[39] Of course, this amount of heat and pressure isn't often encountered outside the laboratory, so Haber enlisted a metallurgist named Carl Bosch to invent devices that could recreate the conditions of his lab experiments on an industrial scale. Together, the chemist and the engineer developed the Haber-Bosch process, involving a giant system of machines that could brew unlimited quantities of ammonia. The first factory opened in Oppau in 1913. The next year, war broke out across Europe.

From the beginning of hostilities, the Germans puzzled over how to apply the Haber-Bosch process to the new battlegrounds crackling across France, Flanders, and Russia. Haber, ever the patriot, lent his talents to the question. In 1914, Germany faced a dire shortage of high explosives. Nitroglycerin, TNT, and indeed all varieties of conventional explosive can only be manufactured with plentiful nitrates, while the sole source on the market at the time was saltpeter from Chilean mines. With the British navy blockading the Atlantic routes, Germany had only six months of ammunition in reserve. And so the managers of the Haber-Bosch factories, instead of manufacturing fertilizer, tweaked a few levers and began to churn out bombs.

Thanks to Haber, Germany now possessed the capacity to build a limitless supply of ammunition, but it had no method of delivering a decisive stroke to its enemies. Directing his mental energy to the quest for a quick battlefield fix, Haber realized that his know-how could, instead of being used to blast men into small pieces, be used to scorch out their innards with corrosive gas.

Even in 1916, this was a sensitive topic. The Hague Conventions of 1899 and 1907 had barred poison from warfare, but Haber believed such treaties were small-minded.[40] After all, poison gas was merely a scientific advance, no more or less moral than a crossbow that could knock an armored knight from his saddle. As far back as catapults and chariots, technology had always trumped tradition in warfare. Besides, his invention promised to clear the trenches of enemy combatants and end the ongoing death and mutilation of Germany's young men. Haber himself oversaw the inaugural uncorking of the cylinders at the second battle of Ypres. Thousands of French and Allied soldiers perished in ghastly agony, and the Germans pushed forward—an entire mile. Shortly thereafter, Haber's wife, herself a brilliant but frustrated scientist, fell into an argument with him over his role in the gas campaign. The conversation ended when she walked out of the family garden, picked up her husband's army pistol, and shot herself in the heart.[41]

Haber survived the war and the loss of his wife, and the year of the armistice saw his name burnished by a prize from Stockholm (although he had to wait until 1920 to actually collect his Nobel). In an otherwise prideful acceptance speech in which he waxed eloquent about the role of scientists in molding "the whole human arrangement," Haber ended on a note of uncharacteristic modesty, saying that, despite the higher calling of knowledge for the sake of knowledge, his work was a small thing and primarily useful for the common good. "Let it suffice that in the meantime improved nitrogen fertilization of the soil brings new nutritive riches to mankind," he said. "And that the chemical industry comes to the aid of the farmer who, in the good earth, changes stones into bread."[42] Despite the toxic uses to which he had directed his research during the war, Haber never lost sight of his original goal, which was the betterment of the world's food supply.

In the years that followed, Haber remained focused on humanity's sustenance, not its choking death, but he didn't abandon his work with gas. Tackling the perennial problem of parasites destroying hard-won crops, he applied himself to insecticides. In the 1920s, he oversaw the concoction of a lethal spray named Zyklon, and then its successor, Zyklon B. But by then, Germany was changing. Although Haber was responsible more than anyone for his country's long endurance during the four years of total war, he died in 1934, homeless and stripped of his precious research positions, a victim of Nazi race laws. It's a mercy that he never lived to see the next, perverted consequence of his genius. But his legacy didn't end in Treblinka.

Today, the Haber-Bosch process is still the choice method of cooking synthesized ammonia—the main ingredient of liquid nitrogen fertilizer and urea, a fertilizer that's also fed to livestock as a protein supplement and appears in everything from plastics to explosives. Factories now brew more fixed nitrogen than exists in all natural sources combined, breaking the ancient threshold of how much protein the earth can produce. China, which uses about a third of the world's nitrogen fertilizer, dumped 31 million tons of it onto its fields in 2006—wheat being the principal beneficiary—while Americans plow 12 million tons of it into the ground each year.[43] In granting us the talent to create food out of nothing but dry ground and a sack of chemicals, the Haber-Bosch process has undone all the old models of sustainability and soil degradation. It's broken our constraints on the natural limits of land and water, on the natural limits of the plants we eat. Today, 40 percent of the Earth's population lives on protein created by the Haber-Bosch process. Three billion people exist on the chemical basis of artificially fixed nitrogen. Our very cells are the products, not of the green Earth, but of factories boiling ammonia in the grey, industrial deeps of Houston, Yinchuan, and Chennai.

Yet even while synthetic proteins build bigger, healthier children in parts of the world once notorious for malnutrition (the Chinese, for example, have reached Western levels of average height after centuries of smaller stature), and while a planet that evolved to support no more than 3 billion human bellies now sees its population shoot toward 10 billion, we face a familiar problem of unsustainable practices.[44]

Soil depletion isn't the killer it once was. Fertilizer has changed the ancient pattern of expansion, overfarming, and leapfrogging to the next stretch of marginal land. But, more than ever, human populations are interconnected. In A.D. 6, when food supplies failed in ancient Egypt, families in Rome went hungry. Today, the entire globe is bound by a chain of dependence and consequence that links us to the Haber-Bosch process. Without artificial fertilizers, we'd have to revert to planting beans to fix nitrogen in the soil, or to digging saltpeter and guano. Corn supplies would collapse. Rice could only be harvested once per year. Meat would slip back to its role as a luxury. In short, without a secure supply of nitrogen, the world would starve.

That's the false solution of Haber-Bosch. It swapped our dependency on nitrogen for a dependency on the process to make nitrogen, which, like so many elements of the modern world, is entirely reliant on fossil fuels.

The educated stratum of consumers knows that the contents of a shopping cart are not created equal. Meat, for example, is profligate with fossil fuels—it costs less oil to grow a field of corn than it does to grow it and feed it to a cow over a period of months, then ship the fattened carcass to market. When oil is cheap, as it usually was for the past sixty years, it makes economic sense to build cattle feedlots and sell inexpensive steaks to a paying urban public. When oil is expensive, as it usually will be in the future, this business model is untenable. The Haber-Bosch process, that miracle technique that sustains so much human life on this planet, requires enormous quantities of natural gas, both for heat and as a source of hydrogen to bond with the loosened nitrogen atoms. Fossil fuels feed us in a very direct way.

We face the choice of having to change our eating habits according to an environmental imperative or an economic one. Either way, our habits are going to change. Our food system—our vast, intertwined world food empire—is dependent on the fuel-soaked Haber-Bosch process. Our dependence on gas invites the cliché of the rising balloon: We have to hold on to the string as we're hauled up into the gusts of swinging markets, government subsidies, and a hungry developing world. But someday, we're coming back down to earth.

THE BIRDS OF PERU

Our landing doesn't have to snap our necks. Farmers are learning to use nitrogen better, which is a hopeful development.

Most plants cultivated by modern farmers absorb about half of the nitrogen that's actually dumped onto them. Even the most efficient methods can only coax the seedlings to swallow about 70 percent of the bonus nutrition. Studies in Europe and Asia have proven that when less than 150 kilograms per hectare of nitrogen are applied to grain crops, the uptake is about 65 percent, but once that threshold is passed, absorption plummets.[45] It's a reasonable guess, therefore, that about half of all nitrogen fertilizer applied to crops today is simply wasted, washing into streams and rivers.[46] In the United States, for example, agrochemicals are to blame for 70 percent of the country's tainted waterways—nutrients leaking off cropland have spoiled 37 percent of all American surface water, rendering it undrinkable by humans and unfit for fish.[47] As well as killing the Mississippi, the Gulf of Mexico, and the Chesapeake Bay, nitrogen is fast poisoning the Rhine, the Yellow River, and the Yangtze.[48]

The damage can't be undone, but there are small fixes. Farmers can increase nitrogen absorption, for instance, by spreading fertilizers at the times when plants are actually growing and can lap them up. They can link tractors to GPS systems to tailor applications to the needs of small areas. Consumers can help by buying grass-fed beef, which cuts corn out of the meat cycle and lowers the demand for fertilizer. Governments in well-fed countries can tax fertilizer used on their own farms and subsidize it in hungry parts of the world where the soils are poor. Everyone needs to spread the nitrogen around in a safer, more sustainable way.

In a strange twist of history, the Peruvian guano deposits are now being mined again. The crust, once 150 feet thick, is only a few feet deep now, and observers speculate that the supply will run out in another ten years. The reason for renewed interest is the cost of oil. Due to gas prices, the cost of chemical fertilizer doubled in 2008, making bird dung suddenly look much more attractive. In addition, organic farmers have a ferocious appetite for guano, and the rise of "natural" foods in the marketplace has meant guano is again a lucrative commodity.[49]

This time, the Peruvians are watching their miners, making sure that extraction doesn't squash the bird populations or disturb their habits overmuch.[50] The government uses appropriate watchwords: sustainability, nesting, habitat. A much bigger threat to our future guano is Peru's thriving anchovy business. Commercial fishing has eliminated much of the birds' food supply—the avian population of the Guano Islands has fallen from an estimated 60 million in 1850 to 4 million today.[51] As always, the food trade has devastating effects.

But even if the guano of Peru were a mile deep, it wouldn't feed the world's population.[52] As the Canadian scientist Vaclav Smil writes,

"Neither nuclear reactors nor space shuttles are critical to human well-being. But [without being able to synthesize nitrogen for plants] the world's population could not have grown from 1.6 billion in 1900 to today's six billion."[53] It's the great challenge for the food trade, and for humanity, to keep these billions from going hungry, from fighting over bread.

CHAPTER SIX

Ice: Preserve Us

Lima, for all its pleasures in fruits and greens, didn't hold Carletti's interest for more than a few months. He and his father sold their merchandise and reloaded their coffers with silver, then boarded a ship north, for New Spain. The first 1,600 miles passed without inspiring much comment, but when the pair arrived in Sonsonate, in modern El Salvador, Carletti observed that people in the town plaza used an unusual fruit as currency to "spend for buying small things." This fruit could be crushed into "a certain drink, which the Indians call chocolate." Carletti immediately formed an addiction to it. "Once one is accustomed to it," he writes, "it becomes a habit. And it is hard to give up drinking it every morning or, in fact, in the evening after supper when the weather is warm and particularly when one is traveling."[1]

Apart from its stimulating properties, chocolate interested Carletti because the natives had developed ways to package it and preserve it from the effects of time and weather. He was impressed at how "it is carried in boxes . . . or made into little cakes that quickly dissolve in water" that the Indians churned with sticks until red and frothy.[2]

Although Carletti had long been swooning over the taste of New World produce, chocolate won his admiration on account of other qualities. Greens, no matter how excellent, had to be eaten more or less on the spot and couldn't survive a week's trouncing on donkeyback, much less a month's sea voyage. But chocolate, having been squashed into dry cakes, could be stored, shipped, and sold for a generous markup. Like beer or cheese, chocolate was preserved, so it could be the stuff of business. Apart from the raw capacity of land to grow foodstuffs, it's decay that limits the breadth of a food empire.

In medieval Europe, food didn't travel very far. The Romans had dealt with decay by building a massive, complex apparatus of storehouses, shipping schedules, and middlemen. They were lucky that the Mediterranean is a smallish sea, letting them avoid the cargo-rotting lengths of the Atlantic. The Sumerians, too, by charting the exact timing of the monsoon, could precisely schedule their trading voyages to the Indus. But without some means of lengthening the shelf life of produce, a food empire's reach will always be constrained to the traveling range of a kernel of wheat ensconced in a dry pot.

Then the twentieth century arrived, and, as in everything from pregnancy to pop culture, we buried all the old assumptions under a pile of industrial patents.

HOW FOOD ROTS AND HOW TO SLOW IT DOWN

Bacteria brew in damp organic matter, so the goal of food preservation has always been to reduce the water in food, robbing the bacteria of a home. Drying, say by hanging a piece of gutted herring in the cold sun, is probably the original way people did this. Another method is to expose food to withering amounts of smoke, which dries it and plugs the molecular structure full of hydrocarbons. Smothering it in salt, too, pulls out the moisture. Fruit responds very well to the addition of sugar, which is chemically similar to the process of jellying—encasing food in a blanket of protective gelatin, as when meat is jugged. Pickling works through the agencies of weak acids like vinegar, brine (liquid salt), alcohol, or vegetable oil.

An alternative to getting rid of the water is to perform a sort of molecular jujitsu with fermentation, using the bacteria for good. It's not the path of least resistance in food processing, since it requires work, but it's historically the most enjoyable. Grain and fruit are the usual foundations for liquor, but herding cultures like the Mongols have also made booze out of milk.

The strangest preindustrial preservative was probably saltpeter.

Scratched out of the ground and smelling like hellfire, it's been used as a fertilizer and as an ingredient for gunpowder. The ancient Indians and the Chinese experimented with its dietary effects, while the Romans noted how it lent a reddish quality to meats. Today, fabricated nitrates are injected directly into hams, sausages, and bacon, bypassing the need for pickaxes.[3]

All of this was useful as far as it went, but human beings cannot live on beer, bacon, pickles, and salt cod alone. Bar snacks do not a modern food empire make. Only ice, which was either a seasonal nuisance or a summertime luxury, could make it possible to supply urbanites with fresh meat and greens. So in the nineteenth century, in the United States, ice itself became part of the increasingly complex food trade.

As Americans left their farmhouses and moved to cities, their diets were no longer rooted in their own gardens. They bought food at city markets, and that food needed to travel. In places like New England, which possessed a wealth of frozen pond water for much of the year, ice could be cut, packed in straw, and used to preserve food from rotting on its way from the field to the street. By August, winter ice was worth hundreds of dollars per ton.[4]

In 1806, a young man named Frederic Tudor looked at the winter ice coating the Massachusetts ponds and saw money. The third son of a Boston lawyer, he had quit Harvard for the excitement of the traditional New England path to wealth: a get-rich-quick scheme involving sea travel. Somehow convincing his investors to buy a brig, the *Favorite,* his idea was to sail a cargo of pond ice 2,000 miles to Martinique and sell it to the sweating natives. Skeptics—including the press—mocked both Tudor's presumption and his grasp of elementary chemistry. "No joke," sneered the *Boston Gazette,* a "cargo of eighty tons of ice has cleared out from this port for Martinique . . . We hope this does not prove to be a slippery speculation."[5] Most people thought the melting ice would sink the *Favorite* before she ever saw the Caribbean.

Tudor didn't drown, but his voyage was a fiasco nonetheless. Nearly all of the ice melted en route, and the remainder went unsold since no one in Martinique had any idea what to do with the weird, evaporating substance. He lost $4,300, landed in a pile of lawsuits, and was obliged to enjoy the hospitalities of debtors' prison for much of 1812 and 1813. But he didn't give up. From his cell, Tudor wrote, "He who gives back at the first repulse and without striking the second blow, despairs of success, has never been, is not, and never will be a hero in war, love or business."[6]

Upon release, Tudor sailed to Havana, where he built a new, technologically advanced warehouse, insulated with sawdust. He also invested in a contraption called an ice plow that could be strapped to horses to cut uniform two-foot blocks, which, Tudor argued to the bemused Boston sea captains, could replace rocks as ballast on board ships. Enough of them liked the idea, however, and Tudor began selling his ice across the hemisphere, opening offices in Charleston and New Orleans. Discontented with mere success, he then decided to export ice to India.

This was a plan of magnificent foolhardiness. The journey from Boston to Calcutta was fifteen thousand miles and, barring bad weather, took four or five months. Tudor's ships would have to cross the tropics and the equator. Twice. And when they reached port, they would dock at wharves that broiled at 90 degrees Fahrenheit.

Tudor addressed these problems by cutting his ice during the cold snaps of January, then loading the blocks onto rail cars that shunted them to the Boston waterfront, packed in sawdust like stones in mortar. The longshoremen topped the ice with a layer of straw and apples, which would (it was hoped) defray the shipping costs, leaving the ice (it was hoped) as solid profit.

The first Calcutta run lost a third of its cargo. But this was still enough to make the journey worthwhile since, thrilled at having cold drinks at last, the expatriate British colonists bought everything Tudor could sell and even helped him build an insulated warehouse. In return, he kept prices low, turning a profit of a mere three cents per pound, so that even the humblest colonial servant could afford a lump of ice in an afternoon cocktail.[7] Ice was now cheaper to buy in India than in London or Paris. One observer noted:

> *It was long before the natives could be induced to handle the crystal blocks. Tradition reports that they ran away affrighted, thinking the ice was something bewitched and fraught with danger. But now they come on board in a long line, and each of them takes a huge*

block of ice upon his head and conveys it to the adjacent ice house, moving with such rapidity that the blocks are exposed to the air only a few seconds. Once deposited there, the waste almost ceases again, and the ice which cost in Boston four dollars a ton is worth fifty dollars.[8]

International trade had triumphed, despite a few setbacks. Tudor's story is illustrative of the changes that occurred to the food trade in the nineteenth century, echoes of which affect our economies to this day. The most notable is that people no longer thought it impossible to deliver fresh apples from Massachusetts to Calcutta. It was a result of a truly global food trade.

Tudor's experiments with ice, while innovative, still relied on the old presumption that ice was a gift of the winter, something seasonal and fleeting. The real shift in food preservation occurred in the late 1860s with the ambitions of another New Englander, a butcher named Gustavus Franklin Swift.

Before the mid–nineteenth century, the only way to move fresh meat between pasture and plate was to walk it. European cultures like the Spanish and the Celts had a tradition of long-distance transhumance (seasonal movement of livestock), and the descendents of these cattle herders brought the cowboy way of life to the United States, culminating in the longhorn drives of Texas. The time during which thousands of cattle marched from the Rio Grande to the markets of Abilene or Oklahoma City was, however, short-lived, no more than a cultural hiccup after the Civil War. Railways soon mechanized the long drives. By the 1880s, cattlemen were marching their animals up to depots and loading them on the hoof onto cars destined for city pens. Urban wholesalers then bought the cows, slaughtered them, and sold them to local butchers. The arrangement saved a lot of money, but astute butchers realized that centralizing meat processing would save even more. The challenge was how to kill a lot of cows in a central facility, dress them, and deliver the parts around the country before they spoiled.

Early solutions came from Detroit, where a small-time meat dealer named George Hammond built the first refrigerated railway car. It was primitive, based more or less on the same principles that Tudor employed on his ships—stacked ice and sawdust. One of the big players in Chicago's meat-packing industry, Nelson Morris, used Hammond's cars to ship beef from the Union Stock Yards to markets in faraway cities. But the real innovation came after the fourteen-year-old Gustavus Franklin Swift got a job at his brother's butcher shop in Sagamore, Massachusetts. Eventually establishing a shop of his own, the young Swift wasn't content with merely selling T-bones to the denizens of Cape Cod. He wanted a food empire of his own. So he moved to the heart of America's butchery scene, the stockyards of Chicago, where he studied the latest ideas in refrigeration. In 1879, Swift unveiled a radical new type of railway car, the "Swift-Chase" car, which held four vented overhead containers loaded with ice and salt. The design worked beautifully, despite several early marketing setbacks, such as when Massachusetts customers refused to buy a cargo of Swift's Chicago beef when they learned it had been slaughtered a week previously. Nineteenth-century shoppers had yet to abandon eons of received carnivorous wisdom.

But technology soon pushed Americans to overcome their prejudices against cold meat. The development of mechanical refrigeration helped, of course, and by the 1890s, mechanical refrigeration ("vapor compression") was coming into vogue.[9] However, the real shift happened thanks to Swift's railway cars. It was through the union of pond ice and the railways that Americans finally accepted that meat was no longer something you ate right after the kill. It was now, like sixteenth-century chocolate briquettes, something you could collect and trade, a commodity. By 1884, Chicago's meat-packing industry needed 1.5 million tons of ice per year.[10]

IT'S A JUNGLE

In 1905, a journalist named Charles Edward Russell wrote a book about the meat-packing industry called *The Greatest Trust in the World*. Although it's far less remembered today than Upton Sinclair's grisly novel *The Jungle*, it deals with the same infernal world of steam, meat hooks, and demonic boilers, although Russell writes from a wider perspective. His concern isn't workers being pulped into Spam, but the consolidation of America's food supply. In it, he notes that Chicago's meat-packing industry had slaughtered 21,712 cows in 1874 but that this number had risen to 2,206,185 cows in 1890. According to Russell, the sheer scale of the operation led to "gentlemanly" agreements between the partners that amounted to price-fixing, economic jobbery, and the undermining of the Republic.[11]

To Russell, the Swift-Chase refrigerated railway car was a symbol of a "cruel and grinding monopoly," forcing clean, unspoiled foodstuffs down the throats of the unwitting public. With the advent of refrigeration, northern towns wanted to buy exotic produce. It was now possible for Minnesotans, say, to develop a taste for fresh fruit and the expectation that they should have it. Russell comments that "where peculiarities of soil or climate gave a region especial advantages for growing any product, that product became there the staple throughout."[12] Regions now had even more motivation to specialize (as in ancient Crete, medieval Europe, and the Fortunate Islands), since the refrigerator car could deliver their peaches and pork chops anywhere in the country. And the meat packers controlled the refrigerator cars.

In 1919, a two-year investigation by the Federal Trade Commission concluded that the meat-packing companies Armour, Cudahy, Morris, Swift, and Wilson were indeed dangerously poised to monopolize the nation's food supply. Between them, they controlled America's stockyards, and they had used this to ruin all the other competition while agreeing not to fight one another. They owned the retailers, too, the inner-city butcher shops that inflated the price of their products by barring "substitute foods" from their shelves.[13]

Henry Ford, himself no stranger to aggressive business methods, was appalled by the collusion between the meat packers and the railways. In his memoirs, he complained bitterly about how the railways snuffed out America's budding canal system so they could institute a system of Byzantine inefficiency and corruption, unnecessarily hauling commercial goods in anything but a direct line between two points.[14] But his worst scorn was for the meat packers:

> *If you look at the maps which the packing houses put out, and see where the cattle are drawn from; and then if you consider that the*

cattle, when converted into food, are hauled again by the same railways right back to the place where they came from, you will get some sidelight on the transportation problem and the price of meat.[15]

But the appeal to men like Swift wasn't that this was a tidy economic arrangement. It was that they owned significant aspects of meat processing *and* railways. By colluding and centralizing, the industrial giants transformed cows into measurable commodities that they could shunt around the country, charging a fee at each step.

Aside from the impact on the consumer, the impact on the environment was terrible. Cows are part of ecosystems, which are more complex and mutable than anything that's sprung from the mind of a financier or, indeed, from the mind of an inventor of refrigerated railway cars. Ecosystems function by recycling the variegated nutrients and elements in a small plot of ground. A leaf drops from the tree and becomes the substance of the next leaf. Refrigeration and transport broke those cycles in the ecosystem, causing the same problems that confounded the Romans and Sumerians. How do you maintain soil fertility when the fruits of that soil—in this case cows as well as fruits—move a thousand miles away?

Industrial meatpacking created other great evils in sewage, animal abuse, worker abuse, and air and water pollution. The Chicago River outside the stockyards earned the moniker "Bubbly Creek" for its noxious brew of effluent, and the horrors of the cutting rooms would one day inspire the formation of unions. But the great meat-packing houses got rich.

THE INDUSTRIAL GARDEN STATE

All the drawbacks of centralization couldn't trump the overwhelming benefit of perennial, perishable foods on the kitchen tables of the nation. Seasonal and regional differences didn't mean anything by the 1920s; families in Maine could drink orange juice at breakfast and eat salad in winter. Consumers and producers were now linked by steam power, refrigeration, and machine processing—by industrialization.

Industrialization, of course, costs money. Refrigerated rail cars, centralized sorting houses, marketing campaigns—none of these could be bought by individual farmers. Capital, in the form of bank leases on industrial machinery, triumphed over the old veneration of sweat. An ancient Sumerian visiting a wheat farm in Illinois might have seen a vestige of the agriculture he knew, but it would have been soon drowned out by the whirr of threshers. Unable to compete with their larger or better-connected neighbors, many farmers sold their land, migrated to the cities (as displaced peasants had in other countries for centuries), and survived by buying the very same industrialized products that had driven them off the land. Capital replaced labor, workers specialized, and the whole system leaped up another notch in complexity, connectivity, and dislocation from the agriculture of past ages.[16]

Modern agriculture reached its apogee in California. Although that state possesses a mere 8 percent of American irrigated cropland, it produces 50 percent of the country's fruits, nuts, and vegetables.[17] It's also a mecca of food processing. California tomatoes, tomato paste, and tomato sauce are the second-largest processed vegetable business in North America (after frozen spuds). About half of American canned vegetables are Californian, and its frozen fruit business, too, is gigantic.[18] Californians also lead the country in "demand-oriented processing," meaning products like potato chips that are fragile and need to be produced close to the point of retail, and "supply-oriented" industries like lettuce, wherein the cost is mostly in obtaining the raw product.[19]

Oddly, California wasn't always America's fruit basket. Until the late nineteenth century, most California farmers grew wheat, which despite the state's fruit-friendly climate, was a sensible crop for the first generation of settlers.[20] Like the Romans, early Californians found wheat to be durable, movable, and easy to grow in the sunshine. These farmers were part of what rural sociologists call "the first regime," settlers who worked the virgin soil for a surplus that they sold for manufactured imports.[21] Surplus grain formed the base for the American economy in the postcolonial years while the British Empire retreated and invested in its remaining frontiers (like Canada and Australia). By the end of the nineteenth century, a world economy had emerged where huge regions had become specialized in growing commodities for sale to other huge regions. Globalization began long before anyone had ever heard of Thomas Friedman.

But by 1900, California's soil had thinned, its organic matter blown away, and the land could no longer sponge up enough water for a bumper wheat harvest. Yields declined, so entrepreneurial farmers began to experiment with irrigation and vegetables. Unlike in Sumer, these farmers didn't need a priest-king's chants or a legion of slaves to irrigate the parched earth. They had credit unions.

At the same time that California's grain farmers switched to horticulture on the basis of four hundred dollar per acre loans, a "second regime" took over the American agricultural economy. These were the rail barons and meat magnates like Swift, who took advantage of circumstances like the Civil War, refrigeration, pro-corn policies from Washington, and the railway. The second regime, although splendidly rich, bred its own slew of ills, such as a tradition of animal husbandry that had less to do with nature than with accountancy. The factory farm was an idea of this time, as was dumping cheap grain on impoverished countries and suppressing the value of rural labor.

So by the mid–twentieth century, food had become a manufactured object, a durable good like steel nails.[22] Giant "vertically integrated" companies like Swift's became the model for the era, controlling every step of the process. Across the United States, farmers applied high-torque automotive engines to pumps that drilled up deep underground sources of water for irrigation. Coupled with new factory-cooked nitrogen and government subsidies, California blossomed with fruit orchards, while a similar process was transforming the land left over from the Dust Bowl into the bread (and corn) basket of America.

In California, the shock troops for this second regime were land developers like William Chapman. In the 1870s, he looked at the exhausted wheat fields around Fresno and saw an opportunity to reinvent the earth. Hiring a corps of engineers to divvy 640 acres into twenty little vineyards, he built a web of canals and ditches to funnel groundwater to a welter of freshly planted grapevines. Then he sold the plots to tired northeasterners, promising them sun, honest labor, and an escape from the East Coast's wilderness of smokestacks. Chapman was one of many such developers—a German consortium dug 450 miles of ditches and 25 miles of feeder canals to irrigate land parcels for amateur farmers; an American group sunk a 30-mile canal to sweeten the deal on 100,000 acres of unplanted orchards.[23] At the end of the nineteenth century, California was very much the cliché of a land of reinvention and opportunity.

The families who arrived in Fresno and Tulare counties in the early twentieth century didn't conform to the ancient model of subsistence farmers spreading into their society's hinterland, like the monastic pioneers in northern Europe or the Minoan woodcutters pondering the sacred heights above Knossos. They weren't looking to eat. Like good Americans, they were looking to sell. The new Californians dug their hands into the western soil with the intent of growing cash crops for middle-class kitchens. Apricots and lemons, not nuggets of ore, fueled the gold rush of the 1900s, which wouldn't have worked without the generous banking that provided the loans that financed irrigation schemes. The new farmers also learned the lessons of the meat packers and saw that, without modern transportation, their agricultural enterprise was doomed.

Around the year 1900, most Californian farmers were still loading their produce, uninsured, onto railway cars for the long haul to the eastern cities. This was a sizable risk, as readers of Steinbeck will recall, and a hiccup in scheduling could leave long trains of lettuces rotting in the sun. But even if the fruit made it to market, the prices were controlled by East Coast processing companies, so growers were at the mercy of both the rail system and the whims of distant corporations.

Enterprising farmers banded together to solve the problem, forming unions that established quality grades for produce, standardized the sizes of boxes, and drew up advertising posters. The Orange Growers Protective Union appeared as early as 1885. Twenty years later, the California Fruit Growers Exchange marketed their collective products under the name Sunkist.[24] Shoppers started to associate the word "California" with the word "fruit," and the connection stuck. America's fledgling canning industry shifted westward.[25]

After the Second World War, more Americans had money to spend on groceries like greens. Lettuce growers organized to adopt a "cool system," whereby they could grow produce in shifts in different sections of the state year-round, so there would always be a fresh stock for the marketplace. They bought or hired fleets of refrigerated trucks, built air-conditioned warehouses, and signed deals with retailers. Vacuum packing, too, helped get the heads rolling.[26] All of this took tremendous infrastructure—it's not easy to shift a vast tonnage of perishable commodities requiring exact temperatures and humidity levels across a continent. But after the lettuce growers had pulled it off, other farmers would copy them.[27]

TRIUMPH OF THE TOMATO

In the annals of human agriculture, rarely has any fruit proved as profitable as the California tomato. Nothing makes a tomato more inherently valuable than, say, an artichoke, but the tomato has been the happy recipient of a flood of public funds, poured into the pockets of growers under the guise of public policy. Governments as far back as the ancient Mesopotamians have controlled agriculture. Tomatoes, and their role in California's propulsion to the head of the twentieth-century fruit business, are merely one of the more spectacular examples of how food is the continuation of politics by edible means.[28]

It happened in a roundabout way. In the mid-1960s, tomato picking in California was performed by hand, usually by low-wage Mexican workers. In 1962, fifty thousand such laborers worked on four thousand farms, most of them growing mixed crops.[29] So, when the University of California unveiled a mechanical tomato picker, alongside a new variety of tomato that could withstand the metal grip of the machine, no one cared. It didn't make sense to spend $25,000 to buy one. Three years after the unveiling, 96.2 percent of California's tomatoes were still hand-picked, but in the early 1960s, the federal government decided to crack down on migrant workers. Fearful of incurring fines and of losing market share to Mexican producers, American tomato growers panicked. Many of them abandoned their farms, setting off a minor land rush and leaving the remaining growers to consolidate and mechanize. By 1973, fewer than six hundred growers remained, employing a mere eighteen thousand workers.[30] Machines picked nearly every tomato in the California harvest. Politics had been the agent of modernization, as had been government-funded land grant universities, established in the late nineteenth century with a mandate to do research on agriculture and engineering. Historically, their research benefited the ledgers of industrial agribusiness, although nowadays they use the word "sustainability" in their press releases.[31]

Where policy leads, private dollars usually follow, and vice versa. Following the consolidation of the tomato business, the federal government decided to plant Interstate 5 over a little dirt road on the west side of the San Joaquin Valley. It's no accident that this patch of Fresno County became the tomato capital of America and that private irrigation, processing, and transportation companies rushed to capitalize on the situation.[32]

American diets adapted to the Californian model. Between 1950 and 1975, consumption of frozen foods more than tripled, effectively severing consumers' connection to their local farmers' markets and dairies. This was the dawn of the aluminum age: of jarred pasta sauce, frozen peas, and canned soup. People across the world learned to eat manufactured foods, sold by corporations that swallowed up the raw produce and cooked or mashed it into an added-value product.[33] California's geographical gifts of mild weather and nourishing soil—along with a very modern mix of industrial organization, policy, and technology—helped turn it into the century's vegetable powerhouse.

The cost of this growth is familiar. As of 2000, 36 percent of U.S. surface water was unfit for animal habitat or human consumption, almost entirely the fault of agriculture. A full 70 percent of the tainted water got that way through chemical runoff from modern farming.[34] Although these are national statistics, as in so much else, California has led the way. Over the past century, agriculture destroyed 89 percent of California's riparian woodlands. Coastal wetlands dried up like sponges in the sun. In 1994, for example, farms in the Pajaro River watershed doused their fields with 5.7 million kilograms of pesticides. Scientists who have monitored the impact of this contamination by collecting water samples observe that this has caused "toxicity in 78 percent of agricultural ditch samples, 25 percent of tributary slough samples, and 11 percent of river and estuary samples."[35]

Everywhere throughout the state, farmers blasted their crops from above with pesticides and from below with chemical fertilizer.[36] It was agriculture practiced at the peak of scientific efficiency, which meant that everyone ignored the fact that the water was turning into poison.

As the water spoiled, irrigation, which had once transformed California from a land of chicken-scratch wheat farms into a horticultural bonanza, was depleting the state's aquifers.[37] Originally, farmers had watered their crops with streams and rivers, but in the 1920s they had learned to tunnel for the deep reserves,[38] using more than rainfall could ever replace. Estimates from the 1980s (and the situation has not improved in the past thirty years) guessed at an average annual decline in California's water table of between fifteen centimeters and one meter.[39] In recent years, pumps have sucked so much liquid from the ground that the actual surface of the earth caved inward. In the San Joaquin Valley, 5,200 square miles sank anywhere from between one and thirty feet since the pumping began.[40]

Of course, farmers' crops need water, but draining aquifers isn't an ideal plan for sustainability. The water will run out, and California will have to change the way it farms.

Runoff and irrigation are only part of the environmental ills of farming. Specializing in particular crops—like tomatoes—was profitable, but it caused unforeseen problems. To pay off the debt they accrued by buying modern harvesters, tomato farmers needed to plant a minimum number of hectares of tomatoes per year. Furthermore, to guarantee their customers a predictable supply, corporate tomato processors forced growers to sign long-term contracts, locking them into methods and harvest sizes.[41] Even if they were environmentally minded, the farmers had no option to use less pesticide or rotate their crops.

This didn't solely happen with tomatoes. The milk business is much the same. By consolidating herds of cows, California ousted Wisconsin as the dairy queen of America. But bigger, more concentrated herds leave a bigger, more concentrated mess. California's groundwater is now laced with a thickening slick of cow dung.[42]

Specialization is always about money; a few cash crops are chosen for their natural advantage, bolstered with lashings of groundwater, propped up with a dusting of pesticides, and then shipped away.[43] Notions of self-sufficiency are irrelevant. Only profit counts. This is nothing new, of course. In the 1890s, when the economy drooped under an economic cloud and the early wheat fields withered, California farmers lobbied for federal bailouts rather than give up their specialized crops.[44] Then, as now, it was better to accept a government check than to put an end to the surreal practice of planting lettuce in an arid, wilting environment.

CALIFORNIA SCHEMING

The world watched California and liked it. Modernizing nations adopted the model of the Industrial Garden State—specialization in crops, massive capital investment in infrastructure, consolidation. And so the world changed the way it thought about agriculture.

The Californian example took a society of small farmers who each fulfilled multiple roles (input supplier, producer, manufacturer, distributor) and turned them into specialists. Now, instead of knowing their way around a toolshed and a barnyard, a modern agricultural worker can be a chemist who boils fertilizer in a factory, or a seed producer, or a machine operator.[45] The complex chain of actions that turns animals, earth, and seeds into a roast chicken dinner is segmented. Political scientists sometimes mutter about the diminishing returns of complexity, meaning that too much of this segmentation causes problems. While some specialization is a good thing, if agriculture is neatly divided for maximum economic returns, everyone depends on all the pieces working as planned. If a single element sinks, we're all caught in the enveloping suck.[46]

Once again, Henry Ford, the man who invented the assembly line mentality that would be writ large across California's landscape, was oddly prescient:

> *A policy of decentralization ought to be adopted. We need, instead of mammoth flour mills, a multitude of smaller mills distributed*

> *through all the sections where grain is grown. Wherever it is possible, the section that produces the raw material ought to produce also the finished product. Grain should be ground to flour where it is grown. A hog-growing country should not export hogs, but pork, hams, and bacon.*[47]

Again, that's not to say that consolidation doesn't have its benefits. To paraphrase Adam Smith, technology and specialization make everything cheaper, while forcing the inefficient producers to stop wasting everyone's time and find other occupations. That's the capitalist theory. Marxists, on the other hand, think that technology and specialization create a malicious cycle. Competing farmers race against one another for the slightest edge, so they borrow money to buy the latest version of Eggplant-Pulper 3.0, leaving the banks as the main beneficiaries. Even more pernicious, a cost-price squeeze of rising input costs and lowering commodity prices means that the workers suffer when their employers inevitably cut their wages.[48] The only beneficiaries in this case are the folk musicians singing protest songs. And since the farmers are broke, they don't want to pay to clean up the environment.

In the United States, late-twentieth-century specialization created a third food regime, supplanting the meat packers and fruit pickers of yore. This regime isn't defined by mere industrialization, but by the creation of huge, unnatural monocultures—massive regions of the planet devoted to single strains of crops, kept alive only by the flowering toxicity of agrochemicals. Rural geographers call this "spatial homogeneity."[49] The natural order—rain that renews nitrogen, for example—is substituted for a can of E-Z-Grow and a contract to sell 3 million bushels of green beans to Japan.

The third food regime is grounded on a presumption that, when people buy a loaf of bread for $2.99, they're not calculating the additional monetary cost in water contamination, deforestation, global warming, and social ruin. Naturally, most people don't notch up these phantom dollars when they read their shopping bills. If the market worked as it's supposed to, then it would transfer those costs to the consumer instead of tricking them into thinking that food is, in fact, cheap. But it doesn't, and it isn't. We just think we're getting a free lunch.

Adam Smith believed that the price of a widget should reflect the toil that the widget maker invested in making it.[50] But usually, as in the case of food, the price tag is very different from the actual cost. This gap between cost and price is what trade is all about, as it gives the middleman a slice of wealth. But the ways in which the gap is hidden is usually much less obvious than a simple markup. Sometimes, as in the case of grain grown on land that's slowly degrading, the true costs may not be apparent for decades. We might ignore the costs for cultural reasons, as the Sumerians ignored their salty fields until it was too late. Government subsidies to farmers lower the end price of food at the cash register, but the bill has to be paid on tax day (American corn farmers have their caps notoriously in hand). The price of most of the food we buy bears only an imaginative relation to its actual cost.

In the modern economy, there's a complex string of minuscule transactions between the moment that a farmer grows a lentil and the moment a consumer eats it. It's very hard to account for all the buried charges in fuel, labor, processing, packaging, advertising, and distribution. It's far harder to account for these costs today than it would have been in Bronze Age China, imperial Rome, or nineteenth-century Chicago. The outlandishly large gap between price and actual cost is due to our newfound ability to store food for unlimited periods and move it unlimited distances with refrigeration, rail, and motor power. Instead of changing the nature of food empires, however, modern adaptations have only changed their scale. The problems that beset Rome and medieval Europe are still with us.

THE ORANGE JUICE QUANDARY

Orange trees are Asian, with a migratory trail through the Middle East and North Africa, entering Europe through the gardens of the medieval Spanish Moors. As of the early 1990s, oranges were the most produced fruit in the world, grown primarily to be smashed into frozen concentrated juice.[51] Orange juice is one of the world's truly globalized foods.

Why orange juice, not apple or guava, came to dominate humanity's breakfasts is a modern food story. In the 1940s, Florida grew more oranges than it could sell. Native sunshine, friendly federal policies, and decades of expansion had created more orange plantations than were practically useful, even in a country stacked with refrigerators. Looking for new ways to move their product, Florida orange farmers hit on the idea of pulping, reducing, and freezing the perishable fruit into something lasting, durable, and easily delivered to faraway shoppers.

Concentrated frozen orange juice was hugely popular with American consumers, and within a few years it became a staple in kitchens throughout the world. But some years, Florida couldn't keep up with demand. In the 1970s, for example, a series of unseasonable frosts ruined the crop. Seeing an opportunity, Brazil stepped into the marketplace, and while Florida remains an orange state, the nexus of citrus shifted south. The American downstream manufacturers like Coca-Cola (through Minute Maid) and PepsiCo (through Tropicana) followed, bringing with them their machines, chemists, ships, and marketing consultants.[52]

To make frozen concentrated orange juice, you suck or boil out most of the water from the fruit, leaving slurry that's then frozen, packed into trucks, and driven to ports where it's pumped into the holds of waiting orange juice freighters. These ship the slurry to buyers throughout the world who simply add water.[53] This universal "reconstituted" breakfast drink has been marketed with terrific success. Brazil, which produces 40 percent of the planet's orange juice and commands 80 percent of the trade, earns $4 billion per year on the business.[54]

Orange juice is a very impressive piece of the world food empire. About 15 percent of beverages consumed by human beings are juices (with China at the low end of consumption and the United States and Germany topping the chart). Poorer populations have a tendency to drink fresh orange juice, since they can't afford the store-bought packaged stuff. (Of course, fresh-squeezed juice is expensive in rich countries, where the squeezing tends to be contracted out instead of being performed by the drinker on the spot.) As incomes rise, people in Malaysia or Zimbabwe will inevitably drink more concentrate. This is very good news for the orange juice industry, so it's very good news for the economies of countries as disparate as Italy, Mexico, China, and, of course, the United States and Brazil.

In Brazil alone there are 800,000 hectares of orange trees, particularly around São Paulo, mostly the property of four dominant companies (Cutrale, Citrosuco, Citrovita, and Louis Dreyfus Citrus), the biggest of which also own large percentages of Florida plantations. Consolidation on this scale tends to tickle the antennae of antitrust officials.[55] In 2006, paralleling the tale of California's tomatoes, Brazil's small growers complained that the behemoths were squashing prices in an effort to drive the little players out of the game.[56] A lot of fruit is still grown by family farms, but they usually sign long-term contracts with the international corporations that control distribution and processing—corporations that own the length of the commodity chain. And again, as with the historical tomato, consolidation among growers seems inexorable. In Brazil, the number of plantations dropped from 28,000 to 10,000 in the past twenty years, while less than half of 1 percent of them own a quarter of the trees.[57]

Concentration, whether in juice or industries, has drawbacks. Frozen concentrated orange juice doesn't taste as good as fresh, nor is it as nutritious. And centralizing production among a few, specialized firms in a few, specialized corners of the world means that pests can devastate the world supply if they crack the barrier of chemicals that shield the orange trees.

"Citrus greening," otherwise known as huanglongbing (HLB), is a bacterial disease spread by an Asian bug named *Diaphorina citri*. About four millimeters long, with a mottled brown body and light brown head, it lays its eggs on the tips of orange shoots and between unfurling leaves, spreading the bacteria that give the oranges wasting disease. The insects also drink the tree sap, killing the plant. HLB entered Florida in 1998, spreading up Highway 1 until, by September 2000, it had attacked thirty-one counties. Today, the bug roosts in trees throughout the nation.

Because of HLB, orange farmers douse their crops with a heavy wash of pesticide. They spray when the trees flower, they spray when the trees bear fruit, and they top off the chemical cocktail with a fungicide to keep mold from spoiling the leaves.[58] As in the areas where California grows tomatoes, these pesticides threaten to turn the environment into a poisonous morass.

Bacterial rot aside, the orange juice business faces a more pressing threat. As worldwide consumption grows, plantations spread and push production into the margins of the landscape—the hillsides of Belize are the latest conquest for the orange groves. Slopes, of course, make for poor agricultural ground, and they erode. More of them will be put under cultivation in the coming years as developing countries adopt a Western taste for breakfast drinks. In 2004, orange groves covered 3.6 million hectares. If every country in the world drank as much orange juice as, say, Germany, we'd need 32 million hectares.

The entire American orange industry would likely teeter and collapse like a tree full of *Diaphorina citri* if it weren't for government protections—a U.S. Department of Agriculture report stated that, in 2001, Brazil's production costs ran to forty-two cents per gallon of juice. Floridian producers spent seventy-five cents per gallon for theirs.[59] The reason Brazil hasn't completely crushed Florida's industry is that the difference in production costs is made up by tariffs and something called the Florida equalization tax. Naturally, the Brazilians don't regard this as fair play, and they're trying to get the thirty-cent-per-gallon tariff repealed. If this happened—not an impossible scenario, by any means—Brazil would increase production, likely put additional virgin land to the axe for orange groves, and continue its long tumble down the rabbit hole of specialization.[60] Add thin profit margins and loud, embarrassing allegations (all of which are denied) about child labor,[61] and you've got an industry that looks, if not outwardly ailing, then inwardly cancerous.

Cancerous is exactly the state of our twenty-first-century global food empire. Whither concentrated orange juice, thither the vast, unmeasured apparatus of commodities markets, shipping fleets, wholesale buyers, and shopping carts. The disparity between cost and price continues to inch apart as the food trade tangles ever-longer threads of capital. It's like a clumping knot into which we're twisting ever-longer spools of string.

PART III

EMPTY POCKETS

Storm Clouds

Shanghai's October drizzle doesn't blur the streets so much as melt them into a sideways wash of colorless, oily light. Even in clear weather, there's no vantage point from which to actually look at East Asia's greatest city. No mountaintop roost or penthouse cocktail bar from which the eyeballs can absorb the whole of the squared, black-and-yellow web cast by urban human life. It's simply too gigantic. The World Bank guesses that the population of the Yangtze Delta megalopolis numbers 75 million souls—many times the mass of Tokyo or Bangkok.[1]

Human numbers have pushed Shanghai out of all possible conceptions of urban planning and into the realm of geology. This is the city as continent, its strata of life piled eighty-eight stories deep.

A groundling's view from the center doesn't lend much perspective. The Huangpu River inches through downtown Shanghai—a channel of earthy soup abutted by the Bund district, a nineteenth-century city hammered together by Europeans after the Opium Wars. Along with the smell of car exhausts, these streets preserve a whiff of London in the brick and cobble thoroughfares laid down by long-dead colonial officials. Ten miles downriver, the Huangpu merges with the greater Yangtze, just before it filters into a buzzing, fifty-mile-long delta that ends in the East China Sea.

Across the water from the Bund is Pudong, an ultra-modern district studded with twenty-first-century trophies. As always in the autumn, a grainy mist washes away the visible contours of the city. It erases the 468-meter-tall, weirdly organic Oriental Pearl Tower with its elephant's legs and piled, bulbous carbuncles, and the twin superskyscrapers of the Jin Mao Tower and Shanghai World Financial Center (one plucked from Fritz Lang, the other a glass monolith with a hole at the top, looking for all the world like God's bottle opener).

Shanghai, like much of China, is emerging from a regrettable hundred years. In the early twentieth century, the city could challenge any grand European capital for bragging rights on sewage systems or electrical matrices. But the Cultural Revolution dragged the metropolis into enforced decay—Mao's anti-urban bias meant that while Shanghai generated 25 percent of China's government income in the 1970s, nearly 700,000 homes in a single district lacked working flush toilets. By the 1990s, when the political straitjacket had loosened, migrants and state investment filled the streets with new life and fresh money. Concrete slathered the land. Earthmovers, cranes, and steelworks gusted and shuddered. They still do. The road to the airport, for instance, is part eight-lane overpass and part rattling dirt track. A common punchline is "China's going to be really nice when it's finished."[2]

Pudong is where much of the new investment rooted, but until 1990 it was simply a 522-square-kilometer patch of low trees and rice paddies. Then, the government marked it on the maps as the "Pudong New Area," giving it the status of one of the country's special economic zones that cut away the mass of entangling taxes and regulations. It became a site for foreign investment, factories, and duty-free imports of coal and chemicals. A spot that once sprouted a few hundred tons of rice was, in a matter of months, paved and wired into a lair for the Asian manufacturing tigers to sharpen their claws. Here, in fast-drying cement, was the soul of modern China.

About seventy miles from Pudong's rhomboid world of glass and steel, lines of tour buses worm toward a relic from a very different civilization—Lake Taihu, a place the Chinese venerate in poetry.[3] In the medieval Tang dynasty, scholars liked to collect unusual rocks from its shores to plant in their contemplative gardens. Generations of Confucians stared at its limestone crags and gentle waters, inking their contours onto Tang objets d'art. Peaceful Taihu—more so than the grinding sea—was where nature revealed her most aesthetic and instructive self.

Today, Taihu is largely known as the source of a creeping infection called algae bloom.[4] The lake, though thirty miles wide and forty miles long, is extremely shallow, at most parts no deeper than a couple of meters. Beginning in the mid–twentieth century, scientists began to notice bursts of green growth spreading out of isolated spots. These growths were a form of algae that choked all other aquatic life and poisoned the water for drinking. Starting in a single bay at the northern end of the lake, the blooms extended every summer, and within fifty years they covered a third of the water surface. Professor Yuwei Chen of the Nanjing Institute of Geography and Limnology has studied the blooms for decades and says:

> Microcystis *(Cyanobacteria) bloom is one of the most serious problems in eutrophic freshwater systems because it forms surface scums that cause taste and odor problems, and even produces toxins that threaten human health.*[5]

The algae make fresh water thicken and stink. A key organism in the bloom is *Microcystis aeruginosa*, a type of cyanobacteria that's highly toxic to human digestive systems and causes a massive public health scare every summer because a million Chinese rely on Lake Taihu for their drinking water. In 2007, the entire city of Wuxi had to switch to bottled water during the bloom months,[6] and in 2008 newspapers ran front-page pictures of the algae being pumped out of the lake and onto fleets of tanker trucks for disposal.[7]

Gigantic algae blooms are the fault of human agency, specifically of farms.[8] The runoff from local food production, approximately forty thousand tons of nitrogen and two thousand tons of phosphorus, trickle into the lake each year, feeding the growth.[9] Of this, manufactured fertilizer plays only a relatively small role. Animal sewage is primarily to blame.[10] Before the past generation started plowing manufactured fertilizer into the ground, the Chinese collected animal waste (both human and livestock) and raked it into the ground.[11] Today, there's too much of it. A single pig is a boon to the soil; ten thousand pigs are an ordure curse. And Shanghai has an appetite for many tens of thousands of pigs.

Industrialized agriculture eliminated chronic malnutrition from

China, but what will the pork-fed citizens of Shanghai do to save Lake Taihu? All the evidence tells us that industrial farming is unsustainable, but the world has been bribed into blindness by a ham sandwich. The global food empire, despite the dire prophecies, is still going strong.

Perhaps the food trade and the affluence it creates will outweigh the shocks of environmental collapse. Perhaps all the millions of healthy, well-nourished Chinese will puzzle out a solution to the grim formulae of carrying capacity, food miles, and erosion. Or perhaps China will follow the example of North America and sweep its industrial farming hells under the carpet, shoving its giant hog farms and eerie tracts of monoculture crops into rural ghettos far from the sight of the cities. This has worked for the past hundred years in the United States and in Europe (how many people in Pittsburgh or San Diego have ever smelled a slurry pond?). Currently, China retains its patchwork character—its heedlessly stitched gardens and dumps and power plants and rice paddies. It still jumbles the good and the dangerous in its food empire, the bowls of stir-fried chicken with a brittle infrastructure, free consumption with the wreckage of unseen land behind the billboards.

Back in the Bund, along Shanghai's riverside promenade, it's impossible to squint through the drizzle at the miracles of Pudong. The precipitation here is unlike the bracing, almost salty damp of a British rain or the steamy exhalation of summer on the American Eastern Seaboard. It can't even be characterized as a dirty fog or smog. It's dusty, as if the water dripped down an old factory wall, and grey particles diffuse the light in weird angles. Everything looks farther away than it should, as if reflected in an automobile's grimy side mirror.

When the rain passes, a perpetual twilight still glowers above the river, but the hawkers come out with their plastic. One popular item is a toy pig that stretches and splatters and then pops back into its original, cheery form, unmutilated. Even though it sells for ten renminbi apiece (about $1.50 U.S.)—three for ten after a moment's listless haggle—it isn't the bargain it appears to be. It's impossible to know if the factory that made it stands on paved-over agricultural ground (almost certainly), if its workers earn a fair wage (only possibly), or if the chemicals used to boil up the plastic trinkets were disposed of responsibly (almost definitely not). Yet the little squeezy pig is so cheap, it requires no thought to buy it, break it, and toss it in the garbage. To squander it away.

If the people who live in Shanghai dislike the perpetual mist, they don't complain about it to Westerners. When pressed about the view of Pudong, they have a habit of giving noncommittal answers, like, "Yes, it is misty, isn't it?" Perhaps they've become inured to noontime murk. Perhaps the pollution is so pervasive that they don't even realize it's hanging in their lungs. It's human nature, after all, to ignore a crisis until we're spitting it into our Kleenexes.

About our food empire, the doomsayers will continue to grumble while the optimists put their faith in technology or God. The pessimists at least have the backing of history. For ten thousand years, human beings have built food empires and whittled them back into parched earth and hunger.

Jia-an Cheng, a professor of entomology at Zhejiang University near Shanghai, sums up the problem with a proverb: "In the olden days, the emperor takes his people as gods and his people take food as the first necessity." In other words, the people stand above the emperor and food stands above the people. Should an emperor neglect his people's sustenance, he would offend the gods. But the modern industrial food empire has no emperor. Its guiding power is the market, which is neither the most pious nor forward-looking intelligence.

Professor Cheng draws on another point, this one culled from folk etymology.[12] "The Chinese character for cooked rice is actually an amalgamation of two other characters. The one for food, and one that can mean revolt. Because without food, all you are left with is revolt."

CHAPTER SEVEN

Blood: The Conquest of Food

In the late sixteenth century, only desperate souls sailed to Asia. But that's what the Carlettis decided to do in March 1596. Francesco is vague about their reasons, although it seems that his father Antonio was again the restless engine to their wanderings. In unsteady health, and with his finances far from secure, Antonio resolved on the course of action most likely to extinguish his bloodline.

Thumbing their noses once more at Spanish law, the pair embarked on a ship out of Acapulco, signing on as the "constable of artillery" and "guardian of the ship." Two other sailors performed these duties while the captain pocketed their wages, but no tiresome immigration officials came snooping to enforce colonial edicts. And so, stowed in the rolling misery of a sixteenth-century oceangoing vessel, the Carlettis crossed the Pacific.

Sixty-six days later they made landfall on the Mariana Islands (where they lost several crewmembers in a rash stab at preaching the gospel to the locals). Then they sailed to Luzon, the largest of the islands in the Philippines, a pearl in the imperial Spanish crown. Spain considered the islands to be part of the West Indies, not the East, and they attracted the same breed of adventurers and priests who had settled in Cuzco and the Yucatán. Manila had recently become the principal gateway between Asia and the New World colonies, and Castilian architecture had begun to sprout among the mangroves.

Francesco Carletti liked the Philippines, especially the local chickens, which, even if cooked fresh after throttling, "were so tender that they seemed to have been slaughtered for ten days or more." He had high praise, too, for the quality of the bananas and breadfruit. But he was most impressed by the Filipino practice of genital piercing. "I should not dare to relate [this tale] . . . if I had not seen it myself, not wishing to be taken for a liar," says Carletti. He's not giggling, or worse, fluttering his morals. "Out of curiosity and to be certain about it, I also spent some money to be showed what I had been told about," says the man of the world, who then expounds on the Philippine method of "arming" a male member with lead studs. It's history's first record of the Prince Albert.

The Carlettis stayed in Manila for nearly a year, enjoying the palm wine and poultry before setting out again, this time for Japan. Francesco's journal doesn't provide details, but it seems that, once they had bought new merchandise, they didn't wish to pay the local Spaniards their customary loading fee for sending it back to Acapulco. Mostly likely, Antonio realized they could cut the greedy Spanish out of the equation entirely by sailing for the Portuguese holdings in China. There were harsh prohibitions against just this sort of dodge, so in the dark of night during May 1597, father and son embarked on a Japanese vessel bound for Nagasaki. The Japanese, being their own masters, had no regulations at the time that barred Italians from turning a profit in their ports.

Japan, though never colonized by Europeans, was at the wayward tip of Portugal's commercial empire. Portuguese sailors and priests maintained an official presence in Nagasaki, although they weren't always welcome: the Carlettis' first act upon disembarking was to take a gruesome day trip to see the crucified bodies of six Franciscan missionaries. Then they settled down for a long layover, taking notes on language, social mores, and particularly on the local prostitutes. "In this sort of venereal pleasures that country is more abundant—as it is of every other sort of vice—than any other part of the world."

Francesco wasn't particularly impressed with Japanese cuisine, which he found lacking in wine and olives, and he disliked the local practice of eating unripe fruit. But they stayed nearly a year anyway before eventually hopping a Japanese smuggling boat bound for Macao, an island outside the city of Canton on the Chinese mainland. A Portuguese enclave on the island ran a profitable business in raw silk, cloth, lead, and quicksilver, as well as in porcelain, precious metals, and "dry groceries." The Carlettis wanted a piece of the action, but having no licenses for travel or trade, they sneaked ashore at midnight and took refuge in the Jesuit house in the colony. By morning, word had spread among the locals that a pair of fabulously wealthy Italian investors had arrived in town with the intent of making a fortune on the China-Japan trading route. Smelling money, the authorities threw the Carlettis in jail.

Francesco writes, "We said we were of the Italian nations and came from a country that was independent, like Japan, and not subject to either one or another Spanish nation, and that moving about the world was a thing allowed to all the nations." But his appeal to the principles of free trade didn't work. The judge fined them two thousand scudi and commanded them to present themselves to the viceroy in India for disposal. This unhappy loss of cash, combined with the stress of the sea voyage, imprisonment, and a case of the "stone sickness," proved too much for old Antonio's health, and he died in Macao that July, "having first received all the sacraments of the Church."

The loss of Antonio nearly broke his son's spirit. His father had been a schemer and a scofflaw, always willing to risk both fortune and progeny on an insanely dangerous whim to, say, ride in an open boat across several thousand miles of storm-wracked ocean. But he had been Francesco's guide in life and his only relation. Brokenhearted, the twenty-four-year-old Francesco buried his father in Macao's church. "Then, left alone, and in so remote a region, opposite to our hemisphere, I gave myself over to considering the unimaginable affliction in which I found myself."

Nonetheless, before long, Carletti's natural cheer bubbled back. Despite the two thousand scudi fine, he still had a good deal of money left, and he felt no particular compunction about disobeying the judge's command to go to India. Eleven days after the burial, another Florentine arrived in port, the first countryman Carletti had met since he left Sanlúcar de Barrameda. This was Orazio Neretti, a globe-trotting merchant who at once stepped into Antonio's empty shoes. Carletti stayed on in China for the next seventeen months, living in the house next door to Neretti's, procrastinating over the voyage back to Europe. Neretti appears to have taught Francesco more about profitable business practices than Antonio ever did, and during their time together, the young merchant invested his inheritance in musk, silk thread, velvet, porcelain jars filled with preserved fruit, and lumps of raw gold.

In his hours away from the haggling tables, Carletti read books about Chinese geography and even studied a few characters in Mandarin, but his real interests were more tactile. He writes with passion about mangoes and lychees, and especially on the subject of native oranges, "which are better and of more sorts than ours, among them being one larger than a football." The variety of edible ducks, too, he finds thrilling, and the size of the oysters astounded him. As for the women, he disappointedly notes that they "are said to be very beautiful and well made, but . . . the men are so jealous of these women that they never allow them to see anyone," concluding his observations with an anecdote about the king of Siam, who caught his concubines "pleasuring themselves with certain appropriate fruits," and punished them by heating oil "in copper pots" and frying them alive. Then he recounts a secondhand report about penis implants in the kingdom of Pegu.

It's tempting to dismiss Carletti as a cheap sensationalist. After all, here was one of the most widely traveled men of the sixteenth century, yet he never seriously questioned the worldview that he carried with him, like a Saint Christopher charm, out of Italy. All the marvels of Asia were, in the end, just a heap of spices and jarred pears, and if the whores of Nagasaki were worth remembering, it was only on account of their difference from the whores in Seville. But that is exactly why he's a fine reporter. Although he was fully capable of shock and judgment, he relished his immersion in foreign parts. He was willing to be impressed. "Every invention for good or for evil, of beauty or of ugliness, must have come from that region," he writes of China. "Not having had it from us or from the Greeks or other nations who taught it to us, but from native creators."

In December 1599, Carletti finally embarked on the homeward leg of his voyage, dividing his now-impressive collection of Chinese goods between two Portuguese ships bound for India by way of Malaysia. Bidding farewell to the grave of his father and to his friend Neretti, and complaining severely about the unchristian squalor of the ship, he sailed westward, with occasional stops for business.

The first of these was the port of Malacca. Here, truly, was the eye of the commercial vortex, where even the humblest peasant stood doused in pepper dust, the stuff of every merchant's most opulent fantasies, as well as nutmeg from the Banda Islands and cloves from the Moluccas. This was the world's central spice port, the key to the Portuguese empire of ships, guns, and, of course, food.

Malacca was Portuguese on account of a bout of hard fighting less than a century earlier, in which the Portuguese dealt an oblique, painful wound to Venice by sidelining her overland spice trade. Perfectly situated to dominate the seaborne spice business, Malacca stands exactly at the point in the Indian Ocean where monsoons and trade winds converge, so sailors from both east and west can reach it with relative ease. Indian vessels, for instance, could sail there in March and return to their home ports in late summer. Chinese traders would arrive early in the year with the trade winds at their backs, sailing back east around June.[1]

Carletti, as usual, took pains to describe the reason for the bustle:

> *[Pepper] grows near a tree, to which the plant clings as peas do, though these grow much larger and have leaves very like those of our beans, but more round. The grains of pepper grow attached to the stalk, like bunches of small grapes, in two rows of grains, and they remain green until they are fully ripe, which they become in the month of January. Then they turn black, though another sort always stays white, and that is the variety most prized by those Indians. While still green, both kinds are fixed in vinegar with salt and eaten as we eat capers, to whet the appetite. And they also have an admirable effect in comforting and warming the stomach.*[2]

In 1511, nearly a century before Carletti's visit, a Portuguese fleet of fifteen ships landed near the port and unloaded a siege crew of fifteen hundred men, among them the young Fernão de Magalhães, known to Anglophones as Ferdinand Magellan. They had come to avenge a defeat inflicted on them two years earlier by the sultan of the city, Mahmud Shah. Even though they were outnumbered twenty to one, the Europeans had allies in the local Chinese and Indian traders, and in the Malaccans who had turned against their sultan after he had executed a popular politician (and his entire family) on false charges. So when the invaders stormed the city, native resistance was less stalwart than the sultan expected.

But the Portuguese didn't care about Malaysian politics, nor about the sixth commandment. They raked the avenues with cannon fire and spared only the lives and property of the locals who had actively sided with them, butchering or enslaving the rest. Then they set to building a fortress with which to lord over their latest imperial subjects. Appalled at the brutality of their new overlords, the Malaccans plotted a rebellion, which was promptly quashed in a season of beheadings.[3]

When Carletti visited the volatile port, he noted that the Portuguese forbade native spice gatherers, who were young and Muslim, from entering the city out of fear that they might incite violence. Carletti called them "courageous and bellicose . . . and by nature treacherous and scornful of death, to which they pay small heed."[4] Under the shadow of European guns, the gatherers dumped their wares outside the city walls, took their pay, and walked back into the countryside.

After cementing the last brick of their fortress, the Portuguese imposed a grossly unfair trade arrangement on the Malaccans. Carletti, being a professional trader himself, explains how the imperial governor bought the spice in exchange for cloth that he obtained from visiting merchants, then sold the pepper to these same merchants, generating a 70 to 80 percent profit "without any capital and without any risk whatever . . . putting into this deal nothing but words."[5] Through the centuries-old text, you can practically hear the whistle of admiration from the observer. This was exploitation at its gilded, shameless best.

Of course, the Malaccans hated that their profits disappeared into Portuguese account books, but with colonialism and food empires the people in power got rich. The producers got calluses and a festering grievance. Although Carletti and his Portuguese hosts didn't suffer a bloody redistribution of wealth at the hands of the spice sellers outside the walls, the revolt inevitably did occur.

REBELLION IN THE SPICE ISLANDS

As well as conquering Malacca, the Portuguese had the good fortune (and navigational skill) to discover the Banda Islands, which lie south of the Moluccas at the eastern end of the Indonesian archipelago, just north of what is today East Timor. In the sixteenth century, the Banda Islands were the only spot on the globe to produce nutmeg. Starting in the fifteenth century, European recipes required handfuls of the stuff—for example, *The Sensible Cook,* a Dutch cookbook published in 1667, includes a recipe for a chicken pasty that's a violent salad of clashing flavors: boiled chicken, cinnamon, cloves, ginger, damson prunes, candied pears and cherries, pine nuts, and heaping spoonfuls of nutmeg.[6] Carletti describes the nutmeg fruit as similar to a walnut but delicious when mixed with sugar and potted into a conserve. Another spice, mace, comes from grating the rind.[7]

The Bandanese made a comfortable business from selling nutmeg, but when the Portuguese captured Malacca, they didn't leave any other buyers alive, thus cornering the nutmeg market. Even as Carletti watched the governor-general cackle over his percentages, however, the Portuguese spice monopoly was coming to an end. In 1599, four Dutch ships had stealthily tracked the Portuguese traders on their way to Malacca, and landed on the Banda Islands. At once, the Dutch tried to make friends with the local sultans and copied the native practice of buying spice from the gatherers, then steeping it in salt and vinegar for a few days before boiling, sweetening, and preserving it for the voyage to Europe.[8] They also bought whole nutmegs and coated them in lime.

Relations between the Dutch and Bandanese started off so pleasantly that the Dutch got the impression that they had charmed their way into monopolizing the nutmeg business. Being meticulous sorts, and having a cultural affinity for legal documents, the Dutch penned a treaty that formally established their right to the entire nutmeg trade. The Bandanese, being agreeable sorts, signed it. But the Bandanese had no intention of ruining their profits for the sake of ink and paper. They continued selling spice to their Dutch friends, but also to the

Portuguese and now to the English, who complicated matters by sending one Captain James Lancaster, of the British East India Company (whom we'll meet in chapter 8), to raise a flag on the islands.

Incensed by what they viewed as the betrayal of a legal contract, the governing Lords Seventeen of the Dutch East India Company sat down to debate their revenge. The more aggressive among them argued that guns were the only means to defend their commercial rights, force the Bandanese to accept low prices, and drive away competitive buyers. Muskets would keep input costs low, profits high, and safeguard the future value of the Company. The more peaceable lords couldn't come up with a good alternative to this. Muskets carried the argument.

To oversee the hostilities, the Company sent an officer named Jan Pieterszoon Coen. Born in 1587 in Hoorn to a sea captain's wife, Coen was no stranger to Southeast Asia. He had signed up with the Company as a teenager and sailed to the East Indies years before with a fleet under one Pieter Verhoeff. After fighting the Portuguese from Mozambique to Goa to Malacca, Verhoeff and the young Coen arrived in the Banda Islands, just in time to hear the angry Dutch spice merchants complain about their breached contracts.[9] Coen was present when Verhoeff opened negotiations with the natives by digging the foundations for a military fortress. The Bandanese, fearful of a repeat of Malacca's fate, lured Verhoeff and his advisors into the forest for a renewal of trade talks. The Dutch followed their guides into an ambush, where Verhoeff and most his men died under a hail of arrows.[10] One of the few to escape the massacre was Coen.

When he reappeared in Amsterdam in 1610, Coen, now a decorated officer, told the lords that the nutmeg cause was not lost. Instead of approaching the Bandanese cap in hand and buying the spice on their terms, Coen argued that the Dutch East India Company should return to the islands as a conquering army.[11] Coercion, said Coen, was the only way to safeguard a monopoly that, despite its unfairness to the actual owners of the nutmeg, was Dutch by right. Besides, honor called for vengeance against the traitors. So the lords gave him a fleet.

In 1619, under his new title, governor-general of the Dutch East Indies, Coen broke ground for a fortress on the island of Java. This was Batavia, soon to be headquarters for the Dutch spice trade. At about this time, he also wrote a brazen but very honest account of his colonial business plan. Its tone is reminiscent of an in-house corporate memo:

> *Piece goods from Gujarat we can barter for pepper and gold on the coast of Sumatra; rials and cottons from the coast for pepper in Bantam . . . piece goods from the Coromandel Coast in exchange for spices . . . from China . . . one thing leads to another. And all of it can be done without any money from the Netherlands and with ships alone. We have the most important spices already. What is missing then? Nothing else but ships and a little water to prime the pump . . . (by this I mean sufficient means so that the rich Asian trade may be established). Hence, gentlemen and good administrators, there is nothing to prevent the Company from acquiring the richest trade in the world.*[12]

Coen's portrait, which today hangs in the Westfries Museum in his hometown of Hoorn, is different from many of the formal portraits of his contemporaries. While other prosperous Dutchmen downplayed their riches by appearing (on canvas at least) in clothes drab enough to shame a Calvinist church mouse, Coen blooms with gold embroidery.[13] In the portrait, he leans back, his prow-shaped beak cocked upward from an ordered brush of facial hair. His hand rests on a golden sword hilt. He looks rich and mighty, a man who enjoys bossing fleets. But despite all the trimmings on his outfit, one of his superiors once described him as "very modest in his living, chaste . . . no drunkard."[14]

Coen's first act as governor-general was to discourage competing spice traders, beginning by sinking Chinese pepper junks and enslaving their crews. He sacked trading towns on the island of Java and blockaded the fort at Bantam. After demolishing an English spice factory and executing a band of Gujarati traders, he finally turned his attentions to the root of Dutch rage—the treacherous Bandanese nutmeg pickers themselves. There would be no quarter for these murderers, these breakers of legal procedure.

In 1620, the last English garrison on the islands surrendered to Coen, but the natives proved more resistant. It took a second wave of soldiers, but eventually the islanders succumbed to Dutch musketry. Scholars estimate that out of an original population of about fifteen thousand, no more than a few hundred survived the attacks. (Coen himself estimated a lower death toll of twenty-five hundred, with three thousand more enslaved.)[15] Most of the survivors went to Batavia in chains, with a handful kept back to teach the conquerors how to grow nutmeg. The islands became plantations, clean of crops, villages, and people.[16] The spice trade had extinguished native life.

Having secured the nutmeg, Coen determined to apply the same techniques to the clove business. Europeans liked these little berries almost as much as they liked nutmeg, and the Portuguese had made an enviable profit on shipping them from their colonies in the Moluccas. Having learned his lesson in the Bandas, Coen needed no excuse for destruction, and he steeled himself to wipe the Moluccas clean in 1621. But the end of the campaigning season forced his fleet to return to Batavia, slaughter undone.

By then, word had reached Amsterdam of Coen's excesses. Perhaps fearing for their Christian souls, the leaders of the Company wrote, "We would have wished for matters to be taken care of with more moderate measures," and they relieved him of his post.[17] Amazingly, this only made matters worse. In Coen's absence, the colonists lost any remaining glimmer of restraint. Anyone suspected of compromising the Dutch monopoly on spice was imprisoned and tortured, usually by having water forced down his gullet until his tissues swelled up. After one particularly gruesome spate of executions (the Amboyna Massacre of ten Englishmen, ten Japanese, and a Portuguese, with the leader of the English being drawn and quartered), the Dutch East India Company panicked and sent Coen back to restore mildness and order.

The next decades were hard ones for the Spice Islanders. The Dutch and the English continued their global gamesmanship, with the natives suffering forcible relocation, imprisonment, or execution. The islanders rebelled unsuccessfully, but within a few decades, neat plantations of spice trees had entirely replaced the original hardwood forests. Spice prices in Europe, which were determined by ruff-collared men in Amsterdam, remained inflated, while prices in the islands remained under Company directive. Coen's tactics of land clearances, enforced serfdom, and iron control of trade had proved a complete success. The Company realized profits of 1,000 percent.[18]

About two hundred years later, a British traveler visited the Banda Islands and commented particularly on the "parks." He noted how the landscape looked like a single, vast nutmeg grove, containing exactly 319,804 fruit-bearing trees. Although neatly planted, the trees weren't well tended by the gardeners—convicts all. A lot of the harvest blew away, uncollected, in the monsoon winds. There was no indigenous population to gather it.[19]

In the still life paintings so popular with seventeenth-century Dutch artists, symbolism is at play among the fruit bowls. Take, for example, *Still Life with a Basket of Fruit* (1622) by Balthasar van der Ast. He finished it the year of Coen's recall for brutality, and, as befits a picture from a maritime empire, the subject is a global bounty. There are tulips, gourds, and grapes, as well as East Indian shells and Chinese crockery. But the fruit is blemished and abuzz. Insects inch along the puckered skin. A grasshopper mulls its next attack on the corrupted flesh and juices. It was a painting that men like Coen might have studied as they sat in a Company anteroom, waiting for news of a captaincy while the North Sea wind rattled against the windows and their minds drifted back to the Indies and the green heat of the nutmeg shore. Perhaps the painting would have stirred memories they had preferred to leave buried in the ruins of Java. But then the riches of the East would beckon, again, in the ink of a Company commission. And they would return.

CHIAPAS

The seventeenth-century Dutch were consummate food traders. Many Dutchmen prided themselves on military and nautical accomplishments or on legal wit, but the spice merchants won the imperial riches that paid for all the soldiery, gunboats, and artists' smocks. And the only way they could safeguard their monopoly on spice was by grinding up the people who actually produced it.

This is a common refrain in food empires. In the historical record from Egypt to the Americas (both pre-Columbian and colonial) to the Soviet Union, dignified freeholders are much less common than serfs. Food production is so valuable to societies that the ruling powers err toward brutality when overseeing the people who grow the crops. When the Spice Islanders rebelled, their colonial overlords dealt with the conflict by exterminating them and designing a profitable plantation. Today, another global food empire is in conflict with traditional farmers who, for reasons of culture or obstinacy or self-preservation, won't cooperate.

On the first day of January 1994 the phone rang in the home of President Carlos Salinas de Gortari of Mexico. At midnight, the North American Free Trade Agreement had gone into effect, binding the continent in a trade pact that guaranteed the open flow of goods and services, ending decades of government protectionism. It seemed a resounding victory for free markets. But at 2:00 a.m., the southern province of Chiapas erupted.[20] A group invoking the name of a long-dead agrarian hero, Emiliano Zapata, had occupied the city of San Cristóbal de las Casas. Calling themselves the Zapatista Army of National Liberation, they declared war on the federal government, saying that their cause was "the dispossessed, we are millions and we thereby call upon our brothers and sisters to join this struggle as the only path, so that we will not die of hunger."[21]

The rebels issued their declaration of war and immediately retreated into the hills, but all the newspapers quoted the rebel leader, Subcomandante Marcos, as saying, "The free-trade agreement is a death certificate for the Indian peoples of Mexico."[22] That's because NAFTA, and the global food empire as a whole, had changed the price of corn.

Over the previous decades, rising living costs had savaged Mexico's poorest farmers. The fast-growing population, particularly the country's new urbanites, wanted to eat meat instead of beans. To feed the growing appetite for *carne picada,* farmers had switched their arable land to pasture, thereby reducing the supply of corn. Improvements in farm machinery further broadened the gap between wealthy landowners and the indigenous farmers scratching out a living on the slopes in out-of-the-way places like Chiapas. In an interlocked global food market, there was no place for a subsistence corn grower.[23] Before NAFTA, these communities had cultivated beans and corn on communal land, using no better technology than iron tools and back muscles. They ate what they needed and sold any modest surplus to the Mexican government at guaranteed (and inflated) prices. From the modern perspective, this was an unproductive and, worse, an expensive way to farm.

Sage economists argued that Mexico should embrace the global marketplace rather than hunker behind a misplaced sentimentality for peasant life. With NAFTA, farmers on the American border would be able to grow crops for sale in U.S. supermarkets, while the hinterland could focus on cattle ranching, which would fetch a neat profit from buyers around the world. The United States, with its huge farms and computerized tractors, could sell Mexico all the grain it needed. Every area would specialize. Everyone would win.

The first steps toward a modern food system happened long before the idea of NAFTA topped a stack of policy papers. Even by the 1960s, 2.4 percent of landowners owned 60 percent of Mexican land. These latifundia owners exported their crops to the global market, lessening local supplies so that by 1980, 90 percent of rural Mexicans were malnourished.[24] The poorest of the poor were the Mayan farmers in Chiapas. They already had a long tradition of seizing municipal buildings and firing guns when angered, but they only indulged in truly organized violence when NAFTA went into effect. The final straw for them was Article 703 of the agreement, which states, "The Parties shall work together to improve access to their respective markets through the reduction or elimination of import barriers to trade between them in agricultural goods."[25]

Innocuous language, seemingly, but it eliminated the government-guaranteed prices of grain for small farmers, who would have no defense against a deluge of high-tech American corn. On the other hand, the growth of Mexican horticulture would mean many farmers could haul themselves out of poverty. So the Zapatistas didn't take up arms against hunger—their casus belli wasn't their bellies. They rebelled against the feeling that other people were making money from unfair rules imposed by a distant, malign government. It was anger at the perception of foreign profiteers, of Yankees growing fat as the Mayan way of life dissolved into the global economic melting pot.

Of course, the Zapatista revolt begs the question, wouldn't a Chiapas subsistence farmer be better off joining the twentieth century instead of scraping a few bushels of worthless corn from his land?

From a perspective of almost twenty years later, it seems that all of the predictions about NAFTA (both the good and the bad) have come true. The bad news for the Chiapas farmers is that the United States is astoundingly good at producing corn. Mechanization, oil-based inputs, and vast fields devoted to a single crop yield 8.5 metric tons of corn per hectare. In Mexico, the yields are 5.8 tons per hectare at best, with ideal levels of irrigation. Rain-fed land, like that in the Chiapas highlands, yields a paltry 2 tons.[26] Once NAFTA went into effect, corn sales from the United States to Mexico went up 240 percent. On the other side of the ledger, however, Mexican horticulture is thriving, and while about a fifth of small corn producers have disappeared, imports of "white" corn (the type used for tortillas, rather than the "yellow corn" that is used as livestock feed) have actually decreased since 2000. The Mexican corn grower hasn't suffered the death sentence that the Zapatistas anticipated. But they aren't thriving, either.

Agriculture is a muddy subject. It's easy to lament the decline of indigenous cultures, but in a world that's crowded with hungry babies it seems irresponsible to waste good arable land on inefficient farming like the style practiced by the Mayans in Chiapas. The more food we can coax out of every hectare under the tractor, the less we'll be tempted to chop down another forest or drain another shimmering bog. Efficiency should be good for biodiversity and the planet, except for the unfortunate truth that food from big, modern farms is practically watered with fossil fuels, which is undoubtedly very bad for the planet. One of the central questions of the twenty-first century is whether we can feed the urban world from small farms using "traditional" farming methods, supplying our cities and our civilization in a sustainable way. The answer will determine the nature of our cities, our economies, our diets, our health, and our very conception of what it means to live and eat.

In 1997, during field research about agroforestry on the Belize-Guatemala border, one of the authors of this book drove along a cracked dirt road, deep into the Mayan highlands. Unlike in wooded country, the sky here was big, as open as the sea. Absent was the high bush of popular imagination. There were no jungle flowers, no huge unfurling crocuses dripping with nectar, no jaguars, no monkey tribes. Occasional patches of pottery poked from the dirt, remnants of the last food empire to grow grain on these hills, more than a thousand years ago. This agricultural land had been worked by the ancient Mayans. After the road disappeared into grass, we walked for hours through empty fields, flesh poaching in the tropical heat until we heard the click of machetes and the swish of leaves.

A cluster of indigenous farmers were hand stripping a field for a late planting. The men bent into the waist-high scrub, their tools swinging like jagged clockworks, tearing out the roots. Swidden agriculturalists, these farmers worked a field until it was exhausted, then they moved on to exploit a virgin patch. In areas of low population density, where the forest is allowed to recover in the years between plantings, this is a sensible, sustainable way of growing food.[27] But once populations swell, the revolving gangs of swidden farmers overplant a diminishing acreage. Fallow land cannot recover. It turns into scrub, land that's neither nutrient rich nor ecologically varied. Twenty years ago, the fields on the Guatemalan border were old-growth forest, a piping kettle of biological diversity. By ten years ago, they had been slashed into ineffective cornfields. Today, they're useless for growing much except thorns.

This is the way most people have fed themselves for the past ten thousand years: slash and burn, plant and uproot. While natural farming like this doesn't infect the land with man-made corrosions, it doesn't manage to keep many people alive, either. Swidden farming is an unrealistic way to grow food in a world of 9 billion mouths.

THE MORAL ECONOMY OF FOOD

When the seventeenth-century Spice Islanders or the Zapatista rebels picked up their weapons to bring down a food empire, their failure was a foregone conclusion. They were attacking a system that, despite social and environmental rapine, delivers pepper to middle-class European stewpots and fresh vegetables to middle-class American grocery bags.

The spice gatherer or native farmer can't sway the unshakable weight of urban shoppers. Only when that weight is shifted, and the urban masses' hunger is no longer satisfied, do guillotines sing and food empires tumble into dust. There is nothing as politically terrifying as a pack of modern urbanites roused to an ancient measure of fury.

That's what happened in France in 1789 and in America in 1917. In a memoir published in 1920, a New York housewife named Marie Ganz wrote:

> *Hunger! That dreadful word, emblazoned in great white letters upon the black flag of the radicals, might have waved over our tenements in February of 1917 . . . In the streets thousands of white, pinched faces told of the specter of want that was hovering over us.*[28]

Marie Ganz was suffering through neither a poor harvest nor an economic collapse. The people in New York during the early months of 1917 were going hungry because of the rising price of groceries. Ganz continues, "The day of the food profiteer had come. Prices had risen rapidly to such figures that many of our ghetto folk were living on only bread and tea, and there were very few among us who really had enough to eat."

American retail prices had, in a matter of weeks, jumped nearly 30 percent because of huge food shipments wending their way across the ocean to wartime Europe. But the real culprit, in Ganz's view, was avarice. Food merchants took advantage of high demand to manipulate commodity prices, tinkering with supply to boost their profits.[29] For the urban poor in 1917, the real cost of sustenance rose to between 40 and 60 percent of wages. Eggs, which cost thirty-two cents per dozen in 1916, now cost eighty cents. Cabbages rose from two cents to twelve. Savings accumulated over lifetimes vanished into bread. The *New York Times* reported that food merchants were driving their supplies away from hungry markets to the richest ones—shops in Baltimore, for instance, missed shipments from dealers who knew they could make a fatter profit in New York.[30]

Thousands of mostly Jewish immigrant housewives, including Ganz, rioted through Madison Square under the banner of the Mothers'

Anti–High Price League. They stormed the Waldorf-Astoria, shouted socialist slogans, and announced a city-wide boycott of groceries to be enforced with beatings at the hands of Jewish mothers.

"We allowed people to buy only certain foods on which there seemed to be the least profiteering," wrote Ganz. "They could buy bread, butter, milk and cereals though surely all these were far more expensive than they should have been and any person who was caught buying anything else was mobbed."[31]

Ganz and her comrades presented such an intimidating front that New Yorkers didn't dare risk angering them. Food rotted on shelves. In a few days, vendors cut their prices to coax customers back into the marketplace. But the rioters didn't waver:

> *Cart after cart [of produce] was overturned, and the pavements were covered with trampled goods. The women used their black shopping bags as clubs, striking savagely at the men whom they regarded as their sworn enemies and oppressors. Onions, potatoes, cabbages flew through the air, and in each instance the target was a ducking, wailing peddler, whose stock had been ruined beyond hope of recovery. Policemen came rushing upon the scene, and they, too, were pelted with whatever was at hand. Surely a thousand women perhaps twice as many were in that mad struggle, long-enduring wives and mothers who had resolved to bear the oppression of the profiteer no longer.*[32]

Profiteering over groceries would not be tolerated in this land of plenty, at least not by the housewives of MAHPL, who were engaged in a sort of food rebellion. Unlike the food riots in ancient Rome or prerevolutionary Paris or Russia, these rioters weren't political. They were simply enraged that their children had to skip meals while someone else—the faceless, paunchy profiteer—drank Champagne.[33]

The same problem happened in 1911 when French housewives rioted over meat, cheese, and eggs, and again in Barcelona in 1918. Europe has a venerable tradition of food riots. Hundreds of them erupted in the seventeenth and eighteenth centuries, often at the instigation of women. A typical attack occurred in Sussex in 1801, when a group of housewives in petticoats, upset at being sold inferior flour by their local miller, marched into his mill and tore up the cloth he was using to dress the meal. Leaving him cowering in fear for his life, they retired to the nearest pub to toast their victory, never to suffer a legal consequence.[34] Often, the riots were spontaneous reactions to overcharging, as in a 1773 raid on the cellar of British wheat merchants who had tried to raise their prices:

> *Seven or eight hundred tinners went thither, who first offered the cornfactors seventeen shillings for 24 gallons of wheat; but being told they should have none, they immediately broke open the cellar doors, and took away all in the place without money or price.*[35]

It's not far removed from modern headlines. And the Zapatistas, too, would have sympathized with the guiding spirit of the violence. The English food riots of the early industrial period happened at a time when ancient entitlements to a day's bread were collapsing under the force of new economic theories. Before the Industrial Revolution, the English food trade operated in a controlled marketplace. Government oversaw markets and tolls, and aristocrats were morally bound to feed their dependents. Even paupers could often rely on meals at the abbey door. Most importantly, a law called the Assize of Bread, the origins of which dated to medieval times, fixed the price of the daily staple. The law regulated the quality of flour, the weight and shapes of loaves, and the baker's fee, so no one would be tempted to exploit the poor for profit. The law governed farmers, too, obliging them to sell grain at markets on stipulated days instead of fresh from their fields, where speculating merchants would have a chance to buy at an advantage, and the urban poor would not. Capital, in those days, was not much trusted.

Middlemen suffered even greater restrictions. They couldn't buy crops "standing" (on contract) or for resale from the same marketplace within a three-month period. The poor, however, could purchase their household grain at the first bell of the market day; grain merchants had to wait for the second.

In short, until the eighteenth century, the Assize of Bread kept grain cheap for individual eating but squashed middlemen or any bakers with entrepreneurial inclinations. But by the end of the century, the idea of laissez-faire economics was beginning to settle into the brains of intellectuals. One would write, "Let corn flow like water, and it will find its level."[36]

In the 1990s, the Zapatistas and NAFTA would fight the same economic battle in an old clash of ideals. The rebels didn't raise their guns against famine, but against the same hazy plutocrats who inspired the housewives of New York to tear apart the Waldorf. So on one side stand the howling protesters, believers that possession of food is a moral affair. Their rallying call is Proverbs 11:26: "He that withholdeth corn, the people shall curse him: but blessing shall be upon the head of him that selleth it."

On the other side are the hazy plutocrats, the retailers and students of Adam Smith who believe that food lacks any moral component. The eminence behind the articulation of free market capitalism, Adam Smith used granite rationality to crush the logic of the Assize of Bread. He argued that instead of helping to feed the poor, ancient protections like the assize actually harmed people by encouraging them to consume in times of scarcity.[37] For Smith, the most benign manner of trade was a free market that would ensure a year-long supply, with some sellers hoarding their grain for the months of want. In this system, prices might rise at first, but then foreign traders would flood the grain bins with imports. The key was free movement, with middlemen regulating the flow of supply.

Smith would have had a convincing argument if food were the same as every other tradable commodity. But the housewives of New York and the Zapatista rebels saw grain as something ontologically distinct from pig iron. They evoked the logic of the Assize of Bread, positing that food is a right, a public good, and that its supply ought to be directed with a moral hand.

This moral element was the concern of a country gentleman who wrote a letter to the British Parliament in 1768 denouncing the illegality of the food riots at the time. Nonetheless, he argued that food, coming through God by his agents of sun, rain, and soil, is in its essence distinct from money. While money may be "lawfully desired and fought over," the writer cautioned against the lure of Mammon, particularly "the oppressive and unjust means used for obtaining it," in which he lumped the business of food trading. The letter ended on a protectionist note, lamenting the scarcity of grain in England when so much was exported to foreign marketplaces.

The eighteenth-century conflict between the idea of food as a commodity or as a moral entitlement, and the letter writer's visceral discomfort with exporting grain while prices soared, is familiar to us today. So is another eighteenth-century innovation—the upscale shopper. Free markets caused prices to rise, but they had also made wealthy men out of the millers and merchants. Bakers, eager to boost consumption among the affluent, developed new, more expensive styles of bread. Instead of baking the few types of loaves that had once been regulated by law, they could devote their best ingredients to making bread for sale to the rich, for which they could charge accordingly. Commoners had to make do with the dregs, often filled with unsavory additives.

Today, commoners still make do with eating the dregs. Academics now talk about "food deserts," urban neighborhoods bereft of fresh spinach.[38] Unprocessed, clean food is, in Western countries, a luxury item. High-income households spend about 12 percent of their food budgets on fresh meat and produce and eat twice as much of it as do low-income families, who spend only 7 percent of their grocery bills on healthy ingredients like raw chickens and turnips.[39] Fresh food is not only more expensive in poor neighborhoods (in both absolute and proportional senses), it is harder to find on the shelves.[40] Retail zoning and access to private cars are sometimes blamed, but education levels are also responsible for the triumph of Yellow No. 5, disodium phosphate, and "cheez."

It's not historically unusual for the poor to eat junk. But whenever the poor have realized that the health of their children matters less than a retailer's profit margin, then, historically, they've started to whistle the *Marseillaise*. A 1795 petition about the Leeds corn market stated that farmers arrived with "no corn to markit but what they carre in thare pockit . . . which cause the poore to groane very much."[41] These "poore" weren't nutmeg gatherers at the edge of an empire, or colonized natives, or even the truly destitute, but urban workers who were struggling to survive on the wages that had once been sufficient to their families. A statistical analysis of the eighteenth-century English riots notes that nearly all of the violence occurred on holidays or during nonworking hours.[42] The protestors were men and women with jobs. This suggests that not all of them were Levelers or Jacobins, but that the food riots were deeply populist.

Hunger isn't necessarily an injustice, but turning a profit on hunger is. Even so, centuries after the English riots, the rampaging housewives in Manhattan weren't starving to death, nor were their children going to perish for a lack of potatoes. As one of the protesters said, she didn't like margarine, and having become accustomed to butter, she wasn't going to go back.[43] The very idea was outrageous. Better to start smashing windows.

THE CLIMATE TRIGGER

Before the greatest of all food rebellions occurred in eighteenth-century France, the ruling powers tried very hard to stem the emergency by feeding the poor. France's famine of 1788—precipitated by urbanization, a global cooling set off by a volcanic eruption in Iceland, and the pangs of the El Niño cycle—ruined the best-laid plans of royal granary officials. Starting in 1788 and continuing until 1796, a succession of El Niño events pounded the world's agriculture, disrupting it to a degree unseen in a thousand years.[44]

William Roxburgh and Alexander Beatson, Scottish scientists who lived at the time of the French Revolution, compiled environmental data collected by ship captains and British East India Company clerks.[45] Their reports show disorderly weather and starvation across the globe. In Egypt, three successive years of low floods plunged the Middle East into famine. In Mexico, a prolonged drought dried up so much of Lake Pátzcuaro that farmers squabbled over the rich land unmasked by the receding waters. Off the coast of Peru, the surge in the El Niño current devastated fish stocks and parched coastal farms.[46] Captain Bligh of the *Bounty,* while sheltered in Matavai Bay, Tahiti, on December 6, 1788, took note of extraordinarily furious winds.[47] Shortly thereafter mutineers set him adrift, and this unprecedented cold spell with its attendant gusts and rainclouds helped him survive 3,618 miles in an open boat.

El Niño's mischief spread to every corner of the world. Canadian fur traders complained about the heat, and England recorded summertime temperatures in January. Winter thunderstorms in the United States hatched plagues of mosquitoes, which spread yellow fever up into the mid-Atlantic region. Thousands died in Philadelphia alone.

In France, the troubles began with a summer drought in 1787. This was followed in early 1788 by a late wet spring that spoiled much of the year's harvest. Food prices rose 50 percent, so merchants traded the reserves, and those who were fortunate enough to have invested in grain made a lot of money. This created the perception that idle merchants and landowners were profiting from other people's hardship. Grain prices continued to surge while sales of other goods, like wine, collapsed, further dragging down France's economy. Raids on bakeries became commonplace. Historian Louise Tilly suggests that people rioted for two reasons. Sometimes they cracked heads in simple marketplace roistering over the price of bread, but just as often they mobbed merchants who, they suspected, were exporting grain out of their towns, particularly by shipping it to Paris. Since the beginning of the seventeenth century, the government had taken tighter rein over the trade of foodstuffs, and Paris's growth as the country's biggest market had skewed prices in the provinces. The economic influence of the city was so disproportionate that the day's prices in the rue Mouffetard set the ones in Bordeaux.[48]

El Niño certainly didn't cause the French Revolution, but it gave a sharp jab to a teetering system. This confluence of weather disruptions and social unrest is a warning for today. Famine is almost always produced by a mix of social factors, politics, and economics, but the weather is often a guilty collaborator, and a starving mob can't take vengeance on an uncooperative sky. They can, however, lynch a retailer.

None of the world's developed economies took fright during the food riots of 2008. In the West, we don't usually empty our pockets when we buy groceries. A typical household spends about 10 percent of its income on foodstuffs, so a rise in prices by 50 percent means we would only be committed to spending 15 percent of our weekly budget on daily provender. But in poorer countries, where families may spend half their income to keep body and soul together, the same price hike of 50 percent would be disproportionate, costing the family 75 percent of their money. Also, Westerners eat a lot of processed foods, the final prices of which have little to do with the actual cost of corn or oil, which insulates us from fluctuations in commodity prices. So if a dollar of the cost of a bag of chips goes to plastic, marketing, and transport, a five-cent rise in the cost of potatoes won't spoil our snack.

The real pains in 2008 struck countries like Argentina, Pakistan, and Vietnam, which declared an emergency restriction of grain exports to safeguard their "food sovereignty."[49] Other countries—like Ecuador, Niger, and Indonesia—bolted in the other direction and immediately opened up their food markets to foreigners, hoping that imports would flow into their empty warehouses. Bolivia gambled on both sides, opting to eliminate tariffs while still banning wheat exports. Street violence broke out in Burkina Faso, Peru, and Russia. In Haiti, one of the protesters told a television crew that "if [the government] can't provide the citizens with its basic necessities, it should resign,"[50] and the crowds ousted their prime minister.

Appalled at the upswell in vandalism, the Indian government shut down the export of non-basmati rice and raised the minimum export price of basmati from $650 per ton to $1,000. This was in spite of India's status as the world's second-biggest rice exporter, and in spite of the reliance of countries like Bangladesh on the Indian supply. Intended to stabilize the crisis, the ban merely toppled another domino in a loop of hysterical markets, further driving up international prices while annoying Bangladeshis. In response, the IMF and World Bank issued dull proclamations about the need for calm, mouthing their faith in open trade.[51] In other words, everyone panicked.

This is very much like what happened in the eighteenth century, except that instead of just a French crisis, the problems in 2008 might have easily shaken the entire world. In 2008, the IMF and World Bank repeated their Nicene Creed in the power and goodness of free markets. Apart from scale, the difference between the eighteenth- and twenty-first-century crises is that today the world almost wholly subscribes to the beliefs of Adam Smith. We've long since abandoned the assurances of the Assize of Bread. There's no going back to feudal safeguards on the cost of a loaf of pumpernickel.

The most troubling fact in the 2008 crisis was that the year's harvest was one of the best since the agricultural revolution, with record crops of American maize, Asian rice, and African cassava. Supply was not a problem. So when fuel prices subsided toward the end of 2008 and economic recession cooled the markets, food prices floated down to less painful levels and the rioting stopped. The question remains, what would have happened if the 2008 harvest had failed? Prices wouldn't have subsided, nor would have the rioters' fury. And what if an environmental catastrophe—like a drought in the American Midwest or in northern China or a rise in global temperatures—were to disrupt several harvests in a row?

In 2008, we got lucky. The sun shone and the rains fell in the right amount and at the right times. But what if the planet had played rough? If our surpluses had disappeared in a burning summer and 6.7 billion people had known the fear of an empty shelf? Then the food rebellions of the past might have looked like very small potatoes indeed.

CHAPTER EIGHT

Money: Tea and Famine

Hot tea, like ocean liner crossings and Received Pronunciation, lost its cachet in the leveling years of the twentieth century. Except in the prissier hotels, tea today is poured mechanically, shorn of chintz and ritual, a blunt delivery of caffeine in a dishwasher-safe mug. Boil water. Drop bag. Douse. Slosh milk and scoop sugar. Maybe add a cookie. It's a ceremony that carries all the social resonance of a microwaved potato.

Like much else in the modern pantry, tea wasn't always so banal. Carletti, one of the first Westerners to see the plant in its native soil, thought it worth remarking that its shape was "almost like that of a box tree . . . it has a fragrant flower in the shape of a damask rose." Of the drink itself, he wrote:

> *It has a somewhat bitter flavor, so that one then washes out the mouth. Upon those who take it good and flavorsome, it produces a very good effect and relieves the stomach weakness because of its warmth. It marvelously assists digestion and is especially excellent for lightening and impeding the fumes that rise to the head. And for that reason it customarily is drunk immediately after the midday meal.*[1]

In the same way that Dutch and German families greet their houseguests with wine, writes Carletti, the Chinese pour this bitter, peppy brew. Tea symbolized friendship and good manners. But if there were a gallery of the world's most notorious vegetables, tea would upstage the coca plant, the nodding poppy, the corn husk, and even the tobacco leaf.

In the nineteenth century, tea killed 40 million people. *Camellia sinensis* savaged the environment of South Asia, started a famine, and doomed an entire civilization to generations of poverty. Not alone, of course. Tea found its destructive partners in the force of international trade and the guns of an empire.

On a clear afternoon in 1843, a Scotsman named Robert Fortune was standing on the deck of a Chinese boat sailing from "Foo-chow-foo" to "Shanghae" by way of the River Min. Even though the crew had lit candles and offered dishes of pork and rice to the gods, they had bad luck. Five pirate junks sped from out of the shadow of an island and were skimming toward them, intent on robbery and murder.

Fortune had spent the day lying in his cabin with a fever, but he had made sure to keep a double-barreled gun loaded and primed next to his cot. "Assistance from our cowardly crew was quite out of the question," he later noted, correctly.[2] At the sight of the first pirate junk putting her helm down to fire a broadside, the panicked sailors bolted for cover, leaving the invalid Scotsman to stand alone on the deck. The pirates' shot fell short by a hundred yards.

Threatening to shoot his two Chinese helmsmen if they left their post, Fortune stood his ground as a second broadside splashed under the stern. A third one tore apart the rigging. Waiting until the nearest junk had drawn within thirty yards, Fortune barked out a warning to his helmsmen. No sooner had they dropped flat than iron shot exploded across the deck, splintering block, line, and gunwale. Fortune leaped to his feet and, aiming straight at the faces of his massed attackers, fired both barrels of his gun. His bullets raked their deck, ripping wounds open and sending bodies tumbling. The pirate helmsman disappeared, and the junk hove off, unsteered.[3]

Despite this rousing scene from his diary, Fortune wasn't a bewhiskered swashbuckler in the vanguard of the empire. He was a botanist. One of his recent positions had been as superintendent of the Hothouse Department of the Royal Horticultural Society's garden in Chiswick, England. But if the pirates had captured his vessel, he would have lost the priceless treasure that had drawn him all the way across the world, a collection of tea plants he had gathered over years of patient fieldwork in the remotest districts of China, often at the risk of injury, arrest, and robbery. On the deck of his little boat, Fortune was fighting not only for his life but for his tea.

More than botanical professionalism fueled his courage. The British wanted to plant tea in India, and Fortune had been the man charged with obtaining the specimens for the project. His adventures ensured that, one day, the subjects of the British crown would have access to inexpensive hot drinks. Also, the resulting tea plantations would cause environmental calamity and suffering on a global scale, laying the foundations for the twentieth century's Third World. This tragedy, however, didn't begin with the greed of nations, or agricultural theft, or even colonialism. It began with an everyday sin: that of a neglectful husband.

A FOUNDATION IN PIRATES

In 1662, Charles II of England married a Portuguese princess named Catherine of Braganza, a Catholic. Facing a hostile court that feared the ascension of a papist heir, the young Catherine may have hoped to soften her landing in England with the help of a generous dowry. One of its enticements was the title to the Portuguese colony of Bombay.[4]

Upon her arrival in London, the infanta asked to be refreshed with a cup of tea. Her new servants dithered. Ale, brandy, and even coffee were ladylike tipples, but the English, unlike the Portuguese and Dutch, owned no Asian colonies and were unaccustomed to drinking tea, at least in quantity. The story says that Catherine went to bed unhappy with a mug of ale, setting a precedent for the rest of her marriage.

However, along with the title to the Indian city, Catherine had brought in her dowry a chest of tea leaves. Charles, his ministers, and the kitchen staff didn't know what to do with either of the gifts—England's navy could not match the might of the Portuguese and Dutch fleets, and, the new marriage alliance notwithstanding, Bombay wasn't very useful unless England floated enough warships to flout Lisbon's far-flung caravels.

Left alone while Charles played with his mistresses, Catherine herself taught the English court how to brew tea. The habit caught on. In 1664, England brought its first shipload of tea from China. Of course, boiling a pot of dry leaves was much easier than figuring out how to exploit a subcontinent. Charles and his ministers sensed that Bombay held opportunity, but they didn't know how to grasp it.[5]

When Catherine arrived in London, the British East India Company had already existed for six decades. Chartered under Elizabeth I and ratified by Cromwell, the company's monopoly over English trade with Asia was extended in perpetuity by Charles.

At its peak the "Honourable Company" (or "John Company," as it was often known) controlled an imperial military apparatus and wielded virtually limitless wealth. It was practically an extension of government. The Company directed England's foreign policy, its finances were the finances of the realm, and its board of directors had the ear of every parliamentarian and lord.[6] At the peak of its success, John Company would have made today's multinationals look thin and provincial.

The Company's original business plan, established in 1600, was subtly different from the typical colonial model. Its primary goal was not to profit from imports but to expand overseas markets for English products. This may have been the first instance where a corporation invested in products that would increase revenue, rather than trying to force homemade goods on remote kingdoms.[7] Their strategy was simple: British captains landed in ports already frequented by the Dutch or Portuguese and read a declaration from Queen Elizabeth:

> *Whearas almightie God in his infinite and unsearchable wisdom and gratious providence hath soe disposed of his blessings and of the good things of this world created and ordayned for th[e] use of man, that the same, however they be brought forth & do either originallie growe and are gathered, or otherwyse Composed & made some in [one] Countrie and some in another: yet are they by the Industrie of man directed by the hand of God dispersed and sent out into all the partes of the world, that his wonderfull bountie in his Creatures may appeare unto all nations.*[8]

The bombast continues in this vein, extolling the virtues of trade and how nations "by their interchandge of Commodities are lincked together in amitie and friendship." Of course, it didn't work. The natives were never impressed enough to forge a trade alliance until a sailor named James Lancaster took the helm of a ship called the *Edward Bonaventure.*

Lancaster was the image of an Elizabethan buccaneer; his portrait in London's National Maritime Museum shows a face angled with a knifing goatee, a severe ruff, and a bone structure as sharp as his rapier. Having learned seamanship as a boy in Portugal, Lancaster returned to England and captained the *Bonaventure* in battle against the Spanish Armada, winning enough garlands to be given command of an exploratory trading voyage to India. In this, he failed horribly. Of his three ships, one sank, one turned back laden with a scurvy-ridden crew after getting caught in the doldrums, and the *Bonaventure* ran aground in the West Indies. Of the approximately three hundred men who attempted the entire voyage, twenty-five returned. Amazingly, Lancaster found both the investors and the gumption to set sail again a few months later.

His second expedition was much more successful, probably because he dispensed with any pretense at higher purposes and simply turned pirate. He attacked the Portuguese holdings in Brazil and captured so much booty—including a carrack laden with spices—that he had to hire more ships to carry his winnings to port. Lancaster's investors were so delighted that they petitioned Queen Elizabeth to legitimize Lancaster's antics by founding a "trading" venture. The East India Company was born.

Five ships—the *Hector,* the *Susan,* the *Ascension,* the *Gift,* and the *Red Dragon*—sailed on the Company's first expedition, with Lancaster in command. Their mission was to gather pepper, cinnamon, and nutmeg. With awful hardship, they did. A quarter of the fleet's crew perished before they reached South Africa, but Lancaster drove the survivors around the Cape of Good Hope and into the Indian Ocean where, for several years, they limped between the ports of Asia, ferrying spice. It was sometimes terrifying work, and Lancaster's journal is a litany of wind, broken rudders, and sailors gawping helplessly at oncoming rocks. This entry, for example, illustrates the awfulness of Indian Ocean sailing in the seventeenth century:

> *We had another great storm . . . which continued all night, and did so beat on the quarter of our ship that it shook all the iron work of our rudder, which broke clean off next morning from our stern, and instantly sunk. This misfortune filled our hearts with fear, so that the best and most experienced among us knew not what to do, especially seeing ourselves in so tempestuous a sea and so stormy place, so that I think there be few worse in the world.*[9]

The *Susan* went down with a hold of pepper and all hands in 1605. The *Hector* left India for the journey home with a crew of fifty-three, only fourteen of whom survived when she foundered off the coast of Africa. For the English, spice expeditions yielded Pyrrhic profits at best. The more successful Dutch and Portuguese invested deeply in building chains of fortresses and ports throughout the East, while the English tended to just float back and forth and pray for luck. But the Honourable Company never stopped trying to coax a profit out of the Asian trade. Realizing that they were losing investments and ships, the directors began to shift their ambitions away from the scented trinity of pepper, cinnamon, and nutmeg and to dabble in other commodities. One of these was tea.

While Lancaster was losing his ships, well-to-do Europeans were beginning to hear about this splendid new luxury from the East. In 1597, when Francesco Carletti reached Japan, he described how government officials searched every boat in order to find "certain earthenware vessels" made in the Philippines. Upon pain of death, anyone carrying them would be forced to relinquish the pots to the king who would pay "five, six, or ten thousand scudos each." The baffled Carletti estimated that these pots should not have been "more than a single giulio," save for their miraculous capacity to preserve "a certain leaf that they call *cha*."

On account of travelers like Carletti, English parliamentarian Samuel Pepys, in his diary for September 25, 1660, was able to write that he "did send for a Cupp of Tee (a China drink), of which I had never drank before."[10] When Catherine of Braganza brewed it for the court a few years later, only cognoscenti may have been aware of tea's existence.[11]

Royal endorsement changed that, and soon after Catherine's arrival, the Company placed an order for 100 pounds of Javanese leaf. Demand increased every year until 1678, when, in a bout of greed, the Company imported 4,713 pounds of the stuff, glutting the shops and kneecapping prices. Seven years later, they repeated their mistake and imported 12,070 pounds, again squandering their profit margin on a wishful reading of the English taste for caffeine.

But the British were steadily forming an addiction. In the early nineteenth century, Robert Montgomery Martin, author, civil servant, and self-appointed spokesman for the worthiness of empire,[12] wrote

> *that the consumption of this innutritious leaf, cultivated on the hills of a distant continent, and manufactured by a people almost isolated from the rest of the world, has increased within half a century from five million to upwards of thirty million pounds weight.*[13]

Tea's popularity made it a tempting subject for tax. The government enacted a punishing rate of 200 percent, forcing smugglers to oil the gears of commerce. By 1720, most of the tea brewed in British pots was contraband, but even so, the East India Company was importing more than a million pounds of tea every year as well as shipping cargoes to the American colonies. During the eighteenth century, the English embraced the drink as ardently as they hated papists, so that by the Victorian years, tea had even edged beer from pride of place at the family table. The reasons for this were reformist Christianity and good lighting.

VICTORIAN HIGH TEA

For millions of years, night necessarily meant sleep—that is, until the invention of really effective light fixtures. Gas was the first modern light source, before anyone meddled with copper and spark. In 1792, a Scottish engineer named William Murdoch made a foray into building a workable gas-powered lamp, and by the early 1800s, inventors in England, Germany, and France had all hammered together machines that turned coal gas into dependable illumination. Pall Mall in London was the first street to be permanently lit. Avenues in Baltimore and Paris soon followed, and by the 1820s, cities throughout the industrialized world had sprouted gasworks. Factories could chug and steam through hours that would have once been lost to darkness. Night receded like an old myth, and people filled the brightened evenings with work, with art, and with life. But mostly with eating late dinners.

As the day grew an artificial extension, it liberated people in northern countries especially, where latitude had formerly imposed a curfew. Winter's short days no longer meant enforced sleep. Fashionable families who owned gas fixtures could now afford to dine at hours that would have once required expensive candlelight, shifting supper from late afternoon to nighttime. But the belly has no tolerance for fashion, and by the Victorian age, even the most aristocratic stomachs began to rumble during the lengthening gap between the noon and evening meals.

Anna Russell, the duchess of Bedford and lifelong friend of Queen Victoria, began the polite tradition of retiring to her chambers in the middle of the afternoon to drink tea served with small cakes and sandwiches. Her status as lady of the bedchamber lent her enormous clout with the burgeoning middle classes, so that by 1882 the duchess's snack had become a rite. Afternoon tea became so popular that Mrs. John Sherwood, a nineteenth-century American writer on etiquette, noted:

> *The only "afternoon tea" that should prevail in a large city like New York is that given by one or two ladies who are usually "at home" at five o'clock every afternoon. If there is a well-known house where the hostess has the firmness and the hospitality to be always seated in front of her blazing urn at that hour, she is sure of a crowd of gentlemen visitors, who come from down-town glad of a cup of tea and a chat and rest between work and dinner.*[14]

Part of tea's popular appeal, particularly among the bourgeoisie, was that it wasn't alcohol. In the nineteenth century, reformist Protestant sects like Methodism had infected a lot of people with abstinence. Temperance gave tea a tremendous public relations boost. Its use as a replacement for strong drink was so widespread that Robert Montgomery Martin's report to Parliament on the tea trade declared:

> *The introduction of this beverage into England, has materially contributed to improved morals and health of the nation at large, by superseding in a great measure, the immoderate drinking of spirituous, vinous, and other fermented potations, while its use as a tonic is strongly conducive to health and longevity.*[15]

Today, high tea is still poured in the more Britannic hotels and sitting rooms of the world. Eaten as a stopgap between lunch and supper, the meal is often a buffet of imperial Victorian treats: imported dainties like lemon for lemon curd tart, chocolate for dipped strawberries, poppy seeds for cake. And, of course, tea.

HER MAJESTY'S DRUG CARTEL

In the eighteenth century, all this tea came from China. The Chinese were as possessive of their *Camellia sinensis* plants as they were of their silkworms, and rightly so. They had made a fortune from the business, since the British were willing to pay huge sums of silver for imported tea leaves—billions of dollars in today's reckoning, amounting to a significant drain on the nation's bullion. Addiction to tea was endangering the stability of the empire's finances, so the British sought another method to settle the bill.

By the 1780s, with Chinese tea imports tripling in a mere twenty years, the Honourable Company tried to finagle a deal. Instead of silver, they offered wool, a commodity in which the British Isles abounded. But the Chinese, like most of the consumers in the Indies, had little use for woolens, finding them too hot for their climate and too scratchy on skin that was accustomed to silk. It was a case of poor market targeting, and the Chinese rejected the deal.[16]

They came to regret it. The Honourable Company had grown into a tremendous commercial and military power. It wasn't willing to surrender the riches of the Middle Kingdom on account of a failed sales pitch. Since the Chinese wouldn't accept wool, the Company decided to give them drugs instead.[17]

Britain's infamous opium trade had actually begun a few decades before, in 1757, when the Company broke a series of agreements with the young nawab of Bengal, forcing him to fight the Battle of Palashi. A famous victory for colonial interests, it ended after a mere eight hours of bloodshed that left Bengal under the Company banner. One of the first acts of the new leadership was to seize control of the region's opium production, commandeering the entire crop and then regulating prices. Years later, when the Chinese refused to buy British textiles, the Company was able to institute a triangle trade. Its ships carried British goods to Bengal, traded them for opium, and dumped the narcotics on a Chinese populace that had already developed an addiction, courtesy of Dutch dealers.

The Chinese authorities didn't like it and declared a war on drugs, the government sentencing both merchants and users to death.[18] A Chinese official wrote personally to Queen Victoria, appealing first to her sense of shame:

> *Some, who, by means of introducing opium by stealth, have seduced our Chinese people, and caused every province of the land to overflow with that poison. These then know merely to advantage themselves, they care not about injuring others!*

Then logic:

> *We have heard that in your own country opium is prohibited with the utmost strictness and severity:—this is a strong proof that you know full well how hurtful it is to mankind.*

And finally justice:

Not to speak of our tea . . . which your foreign countries could not exist a single day without, if we of the Central Land were to grudge you what is beneficial, and not be compassionate [to] your wants, then wherewithal could you foreigners manage to exist?[19]

The queen never answered the letter. Between 1839 and 1860, British troops waged two furious wars to maintain the trade. The Chinese lost both, and drugs poured into their cities.

By 1860, the economic logic of the trade began to dissipate. When the Chinese lost the Opium Wars, the Americans and the French took advantage of the country's weakened borders to kindle their own business ventures. Harboring a deep national suspicion of tea tariffs and sailing fast, modern ships, the Americans could undersell and outrun the Company vessels, bringing tea to Western markets quickly and cheaply. So even in its moment of triumph, the East India Company was losing control of the entire purpose of its narcotics business—the British market for tea.

But worse than Yankee profiteering was the trouble with geography. Tea only grew in China. If the Company could control production on its own terms, replacing the Chinese fields with plantations on British soil, then it would never have to worry about nettlesome foreigners. Even before the Opium Wars, the Company had been investigating ways to cut China out of the equation entirely by growing tea on Company land, cultivated by Company serfs, in India.

That's how Robert Fortune came to stand on the deck of a Chinese boat facing down a fleet of junk pirates on the Min River. During the 1840s, he had traveled through China to collect botanical specimens, including tea plants, and had afterward published the book that ended with the pirate yarn. In 1848, the East India Company sent him back to China with the express goal of collecting tea specimens with which to launch an Indian tea industry. It was a risky plan, but Fortune, having already proven his resourcefulness in traveling incognito through the Chinese hinterland, was the ideal man to carry it off. Disguised in Chinese clothes and a fake ponytail, he embarked by canal boat on a surreptitious tour of the northern tea regions, taking notes and amassing a huge trove of seedlings, eventually numbering some twenty thousand plants, which he delivered to the gardeners of the East India Company.

Fortune's seedlings spread around India, particularly into the now-famous tea region of Darjeeling. The Company also carried them to Ceylon, an island with a miserable history in the coffee trade. In the early years of the seventeenth century, Francesco Carletti had passed by Ceylon on his unhurried way back to Europe, noting that the island was famous for luxuries like precious metals, cinnamon trees, and war elephants: "It proved to be delicious country, well formed of smiling, completely green hills that make as attractive a sight as that of any country that I have ever seen."[20] Between Carletti's trip and Ceylon's pacification by the British in the 1810s (a violent business that cost the colonizers hundreds of casualties), the scene changed dramatically to the desolate.

The British stripped native hardwood trees from the mountainsides and planted coffee bushes, but blight and low coffee prices ruined the venture in the second half of the nineteenth century, and the plantation managers uprooted the coffee and replaced it with tea.[21] Unlike coffee beans, which ripen periodically, tea can be harvested throughout the year, so the British needed a large, permanent workforce to gather the leaves. They found it by ferrying landless Tamils from India to the northern end of the island—a repopulation scheme with aftershocks that are still felt in the car bombs of modern Sri Lanka. Globalization, although no one called it that, had come to India, uprooting traditional cultures and driving the young and capable into low-paying jobs in far-away fields.

For a few years, the Company thought it had finally met the challenge of getting tea into British pots. Then, from 1876 to 1878, a drought struck Ceylon. Thousands of Tamils in the northern provinces of Jafnapatam and Kadavely, removed from the support of family and community, saw their livelihoods dry up. At the same time, a worldwide recession knocked down the price of luxury imports. Low prices meant lower wages for tea pickers, so the Tamils couldn't buy food, let alone return to their abandoned homes on the subcontinent. Devastated by the drought, left adrift by the new economic world order, and unable to eat dry tea, the Tamils died by the tens of thousands.[22]

These deaths weren't all the fault of rapacious corporations. The weather, too, bore a share of the blame.

"IN AMERICA, THERE COULD BE NO FAMINE . . ."

It's a truism that the water in the western Pacific is warmer than in the east. Moist ocean air rises over Southeast Asia and stirs up typhoons, while the air above the eastern ocean, being too cold to hold much vapor, is comparatively arid. That's why parts of Ecuador and Peru are deserts.

In the 1960s, a climatologist named Jacob Bjerknes noticed that, during some years, the waters off Peru turn warmer, causing heavy rains in South America and droughts in Australia and Asia. These inversions are called El Niños. In strong El Niño years, the entire global climate system passes through a looking glass, with North America basking in a mild winter while the tropics parch.

In 1876, the year of the Ceylonese disaster, barometric pressure in Santiago, Chile, dropped from normal August readings to the lowest levels ever recorded. The opposite happened in Batavia. Scientists from Lebanon to New Zealand jotted seasonal pressure records into their journals. Then the East Asian monsoon (always fickle) failed, as did the steadfast Arabian monsoon that drives the annual Nile flood. In 1877, the Nile trickled low, spoiling Egypt's wheat crop. For two years, clouds passed over China's Yellow River basin without a drizzle. People from North Africa to Madras to Brazil starved. Hundreds of thousands died in the Shanxi and Wei areas of China.

It got worse. Toward the end of Queen Victoria's reign, three bad El Niño events upended the expected natural order, spoiling any chance for stricken Asian farmers to struggle back from the precipice. Disease, as always, followed hunger, wracking the weakened populations with malaria, bubonic plague, dysentery, smallpox, and cholera. By the time it was over, perhaps 50 million people had died in a decimation of human capital that laid the foundations for the Third World.

Among the victims were Ceylon's Tamils. Even though El Niños have buffeted Asia throughout history, only in the nineteenth century did they destroy so many lives. This was because the population had become dependent on an imperial, global trading system founded on exporting crops like tea. Had the victims still adhered to their ancient traditions of mixed farming, growing food on a small scale for local trade and eating, the dry years wouldn't have been so catastrophic. Millions would have struggled through the hard times, living to replant and rebuild. Sadly for the colonized laborers, traditional farming had no place in the Victorian trading empire, a system in which British shillings paid for Ceylonese tea, and the produce of empire was shuttled across the oceans to feed the global market.

When drought struck Ceylon in 1876, the Tamil laborers learned, in the most immediate manner, the fragility of the agricultural system on which they lived. If the crop failed or wages dropped, they had nothing to eat or to trade, no village surplus stored away as insurance. Similar disasters occurred throughout the empire. In Fort St. George, deep in India's interior, the British had pushed villagers to quit their traditional mixed farming practices and grow cotton. The colonizers paid cash—the lifeblood of the new, imperial economy—which allowed the villagers to buy grain from neighboring regions. But when the drought destroyed the cotton crop, the farmers found that grain prices had skyrocketed due, not to local demand, but to the demands of foreign—indeed British—buyers. In a hungry global marketplace in which grain was scarce, supplies went to the highest bidder, and the Indians found themselves priced out of eating their accustomed foodstuffs. The free market, which reduced local buying power, created famine. Free movement of foodstuffs hasn't always been a cause of mass death, of course. In medieval Europe, blighted regions regularly imported grain from their neighbors by means of the oxcart. Logically, it would seem that modern transportation methods should only quicken the relief of drought-stricken countries—a *deus ex machina* in steel and steam, delivering food to the hungry in the name of human progress. That was certainly the impression held by former president Ulysses Grant, who toured Asia during the black months of 1877. He believed,

> *In America, there could be no famine . . . unless, as was hardly possible in so vast a territory, the famine became general. If the crops*

failed in one State, supplies could be brought from others at little extra expense in money and time.[23]

All Asia needed was a railway, thought Grant, failing to realize that the very telegraph lines and railway networks he imagined rescuing the agonized peasants were, in miserable fact, actually shunting food away from them. The miracle of modern telegraph lines allowed international grain traders to hear where prices were highest. Then they tapped in their orders and used railways to deliver grain to the richest markets. A letter from Madras to the government of India, dated November 30, 1876, states, "It was apparent to the Government that facilities for moving grain by the rail were rapidly raising prices everywhere."[24] Asian tea pickers were now vying to buy the same food as wealthy Europeans. This easy flow of produce meant that even successful farmers couldn't afford to eat. During the 1896 famine, a local official in the Indian region of Godavari wrote that, despite a good harvest, grain prices were astronomical because they "depend almost entirely on the conditions in other parts of India."[25]

The global system that planted Chinese tea in Ceylon and sold it in Piccadilly wrought its havoc and left environmental destruction, societal wreckage, and tens of millions of people dead. William Digby, a contemporary observer of the 1876 Madras famine, wrote, "When the part played by the British Empire in the nineteenth century is regarded by the historian fifty years hence, the unnecessary deaths of millions of Indians would be its principal and most notorious monument."[26]

Today, however, few people are aware that one of the worst debacles in human history occurred during the Victorian golden age, a period more often associated with Jamesian manners than with mass graves. The world paid a lethal cost when economic "progress" met climatic caprice. It may again.

THE GREAT HUNGER

In 1848, the *Illustrated London News* printed a drawing of Britain's royal family circled around the sheltering boughs of a fir, packages of gifts dangling from its spindly branches. The Hanover clan with its tots in petticoats, prim Queen Victoria and tight-trousered Prince Albert, looked like the ideal nineteenth-century family. Everyone seemed mannerly and pleased, even bourgeois, save for the mother's tiara and sire's aristocratic sash (which were democratically edited out in American publications).[27] Above all, the Hanovers looked like decent people. It would have been hard to imagine such prim creatures lording over governmental policies that only two years earlier, during Christmas 1846, condemned hundreds of thousands of their own subjects in Ireland to die of starvation.

Ireland's moist pasturelands are among the lushest in Europe, and the ancient Irish spent much of their energy in grazing livestock, counting livestock, and killing one another over livestock. The Irish fondness for cows led to a diet that was heavy in milk and butter, augmented by grain grown in small mixed farm plots. But several thousand years of habit changed with English colonization in the seventeenth century. Stripped of their lands and traditional means of sustenance, millions of Irish resorted to potatoes, which had been introduced from the Spanish empire in the 1600s (the original Irish word for potato was, tellingly, *an spáineach*).[28]

Potatoes grew well in the wet Irish soil and yielded more vitamins and protein than corn, wheat, or oats. Served with a little buttermilk or herring, boiled potatoes could nourish a hungry laborer for breakfast, lunch, and dinner. When Napoleon fell in 1815, the world grain markets were no longer buoyed by wartime embargoes and shortages, so the price of wheat plunged. Irish landlords looked at their labor-intensive, expensive grain fields and decided a better profit could be gleaned from beef sold to butchers in England's metastasizing cities, or wool sent to the mills of Yorkshire and Lancashire.[29] They turned arable land over to pasture and shipped the cows and wool to Liverpool, where they fed the Industrial Revolution. Grass now meant money, so the landlords evicted the peasants who once worked the edges of their properties, leaving them to scrape out a living between the rocks and boglands. Shut out of the food trade—and with their cottage industries in tatters as a result of English factories[30]—the rural Irish dropped out of the economic stream. Villages that had once bustled with linen looms and market stalls fell silent as country folk abandoned their old livelihoods for the dismal wages of cottagers.

Culturally, the Irish had gotten themselves into a bind by a disastrously equitable system of inheritance that divided land among all the sons in a family. Given a small lump of property, the Irish married young and reared large families, which in turn sliced the land into ever-diminishing parcels. Even while the means to feed each individual family shrank, the population burgeoned from around 2 million in the seventeenth century to 8 million by 1840.[31]

These new generations needed to eat, and a hectare planted with potatoes would feed twice as many people as one seeded with grain.[32] On the eve of the famine, 3 million people depended solely on potatoes for sustenance. Relying on a single crop is never wise, and relying on a single strain of that crop is a certain disaster. Most of the poor ate Lumpers, a watery spud that grew in bulk under little fertilizer but that was so tasteless and lacking in nutrition that, when first introduced to Ireland, it was "scarcely considered food enough for swine." Other potatoes were available—the "outstanding" Black and Apple varieties, the mediocre Cup—but the Lumper flourished by the ton in the barren, crowded soil on the cusps of the cow pastures.[33] By 1840, there were seven hundred people per square mile of arable land.[34]

Even with valleys full of cows and sheep, and human beings cramming every strip of green land left over, Ireland was still growing grain for export when, in September 1845, a fungus named *Phytophthora infestans* started to bloom. It clung to the Lumpers, blistering fast among the dense rows of plants between the cottages, and the potato harvest—which always just came in the nick of autumn to end the hungry summer—turned into black sludge. In 1846, it rained more than usual. The fungus thrived in the dank, and for a second year the crops dissolved in the fields while the Irish starved by the hundreds of thousands.

In both of those evil years, landlords in eastern Ireland harvested grain and shipped it abroad, while the government fretted about the ethical effects of handing out free food to the poor. Eventually, the British drummed up several famine relief programs, including a public works scheme that employed 750,000 by the height of the famine in 1847.[35] That year, more grain entered Ireland than flowed out of it—although much of this was corn, which the Irish didn't know how to mill and cook. By the time the famine was over, an estimated 1 million people had died, while close to another million fled to Britain, North America, and Australia. Ireland's population has never recovered.

In later years, playwrights and singers would insist that such a calamity could never have happened except through human malice. A scene from George Bernard Shaw's *Man and Superman* boils with righteous fury at the British government's apparently genocidal dithering:

> *Malone: Me father died of the starvation in the Black 47 . . .*
> *Violet: The Famine?*
> *Malone: No, the Starvation. When a country is full of food and exporting it, there can be no famine.*[36]

While the British response was certainly hobbled by smugness and market ideology, the true villain was an antic food market. The world around Ireland was busily selling food for cash, but most of the Irish remained mired in subsistence farming. They had survived through the use of the imported potato, but the blight, another American import, destroyed them (though native to Central America, it had been brought to Ireland on cargo ships sailing from the United States). Having been left out of the food trade, the Irish peasants had focused on feeding themselves and specialized their agriculture to the point where they could be snuffed out by an unlucky, perhaps inevitable fungus. Specialization and a worldwide marketplace had made the Irish situation so precarious that they could hardly dodge an environmental death blow, a tragedy shared a generation later with Sri Lankans, destroyed by the same modern forces.

THE FOOD EMPIRES AHEAD

Today, our landscape is a lot like that of Ireland and Sri Lanka immediately before the famines. We devote much of our earth to a very small number of crops. But instead of relying on prayer, dung, and ditches to coax out a harvest, we use machines, chemicals, and satellite-guided sprinklers. The results overflow our silos, our supermarket shelves, and our waistbands. The Green Revolution of the postwar years created a reality out of Jesus' parable of the loaves and fishes, and food empires, unconstrained by naturally produced nitrogen, or by the speed of oxen or sailboats, now unfold across continents and oceans.

In the mid–twentieth century, scientists started to breed plants that could grow fast and in tight formation, that didn't waste energy on growing too many inedible parts (like roots in a lettuce, or leaves on a broccoli). One of the geneticists leading the effort was Norman E. Borlaug, a native of Iowa's Corn Belt. In the 1940s, he set up shop in Mexico under the flag of the Rockefeller Foundation with the intention of developing new strains of superior wheat and maize. Borlaug wanted to correct a structural deficiency in the wheat stalk, which couldn't support heavy grains, a trait that had stumped earlier geneticists. The most fruitful plants collapsed under the weight of their own seeds before they could ripen. Fertilizer made it worse, since the extra nutrients stimulated so much growth that the plants flopped over even more prematurely. To remedy this, Borlaug's group developed dwarf varieties, thick, short-stemmed plants that could stand up to the strain of bulbous grains. These dwarf species, fueled by artificial fertilizer, increased yield from a maximum of about 4,500 kilos per hectare to as much as 9,000 kilos.[37] Borlaug won a Nobel Prize, and dwarf wheat and rice spread across impoverished rural districts from Mexico to Malaysia.

By doubling the productivity of land, Borlaug had seemingly solved the problem of world hunger. The world responded by specializing, exclusively planting Borlaug's seeds. Fifty years after his first experiments, his cultivars have driven countless traditional plants out of the field and into the botanical encyclopedia, creating huge swathes of monocultures around the world where biodiversity once buzzed and chirped. The effect is called genetic erosion. For instance, China is now a vast "sea of monocultures" dotted with little islands of native rice.[38] Virtually every indigenous wheat cultivar disappeared from Greece between 1930 and 1960.[39] Today, almost every kernel of grain eaten by human or beast is a product of the meticulous field trials of Borlaug and his school.

Genetic erosion isn't the only problem that Borlaug's seeds caused. The more immediate drawback: Borlaug's plants can't survive on a diet of dung. To grow, they need more nutrients than are found on a barnyard floor, so farms with high-yielding crops use lots of artificial fertilizer. As far back as the 1950s, for instance, the Japanese had loaded their earth with Borlaug rice, boosting energy costs for fertilizer by 400 percent between 1950 and 1974. Energy used by farm machinery went up twelve times. The payoff seemed to be worth it, with rice crops increasing by 50 percent, but the math is skewed. Put another way, if every calorie of energy obtained from a rice field was divided by the energy it took to produce, in 1950 the Japanese had an energy ratio of 1.27 calories produced per calorie spent. By 1974, this had dropped to 0.38.[40] Since then, we've started growing lots of hothouse vegetables, which are possibly the worst offenders in the energy ratio game. Most northern countries have done the same. Tomatoes from Maine, for instance, appear regularly in Boston supermarkets in December.

Borlaug's progeny have also sparked an arms race between farmers and insects. Pests noticed when fields started blooming with unnatural abundance, and they wanted their cut. Outbreaks increased, and farmers retaliated with a strategy of chemical shock and awe. For example, in the 1950s, the new crops attracted the attentions of the leafhopper (*Nephotettix cincticeps*), prompting Asian farmers to unleash a rough brew of insecticide that killed not only the leafhoppers, but the spiders who kept the insects in check. The leafhoppers recovered from the blast, but their predators didn't, making subsequent infestations even more tenacious.[41] Worse still, overuse of pesticides, like overuse of antibiotics, creates resistance in the bugs that they target.[42] By the early 1970s, Japan, for instance, had run out of useful pesticides. Chemists have been racing against the genes of leafhoppers ever since.[43]

We wouldn't need supercharged pesticides, however, if we didn't plant monoculture crops. A farm that rations its poisons and grows different plants is most likely to benefit from the ministrations of natural predators like spiders and birds.[44] But that doesn't happen in a purity of wheat stretching to the horizon. The more common strategy among agriculturalists is to try to improve the system that Borlaug built by constructing bigger, stronger, shinier crops.

In the 1950s, Borlaug and his team worked under the scientific shackles of their time. They could only cross varieties; they weren't able to genetically cook up a plant to order. Today, biochemists can select the genes they want and pair them with choices from a menu of specialty fertilizers. For example, as of 2002, Chinese researchers had developed 141 different genetically modified (GM) plant types, among which two strains of rice are currently awaiting regulatory approval before their debut in the Yangtze Valley.[45] These two botanical confections produce their own insect toxins, courtesy of the bacterium *Bacillus thuringiensis* and the cowpea trypsin inhibitor gene. In trial plantings, the rice flourished without any additional pesticides, while their non-GM neighbors fell to the predations of stem borers—a rapacious creature that eats 5 percent of China's annual crop. This would appear to be a true success, a victory for the People's Republic's ingenious men and women in lab coats. Except that the stem borer is yesterday's pest. The leafhopper, scourge of the Japanese, is making a comeback and is likely to be the recurring villain of the upcoming seasons. It's naturally impervious to the defensive toxins spewed by the new Chinese rice. When the crop is planted, the leafhopper smiles, twirls its mustache, and wraps a bib around its mottled neck. A well-known scholarly journal has called the Chinese GM rice program "ham-fisted," unschooled in the subtleties of ecology.[46]

But who really is schooled in them? In the decade after Borlaug accepted his Nobel Prize, a group of ecologists started to wonder why ecosystems sometimes collapse under the weight of a pestilence, while at other times the same ecological disturbance doesn't cause lasting harm. Studying places as diverse as the Florida Everglades and the boreal forest of northern Ontario, the ecologists drew up a list of three warning signs for imminent, catastrophic ecological collapse—a sort of diagnostic kit for environmental death. It's an elegant list, so simple that it seems intuitive.

The first danger sign is when an ecosystem has too much biomass. A place stuffed to the rafters with leafy greens and wood is likely to catch either fire or the interest of a vicious beetle. Less productive land lacks fuel and bores bugs. So lush ground is more vulnerable than rocks.

The second cause for alarm is connectivity. If the plants jumble together in a promiscuous thicket, flames and beetles can spread quicker.

The third danger is exclusivity. If the thicket is made up of a single breed of fern, a fern-eating bug will gobble the entire growth, not just nibble at a few unlucky individuals. So as biodiversity goes down, vulnerability goes up.

One of the ecologists who articulated this list of signs was Buzz Holling of the University of Florida. A man of towering intellectual and physical stature, but with a startlingly mild voice, Holling explains his systems theory, which argues that an ecosystem where biomass and connectivity are both rising but diversity is falling faces an inevitable collapse.[47] It will lie down and die at the first sniff of smoke or the first chirp of a hungry cricket.

Holling is mostly talking about "natural" ecosystems, but his list applies just as well to Ceylon or Ireland during the Victorian famines. It's an accurate depiction of agriculture in general, since competently tilled fields are by definition high in biomass, tightly packed, and specialized.[48] Borlaug's hybrids only made the process more extreme. As the Irish also discovered in 1845, a highly productive, densely planted potato field is no security against hunger.[49] Not when the weather and a malignant fungus are against you, and government policies promote exports over food security.

Genetic modification is a tool, just like irrigation, artificial fertilizers, and refrigerants, all of which have made it possible to feed our civilization and to keep 6 billion bodies and souls together. When misused, however, these tools become bludgeons—they miss the nail and crush the thumb. So while we've built our food empire with these tools, we've also used them to invent landscapes that fail Buzz Holling's simple test.

Biomass. Connectivity. Lack of diversity. The result is always the same.

CHAPTER NINE

Time: Fair, Organic, and Slow

On his ten-year ramble back to Ithaca, Odysseus famously loitered with a nymph. At the turn of the seventeenth century, Carletti loitered with a subcontinent. Of all the breaks in his itinerary, his stopover in India was the longest and, judging by the pitch of his descriptions, the most pleasurable. He spent a full twenty-one months in the Portuguese colony of Goa, waiting for a favorable monsoon to carry the larger share of his merchandise through the Straits of Molucca. Carletti took a natural liking to colonial life: its mix of diluted exoticisms and primitive luxury, its truant feel of getting away with a scam. As in Cape Verde, he was particularly interested in the mixed-race wives of the Portuguese settlers, "the most desirous creatures imaginable." His enthusiasm runs to nearly a dozen heated pages on the sculptured appearance of a sari-clad torso, the lasciviousness of native ladies, and their "very well-proportioned members."

Somewhat more reserved on the subject of Indian cuisine, Carletti still commends Goa for its variety of chickens. "The country abounds in fowl," he writes, observing that the birds are sometimes preserved in sugar and cooked whole, or filleted, boiled, and then roasted, "a thing no less marvelous than flavorful." Conserves, too, are cheap and plentiful, although bread isn't very common, since rice "pleases more and is more easily eaten" in the sweltering climate. Best, though, is Indian fruit, because it is sold on the street not by grocers, but by prostitutes. "There is no other region in the world in which it is possible to live better and more lavishly!" burbles the son of Renaissance Florence. Then he writes three pages on the culinary and therapeutic qualities of the coconut.

When at long last Carletti's remaining Chinese swag arrived in port, he had no excuse to linger, so he sold his textiles and knickknacks for a small fortune, and bought himself passage on a pepper ship bound for Portugal. They sailed on Christmas morning 1601, almost seven years to the day after he had embarked from Sanlúcar de Barrameda. He brought with him three servants ("one of the Japanese nation, a Korean, and the other a Mozambique Negro") and a hundred hens, along with his money and remaining luxury goods. For two and a half months they sailed in peace, rounding the Cape of Good Hope without trouble from sea or weather, until the fateful day of March 14, 1602.

The captain of the vessel, Antonio de Melo de Castro, knight of the Cloak of Christ, had ignored his passengers' impatience to reach home, and rather than setting course directly for Lisbon, put in for a rendezvous with a convoy of friendly merchants at the island of St. Helena. When they arrived at St. Helena, however, instead of merchants he found the cove jammed with Dutch warships. Terrified, the captain fired a cannon at one of them, and the Dutch responded "at the ratio of one hundred to one," blasting the Portuguese rigging to pieces and killing about fifty sailors. Carletti watched, horrified, as the Dutchmen holed his ship below the waterline. De Melo de Castro determined to stand fast, even though his passengers were baling out the hold with kettles; the bilge pumps had clogged with all the loose pepper floating in the water. Drowning seemed certain. The Dutch sent out a boat to discuss surrender, de Melo de Castro swallowed his pride, and the Portuguese yielded to the horrible math of three enemy warships and a thousand fathoms of South Atlantic deep.

The Dutch turned out to be Zeelanders sailing under the colors of the States-General of the United Provinces of the Low Countries of Southern Germany and Count Maurice of Nassau. They were privateers, not stateless pirates, and while their letter of marque gave them license to attack Portuguese ships, they had no legal right to terrorize citizens of Florence. So, for the bribe of two thousand ounces of musk, Carletti convinced them to accept him onto one of their ships, leaving the miserable Portuguese to weather the night in their sinking vessel. No one expected them to survive until morning.

But the food trade saved them. The pepper that had clogged the bilge pumps during the cannonade also prevented the water from flooding up and swamping the ship; the shivering survivors stayed afloat that night on a thin scum of spice. The next day, the Dutch began to repair the damage they had wrought, removing the Portuguese to the other ships (and drowning or stabbing a lot of them in the transfer). Carletti, however, kept his wits and some of his treasure, and he finagled a place among the more coddled prisoners on the Dutch flagship. Even so, he sat crammed in a tiny cabin with fifty other captives, given barely enough water and fetid rice to survive, eking out his rations with a jar of preserved Chinese pears he had smuggled aboard. They landed twenty-three days later, stewing in misery, on the barren island of Fernando de Noronha, which contained nothing but a brackish stream and clouds of fishy-tasting seabirds.

The privateers left the Portuguese there with a mound of rotten biscuit and rice, a rickety boat, and the advice to sail westward for three hundred miles to reach Brazil. As for themselves, they were heading home to Zeeland with their prize. Carletti, being Italian and rich, could go with them.

"You are placing yourself in great peril," warned de Melo de Castro. "Watch out. They will throw you into the sea."

Carletti thought that Dutch mercy was a more reliable bet than three hundred miles of the Atlantic in an open boat. He went with the Zeelanders and even took pains to ingratiate himself by teaching the sailors how to cook the vile-tasting seabirds on the island (marinated in saltwater, then filleted, and fried in butter with handfuls of Indonesian spice).

It took two more months for Carletti and the Dutch to sail up the Eastern Seaboard of North America, across the Atlantic using the Westerlies, and then into the English Channel. The privateers did not murder Carletti (although later, many Dutchmen expressed surprise that the captain hadn't thrown him overboard to avoid dealing with the paperwork), but when they anchored at Middelburg, on the island of Walcheren, they divvied up Carletti's gems, spices, and Eastern treasures, and even broke up the Portuguese ship to sell for timber. The sum of the haul exceeded 600,000 scudi. It was an extraordinary prize, far richer than they had guessed until they had unloaded the deepest bales of spice from the hold. Carletti, at the end of his great adventure, had lost everything.

"Many who had been poor became rich, whereas the rich became beggars," he notes, grumbling that he would have hidden more pearls in his stomach but for an untimely dry throat.

There was nothing to do but look for a lawyer.

THE MEANING OF FAIRNESS

The Dutch who robbed Carletti in 1602 were men hardened by wars of independence and religion. They hadn't yet slipped into the long regret that colors modern Europe. Fittingly, it was a nineteenth-century Dutchman who led the European charge headlong into postcolonial guilt. Eduard Douwes Dekker, who served in the Dutch East Indies, was a career civil servant.[1] A sea captain's son (like old Jan Pieterszoon Coen, the terror of Java), he had arrived in the East Indies as a youth and stayed there, off and on, between drinking binges and bankruptcies, eventually landing the job of assistant resident in the town of Lebak in West Java in 1856. By then, the Dutch Empire had long since faded, but there were still a few guilders to be scratched out of Indonesian sweat and soil.

Dekker had a taste for cards and liquor, but he also had a Calvinist's sense of righteous indignation.[2] The Dutch worked their islands under *cultuurstelsel* (cultivation systems) that obliged the peasantry to grow export crops, especially coffee, for Dutch markets.[3] This arrangement paid for an entire third of Holland's overall revenues and fueled a nineteenth-century economic revival in the Low Countries. The plantations, however, kept the Javanese coffee farmers enslaved in everything but name. And Dekker was an idealist. Appalled at the natives' conditions, the new assistant resident began gathering evidence of corruption, pointing fingers at local potentates, and clamoring for justice. Naturally, they fired him.

Dekker returned to Holland disgraced, penniless, and steaming with holy fury. After years of dragging his family around Europe in a fruitless search for steady work, he settled at the Au Prince Belge hotel in Brussels. There, under the nom de plume of "Multatuli" (from the Latin for "I suffered much"), he wrote a novel drawing on his experiences as an administrator in Java. It was called *Max Havelaar, or, The Coffee Auctions of the Dutch Trading Company,* and it drew an awful portrait of the merciless exploitation—piracy, really—at the heart of colonial economics. Profits, writes Dekker, "can be made in no other way than by paying the Javanese just enough to keep him from starving."[4] He adds, "One must be convinced of the effectiveness of this policy, even though one cannot consider it noble."[5]

Max Havelaar was a sensation. In the centuries since their freebooting ancestors had carved out a foreign empire, the Dutch had grown a delicate social conscience. They didn't like to hear that their government was enslaving anyone. A liberal wave swelled up in the coffee shops of Amsterdam, and Europeans began to notice the true bitterness in their cups. The popular will to make amends ran so deep that, by the turn of the twentieth century, the government enacted the Ethical Policy, giving the colonized peoples at least a few nibbles from the fruits of the empire: education, banking, and investment in infrastructure, like irrigation ditches.[6] The economic development project, for better or worse, had been born.

This early attempt at ethical trade, and the whole colonial trade system in general, fizzled in the tumult of the early twentieth century. Not even the international food empire could survive the squeeze of the Great Depression and two world wars. Victory gardens are the epitome of the "Buy Local" movement, and the immediacy of blitzkriegs drove away people's guilt about coffee workers in Java. Only with the Bretton Woods trade agreements in 1944 did the food trade recover, and then it stormed, snorting and pawing, into the marketplace of the new order. Starting in the second half of the twentieth century, the free trade of foodstuffs was again an inviolable fact of global economics, shielded by an agreement called GATT.

Along with inventing the World Bank and the International Monetary Fund, the Allies used the Bretton Woods talks to concoct this GATT, the General Agreement on Tariffs and Trade. It was a new set of rules governing international trade, and hence the future global food empire. Using the smoking wreckage of several continents as a cautionary example, the Allies wanted to create mechanisms like GATT that would replace genocidal warfare with nice things to buy. If countries got rich making office furniture, stiletto shoes, and yogurt, then they would forget to make tank divisions.

Critics of the scheme—Edward Douwes Dekker's ideological descendents—howled in protest. Wasn't GATT (and the raft of commodity trading agreements that were signed around the same time) simply ancient, bloody colonialism with a bland banker's face? Perhaps this sounded like leftist zealotry, but Dekker's followers, by this point known as the "Fair Trade movement," raised a salient point: they reminded Westerners that commodities grown far from the financial strongholds of the world—foods like spice, coffee, tea, sugar, and chocolate—were often the products of brute force, with middlemen reaping huge profits at the expense of farmers. The only difference was the guns that had enforced the chains of the colonial empires were now replaced by the paper on which the trading agreements were inked.

The modern Fair Trade movement got its start in 1946 when an American Mennonite named Edna Ruth Byler took a holiday in Puerto Rico. Shocked by the poverty of the natives, she bought a box of mercy souvenirs, a trunk of handicrafts that, apart from looking darling on her mantelpiece in Pennsylvania, might do some Christian good. An ardent believer in the free market, she understood that, if a Puerto Rican artisan sold a piece of hand-embroidered fabric to an American housewife, there would be one fewer hungry family in the world.

Today, her business is an international retail chain called Ten Thousand Villages, and in 2009 its retailing and wholesaling sales were valued at $24 million.[7] Its stores crop up in places like Toronto and Pasadena, wafting with Tuareg music and myrrh. African proverbs scroll across the walls, and the clerks shill onyx candleholders from Pakistan, paperweights from Vietnam, greeting cards from Thailand. The whole ambience is three parts suburban boutique, one part badgering activist with a clipboard. And, of course, one of the big sellers in the stores is coffee.

For decades, the Fair Trade movement nibbled at the fringes of popular consumption.[8] They sold a few products (coffee, mostly) out of specialty shops in politically friendly enclaves, or among ardent

Christians. Then, in the mid-1980s, the spirit of Edward Douwes Dekker again stirred in Amsterdam, and Fair Trade went global. It started when a group of indigenous Mexican coffee farmers decided that Fair Trade had exhausted its reach. They had been selling their beans to American and European markets through specialized "world" boutiques, but the middling volumes weren't putting their coffee into enough pots. The growers wanted to sell more but didn't wish to chain themselves to a multinational coffee roaster and betray their ideals. Or their bank accounts. So they approached a Dutch company with an offer to concoct a Fair Trade label that could compete against the intimidating market share of Maxwell House and Folgers. The name the company chose was "the Max Havelaar Foundation."

Timing was on the side of the Fair Traders. In the 1980s, the world was abuzz with optimism about the power of free trade. Asian tigers strode across the financial pages, movies were full of images of fat cats snapping their suspenders, and the protectionist mantras of the 1970s had come to sound scratchy and out of date. The principles of free trade trickled down into theories about developmental economics. Since developing countries have economies that generally rely on agriculture, free trade and food seemed like the twin engines that would rocket the world's poor into Reaganite and Thatcherite splendor. Max Havelaar's time had come.

By 1986, GATT, that aging product of the postwar Bretton Woods conference, seemed rusty and overweight. The world's economic brains had decided that the market needed to be cut free. Talks on how to do this began in Punta del Este, Uruguay, and lasted seven and a half years.[9] This Uruguay Round, as it was called, included 123 countries, took more than twice the time originally scheduled, and ended up being the largest negotiation in the history of trade. For their pains, the negotiators boasted of three grand accomplishments. First, they buried the name, "GATT," and replaced it with the moniker "World Trade Organization." Second, they concocted a closed, completely undemocratic tribunal for settling trade squabbles. Lastly, they hauled food products into the arena of global regulation. This, in particular, was new. GATT had covered agriculture, but it was hampered by a rampart of import quotas and subsidies shielding American and European farmers. Uruguay changed that. Food was now, in theory, no different from automobile gaskets. Subsidies would be hacked away and Western markets thrown open to the cleansing light of pure commerce. The idea was that, since developing countries could use their cheap labor to grow coffee or bananas, rich nations would soon be awash in bargain foodstuffs while the profits sluiced southward, into the callused palms of the needy.[10]

The critics of globalization howled the usual catchphrases about labor rights and environmental rape, crying that the entire developing world would be staked out as a vast, fragile plantation, soupy with agrochemicals and enslaved to the Western gullet.[11] The free traders replied with their old line that rising tides lift all the boats. Into this mess stepped the Mexican coffee growers and their Dutch marketing consultants waving their new Max Havelaar label. By trying to tap into world markets, they were implicitly agreeing to the Uruguay Round's insistence on open food trade between nations. But they didn't like the rules.

The coffee growers and their allies thought they had a new solution to the ancient inequities created by food empires. Instead of competing with the giant "canned" roasters, they would establish a label that any producer or roaster could use so long as they met certain social and environmental standards. More than a label, this would be a license promising that the buyer was getting coffee that, regardless of its taste, was of premium ethical quality. It would come at a premium price, but the consumer would be assured of a long list of happy thoughts: that the coffee farmer was receiving a guaranteed payment above the world market rate, and that some of the proceeds funded schools, hospitals, and infrastructure in the farmer's neighborhood. To offset the eternal problem of getting credit to pay for farm inputs like seeds and buildings, the Fair Trade farmers received a cash advance. Instead of plantations owned by grasping absentee landlords or accountants, farms were meant to be small family affairs. In short, coffee production would be respectful, dignified, and, above all, fair.[12]

Max Havelaar was only the first of many Fair Trade labels, and since its launch in 1988, the world market for fairly traded commodities has ballooned to encompass rice, cocoa, sugar, honey, orange juice, fresh fruit, cut flowers, cotton, and soccer balls.[13] All this ethical business added up to $3.4 billion in 2007.[14] But while most development economists agree that Fair Trade has improved conditions in certain corners of places like Guatemala and Kenya, there's a paradox in its success.

The Fair Trade label is a license, but licenses are useless unless they're enforced. Back in 1601, to his dismay, Francesco Carletti learned that, while a Dutch privateer's license may have prohibited the despoiling of Florentines, the letter of the law didn't count for much in the empty blue of the South Atlantic. If a system rewards greed, as it did on the seventeenth-century high seas, greed will find a way to thrive.

In 2000, the American café franchise Starbucks starting brewing Fair Trade–certified coffee.[15] At first, idealists rejoiced, applauding a happy union between big business, consumer pockets, and the Rights of Man. Perhaps the global food empire could actually be a force for virtue. But a decade on, the experiment remains inexpertly mixed at best.[16]

Despite the press releases of 2000, Starbucks management didn't storm the warehouses and bulldoze their unclean beans to clear the way for ethical French roast. There were supply chain hiccups and dithering over the public's taste for a flavor shot of morality. By 2007, only 3 percent of all Starbucks' coffee was certified as Fair Trade. In the autumn of 2008, the company announced that it would double the percentage of fair beans its U.S. operations would buy.[17] (Starbucks in the UK and Ireland had more ambitious targets. Today, all of their espresso beans are purchased from Fair Trade sources.) But this is still a mere drop in the scalding Venti cup. According to the corporation's website, in 2009

> *Starbucks global purchases of Fair Trade Certified coffee totaled 19 million pounds (nine million kilograms) . . . This equaled five percent of Starbucks total coffee purchases.*[18]

In its defense, Starbucks argues that it has always paid a premium price for its beans, and anyway it doesn't matter because it has proven its social credentials in other ways like conservation, while it continues to make progress on the ethical bean front. Still, it's hard not to think that, after almost ten years of a highly publicized commitment to fair trade, there are limits to patience. Instead of asking how Fair Trade influences Starbucks, though, a more salient question is how have companies like Starbucks influenced Fair Trade?[19]

Even at the beginning of Starbucks' flirtation with ethics, some die-hard activists muttered darkly about Matthew's 6:24 argument that you can't serve both God and money. Before Starbucks inked its deal with the organizations that establish the rules of the Fair Trade movement, coffee roasters and sellers needed to buy at least 5 percent of their beans from Fair Trade sources if they wanted to slap the Fair Trade logo on their packaging. But the American Fair Trade consortium, TransFair, made an exception in the Starbucks case. Despite the fact that until recently the latte colossus bought considerably less than 5 percent of its coffee from Fair Trade sources, Fair Trade posters cropped up in their stores. The argument was that Starbucks, being so big, needed to be coaxed into the fold. Besides, 3 percent of Starbucks was countless times bigger than 5 percent of one of its smaller rivals. Even so, more than one scowling idealist shook a fist in anger at the coffee shops of Cambridge and San Francisco.[20]

It is important not to be too cynical, however. Starbucks' engagement in Fair Trade coffee has undoubtedly been a good thing for thousands of poor coffee producers. Despite its problems, Fair Trade is helping make the world economy more equitable, and Starbucks is a powerful ally.

The problem with Fair Trade is its own success. From its beginnings, Fair Trade organizations removed middlemen from the chain of distribution, helping small farmers sell directly to retailers without any intermediaries taking a cut. The lack of a middleman meant that farmers could sell beans at a premium price and, it was hoped, invest the extra cash in community projects. This worked nicely, for a time. But as the Fair Trade idea gathered commercial steam, it evolved into a technocratic accounting exercise rather than a grassroots mechanism for reform.[21] The ideals of the movement—empowered workers, a social premium plowed back into community projects, a respectable minimum price—have gotten cloudy.[22] According to Dr. Anne Tallontire, a British specialist in Fair Trade from the University of Leeds who has extensively studied the Kenyan agricultural market, "With Fair Trade, the outcomes for 'empowerment' [of the producers] depend very much on who is doing the buying and how much they share the values of the fair trade pioneers."[23]

For example, Fair Trade coffee has always been produced on small family farms. Today, however, the labeling organizations are under pressure to relax the "small" condition and accept plantation beans. After all, this regulation was relaxed years ago for other products, and Fair Trade bananas, tea, and wine are all plantation goods. Big tea producers don't buy from family farms. An army of small-time operators could never grow enough bananas to fill the West's fruit bowls. So to meet the popular demand for Fair Trade food, the movement relaxed its rules for these products. Instead of solely certifying small cooperatives and family farms, the American labeling body TransFair suspended the dictum that certified producers must be farmers "who are not structurally dependent on permanent hired labor."[24] Today, TransFair and the Fairtrade Labelling Organizations International (the premier European label) no longer turn up their noses at goods bought from farms that are "structurally dependent on waged labor." Plantations—the bugbear of sustainable agriculture since the Stone Age—are now certified as "Fair."

Relaxing the rule on plantations has extracted a toll on the label. According to Catherine Dolan, an academic from Oxford University who has studied Fair Trade tea production in Africa, there are two problems. The first is the obvious fact that one of the points of Fair Trade is to guarantee a minimum price for farmers. Kenya's Fair Trade tea industry, for example, may not actually do this, because all the tea in the world is sold at large auctions in which prices are set by the day's global commodities market, regardless of any promises made to particular tea growers.

Dolan's second problem has to do with the social premium—another cornerstone of Fair Trade. When the label only certified farms "not structurally dependent on labor," the social premium went to projects collectively determined by farmers who were, culturally and economically, equals. They shared the same fears, the same ambitions, and the same amount of leverage with the local bank. Plantations, however, introduce management and labor. Hierarchy. And very often, the decisions of management don't necessarily accord with the ideas of the needy.[25]

So Fair Trade plantations not only fail to guarantee minimum prices, they may also discard democracy as so much cumbrous hokum. By definition, they create landscapes of monocultures. The picture is a familiar one, of course, but the marketing is something new.

In the past twenty years, Fair Trade has undoubtedly freed many people from a miserable cycle of poverty, wage slavery, and exploitation, but it hasn't reinvented the food empire. Historically, we're still hauling ourselves up the economic hill, then sliding down its broken slopes into social and environmental wreckage. At its most successful, Fair Trade has made life better in places where it used to be intolerable. But it hasn't stopped the cycle.

It can't. Not alone. But it has, at least, given a great many people the idea to view their food through a prism that isn't simply cost or appetite. And that, alone, is revolutionary.

GREENER PASTURES

Not long before indigenous Mexican farmers rallied under the banner of a fictitious nineteenth-century Dutchman, another food term seeped into the popular lexicon. In the United States, "organic" once meant a type of chemistry class. But after the 1962 publication of Rachel Carson's environmental alarm, *Silent Spring,* the word took on a cluster of new meanings.[26] Because of this chronicle of the ecological devastation caused by chemical pesticides, especially the destruction of songbirds by DDT, Carson is often credited with launching the modern American environmental movement.[27] Soon after the book appeared, the restaurant review columns of California started using "organic" as shorthand to mean food that hadn't been laced with sinister industrial potions. By the mid-1970s, Western states created the first organic food certification programs.[28]

That the U.S. manifestation of the organic food label should originate in California is an oddity, on the surface.[29] From the early twentieth century, California was the epicenter of industrial horticulture (see chapter 6), its fruit farms at the vanguard of intensive land use and mechanization, its land drizzled with artificial fertilizers and corporate money. But perhaps it's natural that such a powerful brew would have side effects. When the cost of pesticides and fertilizers went up during the oil crisis of the 1970s, farming without chemicals came into vogue.[30]

But while Carson's book and the oil crisis focused early organic pioneers on the need to cut chemical inputs, organic farming has always meant more than whether the nitrogen on a field originates in a factory or a cow. Organic farming, according to popular understanding, embodies other words like "sustainable," "respectful," "diverse," "balanced," and, most loaded of all, "holistic." It's not a new conflation. In the 1920s, Rudolf Steiner, a radical educational reformer, established the principles of "biodynamic farming,"[31] in which he argued that a farm should be a "self-regulating organism that . . . mimic[s] nature and function[s] in harmony with its environment."[32]

There are many small steps that farmers take to be biodynamic. For example, leaving a hedge around a field creates habitat for the birds that keep insect populations low. Low insect populations mean less need for insecticides. Similarly, by planting nitrogen-fixing legumes along with nitrogen-greedy grain crops, the soil keeps its healthful chemical balance and needs fewer fertilizer supplements. Steiner was writing in the 1920s, in the period immediately before the widespread use of synthetic farm inputs, so his philosophy isn't necessarily "organic," but Steiner elucidated a way to view a farm as part of an environment, rather than as a machine for churning out bushels of identical crops. The view ensures that the farm can continue making food in the future.

A typical organic operation in California today looks like Dry Creek, a tomato farm near Pescadero on the gusty surfers' coast south of San Francisco. "We don't use much water because the fog comes in and the tomatoes sink deep roots," explains an attendant at the Dry Creek farmer's stand in the metropolis's civic center. "It works because we're close to the sea." In other words, the farm is able to grow organic crops because it acts in harmony with its specific environmental conditions.

Dry Creek is grounded in a bowl of rock and Douglas firs across the road from Butano State Park. Most of the neighboring properties are ranches, since the hills are too steep for planting anything more delicate than the more rugged styles of livestock. A humble blue farmhouse fronts a barn with a roof gone concave from age and weather. It's a scene of chipped paint, flowers drying in bunches, and washing hanging on the line. A satellite dish is the only touch that keeps it from sinking into the pages of Steinbeck. This is an unusual spot for a tomato farm, and, in fact, most of the land is given over to corn. The soil isn't hugely different from the sand kicked up by the surfers on Pescadero Beach six miles away—it's gritty, grey, and flecked with stones.

But Dry Creek Farm can profitably sell tomatoes in downtown San Francisco. In the 1990s, organic farm production in the United States leapfrogged upward by 20 percent per year, with organic cropland doubling just between 1992 and 1997. This increase wouldn't have happened without marketing, and by the end of the decade, organic label milk and tomatoes were as unsurprising as Chilean wine or imported salami. By 2000, Americans bought more organic food in supermarkets than from farm stands or specialty shops. Marketing alone doesn't account for this shift. It took the strong, often controversial arm of the law to push this trend into the public embrace.[33]

The story of American federal organic legislation begins with the 1990 Organic Foods Production Act, a law intended to streamline the chaos of competing labels and voluntary standards that had rendered the term more or less meaningless in the 1980s. It took another ten years of acrimonious debate to sort out how it would actually be implemented, but on April 21, 2001, Americans entered a bold new world of eating, where "organic" ceased to be an adjective of opinion and became one of law.[34]

In reaching mainstream acceptance, organic food took a similar trajectory to the one followed by Fair Trade. From its roots in countercultural ideology, organic production has sprouted so many certification boards and lobbying groups that the old green hippies holler treason.[35] They're often right. In the original guidelines proposed for the Organic Foods Production Act, the government insisted that food treated with sewage or radiation, not to mention genetically modified organisms, could qualify as organic. Aghast, activists argued that this was a cynical move by industrial farming to co-opt the organic name to sell more groceries. By the time the legislation passed, the provisions for sludge, gene splicing, and loose gamma rays had been squashed, but Rudolf

Steiner's intellectual descendents are still fighting a running battle with agriculturists who insist that "organic" should solely refer to the inputs used on a particular piece of food and nothing else.

The debate reached a boiling point in 2005 over accusations that dairy cows in the certified Aurora Organic Dairy in Boulder, Colorado, were living a lie. The media printed claims that the cows lived in outdoor pens and ate a diet that included intensively-farmed grains.[36] Organic purists wanted milk to come exclusively from ambling, grass-fed animals. They felt that an industrial lifestyle, despite these cows' organic feed and lack of injections, betrayed the spirit of the label, if not the letter of the law. A high density of animals confined to a small space, complained the purists, degraded the environment, spewed floods of methane and manure, wasted energy, and spoiled the water. Surely organic meant something nobler than this?

It's the old Starbucks quandary, rehashed. Starting in the 2000s, Americans wanted to buy lots of organic milk, and the grass-fed method of raising dairy cattle wasn't supporting big enough herds to meet demand. Farmers could sell to mass market operations like Walmart, Target, Safeway, and Costco if they increased production, so they opened the barn door to large-scale dairy business (Aurora kept 5,700 cows in 2006). When questioned on confining his animals, Mark Retzloff, Aurora's president and chief organic officer, stated, "We don't have a lot of water that produces pasture. Here in Colorado, we like to use our water to grow higher-value grains and proteins."[37] Hence the locked pens and buckets of feed.

In Aurora's case, the United States Department of Agriculture showed up at the farm, threatening to revoke its lucrative organic name.[38] Lawsuits flew, and the media ran with a story about the greatest scandal in the history of organic food.[39] A consumer group called the Cornucopia Institute accused Aurora of "fraud, negligence, and unjust enrichment."[40] Lawyers' pens flashed from their scabbards and Aurora denied wrongdoing. But the dairy sold some of its cows before the tumult subsided.[41]

The problem from the start wasn't that Aurora had broken the law, but that it had belied popular conceptions.[42] This happened because, from the beginning, the organic movement had a subtly different marketing strategy from the one used by the Fair Trade movement. Both labels aimed for the wallets of thoughtful shoppers, and both played on consumers' sense of justice, but the organic industry one-upped the Fair Traders by also appealing to people's biological self-interest. Eating organic, they said, would spare you the chemical coating slathered over conventional foodstuffs, not to mention their weird hormones and zombie genes.

It's a compelling argument. E. Melanie DuPuis, a sociologist at the University of California, Santa Cruz, estimates that the rise of organic dairies is directly linked to the moment when the USDA approved the use of growth hormones on dairy cows.[43] Recombinant bovine growth hormone, or rBGH, is a synthetic hormone (originally derived from pituitary gland extracts) that, when injected into a lactating mammal, causes it to erupt in a font of cream. Since the hormone doesn't cure disease or fight tooth decay, its effect is purely commercial and of no benefit to anyone drinking it.[44] So when the agri-input conglomerate Monsanto started injecting it into American's milk supply, educated consumers became alarmed.

To make sense of this debate we have to remember that there are, in fact, two sorts of organic foodies. One group wants to save their own bodies from the chemical attack of a modern salad. The other group thinks that industrial farming means that modern salads are wicked in principle. Most organic buyers probably fall between the two categories, but when the USDA finally wrote the definitions of organic foodstuffs, they focused on concerns over inputs rather than on the broader issues of sustainability. Organic came to mean what a farmer uses to fertilize a field, to feed an animal, or to kill a pest. Something as obviously unnatural as rBGH was prohibited (a synthetic hormone is pretty much the definition of an additive), but the rules didn't say much about a cow's domicile. So the Aurora dairy was considered organic.

"Organic"—as defined by the U.S. government—has never meant the same as "sustainable." Nevertheless, for many farmers in the Rudolf Steiner mold, sustainable is inseparable from organic. The Steinerites oppose cattle operations like Aurora, arguing that an "organic" herd fed on grain and living in a pen is, for all practical purposes, conventional. The problem with the U.S. certification program is that it took a host of ideas and problems—health, sustainability, animal welfare, climate change—and compressed them into a rigid list of inputs. In writing the standards, the U.S. authorities essentially asked farmers a single question: Are the inputs you use from a factory or from an organic source? It's like reducing the entirety of *War and Peace* to the line "Napoleon was a product of historical determinism."

The result today is a field of organic products so broad that they include tomatoes grown on monocropped fields, picked by migrant labor, and sold through conventional supply chains to giant supermarkets.[45] The only difference with industrial agriculture is that the fertilizer wasn't cooked in a lab.[46] It's a long way from farming in nature's image, from maintaining a fertile soil balanced with carbon and nitrogen and circulating with clean water.[47] This is assembly-line farming with all the ills of the food empire—long distance travel, processing, packaging, *energy*—still attendant in the organic court.

Even so, times change, and so do laws. The first generation of U.S. organic regulations wasn't perfect, but it legitimized the idea that conventional food was somehow flawed. Millions of American shoppers today are familiar with Ben & Jerry's ice cream and Annie's organic macaroni and cheese—products packaged in recycled materials and festooned with pictures of cows and bunnies. Although they skirt the edge of twee, they make it easy for a hurried consumer to "do something" for the planet without any effort.

American organic law is evolving, too. In December 2008, the USDA ruled that organic dairy cattle "must receive 30 percent of their dry matter intake (DMI) from pasture," while "all animals over the age of six months must be on pasture throughout the growing season."[48] Pebbles rolling down a mountainside, yes, but the boulders have begun to budge. Or they would, if organic farming could break free of the model of the food empire and its millennia-old rut.

THE SNAIL TRIUMPHANT

Carletti never got back his money. For more than three years, he fretted in the Low Countries, an unwelcome presence in the waiting rooms of genteel burghers, reminding them of their piracy. After his years in the blazing colors of the tropics, Holland seemed a sodden mush of a place, all tin skies and flat water. He disliked it immensely, although he couldn't help but admire the seamanship and technical rigor of his robbers.

Despite the justice of his claim, Carletti's treasure proved too tempting for the Calvinists, who wouldn't give it back, even though Carletti wrote letters to everyone from the minister of Rotterdam to the queen of France. He shuffled through trials and retrials and wheezed under the weight of a malign bureaucratic machine. Once, on the way to Sluis to petition the States-General, he was assaulted by a crew of soldiers who would have murdered him for his jewels had he not stripped off his clothes to prove that he was, in fact, penniless. He was also miserable and even lonelier than he had been in Nagasaki or Macao. "One might go mad, as I was on the verge of doing, finding myself at one and the same time deprived of so much goods and in a country so foreign." But he never entirely lost his good humor. On a sightseeing visit to Gravesande, he marveled at two copper basins that had been reputedly used to baptize the Countess Margaret's 365 children, and he took long, involved notes on dike construction. He was, to the end, a tourist.

The end came on April 18, 1605, when a retrial court of the Council of the Admiralty decreed that the "Company of Merchants Dealing with East India" would pay Carletti 13,000 florins, closing the affair forever and absolving the court from any further responsibility in the matter, or any like it. Then they made him buy a big dinner for the judges, with "many flasks of wine." The eating lasted three hours, and the drinking carried through the night, during which the judges tried to console their host "with beakers in hand." They all knew that the 13,000 florins was a sop. Carletti was ruined.

Carletti's first impulse was to sail back to Asia and start all over again, but a detour in France and a letter from the duke of Tuscany convinced him to abandon that suicidal idea. And so, hardly richer than when he had set out, Francesco Carletti returned home to Renaissance Florence.

Today, Carletti's Tuscany, and more broadly the entire Italian peninsula, is where American food writers go to be consecrated. Scarcely a vineyard in Umbria or a Piedmontese cheese shop is unclaimed by some expatriate as Damascene ground where a writer's eyes opened to the transcendence of "real" food, conviviality, and the well-lived life. Of course, the locals sniff that *Under the Tuscan Sun* is "saccharine, inaccurate and boring,"[49] but they're thrilled about the villa rentals.

Italy has been the center of two far-flung food empires. The ancient Roman taste for wheat once shaped the landscape of Europe and a sizable slice of North Africa. The legions had marched, in part, to conquer and defend grain fields (see chapter 2). Centuries later, Venice was the hub of a food empire that snaked across the Mediterranean, down the Red Sea, and up the Himalayas, with its tips in the green jewels of the East Indian Ocean. Spice paid for the marbles on the Grand Canal. There was spice in Tintoretto's oils, and spice in the cannons at Lepanto. The palaces of Venice, like Carletti's sinking ship at St. Helena, stayed afloat on a bed of pepper dust.

Today, Venice is the hub of a different sort of food empire, a cultural one called Slow Food that trades in newsletters and symposia instead of bales of nutmeg. An "eco-gastronomic" organization that aspires to create a counterrevolution to the industrial food system, the movement's steering intellect is Carlo Petrini, a former folk music festival organizer who founded Slow Food International in 1989 and who remains its patriarch, its chief spokesman, and its seer.[50] His followers consider him to be a modern Luther nailing his theses to the door of the supermarket, and when fifty thousand people convened at the 2008 Slow Food Nation festival in San Francisco, the sense of righteousness was as sharp as the air in the Pickles and Chutney Pavilion.

Petrini launched his movement as a crusade to dislodge McDonald's from its foothold in the Italian market, arguing that industrial fast food not only stifled good taste and conviviality, it destroyed culture (today, Carletti's Florence is home to precisely nine McDonald's restaurants). Petrini wasn't only worried that traditional recipes, such as that for a homemade peperonata, would be lost under a cheap onslaught of Big Macs, but that traditional food products themselves, the local varieties of peppers or pigs that went into cooking ancestral dishes, would perish.

Slow Food is a conservative philosophy, carrying the Luddite flag against the beeping microwaves of modern eating. It calls for an end both to frozen beef tacos and to the industrial cattle operations that produce them. Food is necessarily political, it tells us, and we must fight the good fight against corporate agribusiness (and the capitalist oppressors who own it).

Many Slow Foodies are drawn to the movement's demand for "suitable doses of sensual pleasure"[51] and then stay for the politics. But eating is always at the stomach of the agenda. Slow Foodies may clamor to preserve the small family farm for the sake of workers' solidarity, but their hearts are in the heritage cabbages in the garden. One of the organization's most fascinating projects is its Ark of Taste, in which endangered foodstuffs are cataloged for promotion, and hence for survival. So we get entries on the Gilfeather turnip, the Hutterite Soup bean, and the Tennessee Myotonic goat. All of them are probably delightful in a cassoulet, but they are hardly the raw contents of most people's shopping baskets.

On a Saturday morning in August, Petrini sat in the sun-bleached lobby of the Hotel Vitale on the Embarcadero waterfront in San Francisco, his fingers wrapped around the day's *Corriere della Sera*. Although he was wearing woolly, professorial tones, his tailoring was far too crisp to belong to an academic. Even his beard looked neatly creased.

"As all the environmental, health, social, and political disasters have come to the surface, the key issues of our movement are now being felt," he pronounced. And Slow Food's response to global warming, social disruption, and a future food crisis is, actually, very simple. "Our solutions aim at promoting a local versus global economy."

The idea of local food—of living off the carrying capacity of the land by buying seasonal, organic produce and boutique-farmed meat—is at the heart of Slow Food's dream of a "new rurality." The ideal is nothing short of a renunciation of humanity's long, twisting history of trading food.

But contradictions abound. For example, while Slow Food champions the idea of regional distinctions—rival cheeses in Campania, for instance—such distinctions aren't static and never have been. Ideas of eating are as fluid as the Valpolicella poured at a Mexican restaurant in Vermont. Apart from inside a patch or two of Amazonian bush, or up a forgotten New Guinean gully, there's no such thing as a purely regional cuisine. Promiscuity in foodstuffs is part of human nature. Recall the Stone Age merchants who trucked Middle Eastern wheat across the breadth of Asia and laid the foundations for four thousand years of noodles in China (see chapter 4).

Take *zuppa del contadino* ("peasant soup"), a traditional dish from Petrini's own home ground of Piedmont. It's a cluster of rude imports. The chickens that make the broth came to Italy from China by way of India. The tomatoes that give it zing and color are famously South American. Even the garlic—southern Europe's lordly old flavoring agent—is an immigrant from Central Asia.

What, then, is authentic? Surely the very concept of a peasant "tradition" is ridiculous if you take history into account.[52]

But Petrini is used to critics. "Trade will always exist," he admits. "It is necessary in order to maintain relationships with other people and consider them as neighbors. My concept of local economy is based on a systemic approach to people's lifestyles, including the search for renewable energy, the safeguarding of the environment, use of waste, and a more democratic participation of people in this process. It's a method to make us stronger and fight against the globalized economy that has deprived us."

Another contradiction: Slow Food is ostensibly about sustenance, fellowship, and democracy, but its public face is the truffle-sniffing snout of the eco-foodie. Across the street from Petrini's hotel is the Ferry Building, a mall devoted to the cult of high-grade hors d'oeuvres. Fit Californians with good credit ratings shop for pawpaws, Bronx grapes, and aristocratic cheese. "Natural" butchers hawk organic salamis, grass-fed beef that practically drips with chlorophyll, and pork chops as pink as carnations. A chalkboard beside an organic vegetable stands reads "Slow Food Mushroom Basket $30." Even the smells—extra virgin olive oil, fried crab, ATM machines—are expensive. But to most Americans and the rest of low-wage humanity, a pound of pink tree oyster mushrooms is as attainable as a moon rock.

Petrini scorns such comparisons. "Saying our movement is elitist is not true," he insists. "We are present in Ethiopia. In the Rio de Janeiro slums. People accuse us because we support the right to pleasure for everyone, and many people consider suffering to be [the natural state of the poor]."

Despite this populist rhetoric, five minutes at a Slow Food event makes it clear that the epicurean value of food ("Try a slice of the Bazzone prosciutto. Note the musky aroma of chestnuts.") outweighs its material importance ("If I eat ham, I won't starve."). That's the power of marketing, in which Slow Food is proficient. But as many economists (or nutritionists) will tell you, eating is the purest mode of consumption. Our purchases are statements about our social class, our friends, and our beliefs. Buying something as continually necessary as food is an ongoing act of self-definition. It's not the vitamins or calories we're purchasing, but the cachet we get from tossing a pound of imported Irish butter into the cart.[53]

Slow Food, of course, isn't simply an international conspiracy to sell expensive cheese. Its motto is "good, clean, and fair," and it takes itself seriously. Its products are invariably better for the planet than are their equivalents grown in the industrial system. This justifies the "clean" part of their motto. As for the "fair," visit the coffee or chocolate stand at a Slow Food convention and count the familiar logos on the posters.

The "good," as in teaching people to enjoy the taste of, say, artisanal sauerkraut, is harmless, or even laudable. One of Petrini's favorite semantic schemes is to call food shoppers "co-producers," with the hope of changing the way people think about their relationship with their lunch. He wants to extend the principles of Fair Trade into every transaction involving food, which should at least educate people about the need for change. "The food industry played a positive role in the beginning," said Petrini. "But as time went by, it became more and more invasive and controlled more and more natural resources. The result is that we produce enough food for twelve billion people, but we're six billion. There are eight hundred million hungry while millions suffer from too much eating. We must be ashamed of that. The problem isn't production, but distribution."

Is Slow Food a solution to the millennial problem of the food empires expanding and collapsing? Perhaps it is, partly. In his book *Slow Food Nation,* Petrini suggests that we feed the world's metropolises through a *simple localization of products, with the search for the closest products (as in the research into the impact of food miles) through the creation of direct buying groups, formed in conjunction with farmers (community-supported agriculture, called CSAs), or with the creation of more farmers' markets."*[54]

This is good, but it's like firing a squirt gun at a burning house.

We can't expect a well-meaning dining club to feed tomorrow's hungry billions. But Petrini has done more than anyone to teach the world that there are alternatives to the tottering chemical mess that is the modern food empire. Slow Food has rung an alarm, jarring people into thinking about what they eat. It's given them ideas. And while Petrini's pronouncements have a tendency to deflate under scrutiny, his message is sound:

We need to make things better.

Conclusion: The New Gluttony and Tomorrow's Menu

To be a glutton in America today takes effort. A generation ago, you only needed an addiction to loaded nachos, but the New Gluttony is as much a test of education as it is of gastric power. New Gluttons read magazines. They post on message boards about *banh mi* sandwiches and the right way to blanch tilapia fillets. They fight over the reputations of cheesemongers. Excessive refinement in eating—what Thomas Aquinas called daintiness—has replaced gargling milkshakes as the definition of gluttony. A New Glutton would feel queasy at the thought of eating a pound of cold cuts in one sitting. Unless it happened to be *pata negra* Iberian ham.

Not long ago, a magazine writer pitched an article to one of the authors of this book. The article's theme was "pork bellies are the new short ribs." As a measure of the times, the author rejected the article as too done, too obvious. It was too much the established wisdom. Everybody was already well aware that pork bellies were the ingredient of the moment, as fresh herbs and sea bass had once been. To millions of New Gluttons, food is fashion.

But New Gluttony misses the point. Food isn't fashion. It's survival—for individuals and for civilizations. And the New Gluttony habit of turning food into a fashion statement risks undermining the critical danger we face. It's easy to dismiss the fear that our food system is threatened—after all, our minds are already too crammed with time bombs. If loose nukes aren't ticking down to Armageddon, then the glaciers are. Or the banks. Why should we fret about a five-dollar rise in grocery bills when we spend as much on an amusing ringtone? Surely, we'll all be dead from rogue viruses or nanotechnology long before we'd ever quake in existential fear at the sight of the last quart of milk on the supermarket shelf.

Still. The Roman recipe collection, *De re coquinaria*—attributed to the apocryphal gourmand Apicius—appeared around the beginning of the fifth century A.D. It was an exhaustive celebration of dainty eating, just the sort of food porn that might grace a New Glutton's kitchen shelf today, and it was written just in time for the last splutters of the Western Roman Empire. Then the world ended.

There's something similarly millenarian about the New Gluttony in America, a yearning for lost "authenticity" and less complicated times, when everyone had rough hands and long lunches. When the air smelled like hearth-baked peasant loaves and chickens came in feathers instead of shrink-wrap. Before we lost paradise and replaced it with a canning factory.

Tempering this nostalgia is a streak of nihilism. Eat yellowtail with ponzu glaze and be merry, for tomorrow we shall starve. That, more than sheer perversity, perhaps, is why urban diners commonly pay thirty-five dollars for a plate of fish. *Carpe carpem.*

In 2009, Professor John Beddington, chief science advisor to the UK government, told the press that by 2030, world demand for food would spike by 50 percent, and water by 30 percent, as the population topped 8.3 billion. "It's a perfect storm," he said. Lately, even the more conservative journals have agreed that estimates of how much food the earth will produce under climate change are too sanguine. Not that we'll notice, at first. Many current projections claim that the global larder will actually grow bigger, with longer growing seasons in the upper latitudes. And then, after the earth warms by more than two degrees, which is likely, everything will crash into mosquito swamps and bare ground.[1]

Now even the short-term boost looks unlikely, considering new models that add ozone poisoning to the tally.[2] And, of course, people are still having babies. Before 2050, then, world cereal consumption is set to rise by 56 percent and livestock consumption by 90 percent.[3]

But as the pendulum swings, this food culture of ours, as much as our production methods and distribution channels, as much as our food empire, is transforming. Locavores—the Luddites of gastronomy—haven't seized the machinery, but they now run the front offices in the factory. Marching outward from Chef Alice Waters's Californian enclave of Chez Panisse, they've planted their mark on every fine dining menu in the land. Today, any restaurant worth its Zagat rating wouldn't dare serve unsourced salmon. You can eat "natural" pepperoni at Pizza Hut. Even the chef in the Obama White House is vocal about food miles and sustainability, while government websites publish maps of the president's organic kitchen garden. In Britain, Paul McCartney launches a campaign for meat-free Mondays while Prime Minister Gordon Brown hires the celebrity chef Jamie Oliver to cook a "responsible" banquet for world leaders at a G20 summit.

This is good, but fashion alone won't keep us from starving.

Our food systems are bound together by more than history. Modern agribusiness has the potential to translate a dry month in Brazil into red ink on a ledger in China into an empty shopping cart in New Jersey. There are no buffers left, no Pharaoh's hoard of corn to tide the world over when the bad years come. Margins are thin now that the earth has been washed clean of its native cover, the ancient netting that anchored the soil in place. Our system reels under its addiction to fresh water and refrigerants. And if our plump laboratory crops disappear in clouds of insects, there will be no replacing them.

The United States Department of Agriculture frets about crop yields in the tropics,[4] and the *Proceedings of the National Academy of Sciences* expects up to another 170 million empty mouths on the planet by the year 2080.[5] Forecasters live in terror of the day that the last tank of gas boils away, when our cities clunk back into the Iron Age as the power grids fizzle. But even the most ardent peak oilers tend to overlook the fact that fossil fuels make our food. Should the derricks stop pumping crude, the loss of fertilizer would drop crop yields by half. Three billion people would lose their daily sustenance.

Heat will make food prices go up. They'll float up steadily at first, like a balloon with a long string. Then around 2050, the string will be let go, and they'll soar. Rice, for example, will possibly cost—in real terms—80 percent more than it does now.[6] We're used to hearing that climate change heralds disaster, but we're not used to thinking of it in the form of a cup of long grain.

As the pendulum of plenty and dearth comes to the tip of a trajectory, it slows, stills, then it plunges backward. We don't know for certain if we're at the end of the arc. It may take another decade or a generation for the historical push to swing back into a pull. As a species, we humans make bad prophets. In 2007, nearly every economist in the developed world saw a path of gold stretching toward the horizon, failing to notice the wrack and ruin a mere flip of the calendar ahead. But to anyone who doubts that the cycle of agricultural peaks and collapses will repeat—to anyone who doubts history—the clinching argument is nature. None of our technological enchantments has been able to conjure away the limitations of earth, seed, water, and light. We can ape them. We can hammer together greenhouses and loop new strings of DNA. But the miracle of the loaves and fishes remains just that: a miracle.

Unless we change the way we work our land, our answers—alchemical crops, blizzards of coolants, Niagaras of water pouring onto the fields—will only exacerbate the problem. Yet if we hadn't chosen industry over nature, there wouldn't be 6 billion people alive today (soon to be 9 billion), and those of us who had been born would spend our leisure hours pottering among the family onions or dunking summer berries in pectin so we could have food come winter. We'd watch our calendars for the day the geese would splash down in the neighborhood pond, taking their rest on their annual crossing, and wait among the rushes in the predawn damp, our shotguns primed for Christmas. We would live and eat as our grandparents did. We wouldn't have built a civilization in which people published books like this one, since we'd be too busy nosing in the grass for rhubarbs.

That's what we would have done, at least, until the planet's easy sources of nitrogen and groundwater ran out, probably by the 1980s or so. And then many of us would have starved. The utopian visions of freegans and anarchists have always been predicated on the annihilation of about half of the human population.

Industrial agriculture once gave us our world on a platter, but that doesn't mean it can do so forever. The nature of the global economic system means that an environmental tremor in northern China could unleash a catastrophic rise in food prices, which will make the current worldwide rumblings look as insignificant as a craving for an after-dinner mint.

Again, imagine that China went thirsty. As apocalyptic disasters go, it's not a stretch. Unlike earthquakes and terrorism, this is a quiet, even pedestrian nightmare. It shouldn't be hard to picture. The rains stayed away in 2008–9, and many climate change models project that by 2050 the sky in northern China will become much drier.[7] Now recall that China's hunger for grain has already driven the government to divert all the country's major rivers into irrigation.[8] In a future dry spell, the reservoir that sits behind the Three Gorges Dam will drop. There will be no more sources to tap. The Yellow River is particularly worrying: as of this writing, it's lost 60 percent of its volume to irrigation, industry, and drought.[9] For 227 days in 1997, it didn't even manage to trickle as far as the sea.[10]

When the inevitable parching comes and the rice paddies crack with stony mud and the grain fields bake into straw, it may not be the Chinese who starve. They'll be rich enough to buy food from Vietnam, Indonesia, and America. But the Africans won't. They are always the losers in the world's economic games; their rice deliveries will veer into Chinese ports. Even in 2008's relatively minor food crisis, Africa was the first to suffer a cut in exports.

Possibly, hunger will make China even bolder than does its hunger for economic expansion. Instead of buying food, perhaps it will shrug off its customary borders and look northward toward Manchuria and Siberia, pitting itself against nuclear Russia and setting off a cascade of events that will touch even countries with the most fashionable addresses.[11]

It's also possible that the Mississippi basin and Great Plains will "suffer huge losses to its food production"[12] and that the United States will cease to be a food exporter. If this comes to pass, Western governments, desperate to keep grocery bills within reach of voters, will use multinational food contractors to drive down wages for farmers in the tropics—a shadow of the Roman bent for provincial plantations manned by slaves. Colonialist exploitation will be manna for terrorists. Bombs will burst, and future Pompeys will seize extraordinary powers to sweep the devils from our seas and airports. Over the qualms of civil libertarians, war will keep bananas cheap in the short term. But the problem won't go away. It will fester and sometimes bloom into a whirlwind of fire and blood inside the world's remaining privileged enclaves. We're all connected, after all.

There's no reliable forecast to tell us how the current crisis will play out in the next few decades.[13] We have to thumb through history books and weather reports and guess that, by the lessons of the bad years in the 1870s, Africans will starve by the tens of millions while tides of immigration swamp the thin borders of Europe and the Middle East. Many immigrants will be seething with resentment and vector-borne diseases, hardly a recipe for public health, racial harmony, or peace.

Our agricultural-industrial complex may chug ahead for another generation or two, perhaps sipping a little more cautiously at the oil well, perhaps hammering a few more No Pesticides signs on the edges of soybean fields. But the momentum of the pendulum won't be stilled. Our food system is going to change.

We may not even notice it happening. It took about two hundred years for the ancient Romans to whittle their numbers in half. There are no mass graves along the Via Sacra. In Mesopotamia, the slow winnowing of the soil happened over the very centuries in which the great cities of Ur and Nippur strutted upon the stage. Atrophy doesn't make for a particularly stirring exit, but it's the way that food empires usually die. We'll become accustomed to bad processed foodstuffs, their nutrients padded with filler. We'll learn to swallow the nitrogen in our water and the slick of hormones in our meat. The marketing for our food products will be splendid—we'll feast on images of salads bejeweled with neon tomatoes and tacos adrip with hot cheese. Madison Avenue strategists will hatch their subtle plots and spring exciting new products on the public, all of them spun out of partially hydrogenated corn oil and fructose. Instead of famine, our tottering food system will first deliver a spike of cheap, nutritionally bankrupt calories, masking the loss of gastronomic diversity, health, and flavor. And then it will slump.

Cheap food is not only a historical quirk, it's not even cheap once the bill is reckoned. Grass-fed beef, organic beets, Fair Trade coffee—their prices aren't more expensive, they're simply more honest. We ought to buy them, but that's not enough.

Slow Food is right about getting people to obsess over their food. Change will come from the skeptic at the fish counter, the bag of celery from the community-supported agriculture truck, the metastasizing e-mail petition to Congress. When the food miles, provenance, and cleanliness of a char fillet inspires as much interest as the day's stock readings or football scores, then we'll see things get better.

But until there's a public outcry for tax incentives directed at promoting sustainable agriculture, the best we can do is start hoarding against the future. Not by stacking cans of beans in our cellars, but through loading silos, enough to stave off hunger for more than just a season. We need an economic plan that counts for a day when the whole world needs bread more than it needs circuses. That, at least, would help us through the first dry spell.

For seven thousand years, food empires have expanded as far as transport and topsoil and markets would allow. Then they slunk back to lick the dregs of their empty storehouses when their farms fell into dust. Every food empire—the network of specialized farms that survive and support urban civilizations through trading—overextends itself. So will the modern one, for all its technological talent.

How then do we avoid repeating the mistakes of Mesopotamia, of Rome, and of the nineteenth century? There's no chance that the modern world could abandon specialization, much less go without trade, but it's worth imagining what self-sufficient cities would look like. Their citizens would be flimsy creatures, stunted on diets of stale grain and whatever greens they could scratch from parks and victory gardens. And there wouldn't be many of them. A city the size of London, Rio de Janeiro, or Johannesburg could never feed itself on the proceeds of its hinterlands. Even if a city solely bought local, it would be foolish to do so. Without the food trade, a local drought or crop blight becomes a death sentence. Having the world as our breadbasket is an excellent means of insurance.

Fair Trade offers a lesson in tamping down the excesses of food empires by enforcing the revolutionary principle that everyone is entitled to food and a living wage. Organic crops rid our fields of fossil fuels and, hopefully, recycle the soil's nutrients so that we learn to farm in nature's image. Hedgerows, trees, and legumes alongside the corn, and a healthy dash of wild fowl. That's the best model for a twenty-first-century agribusiness.

Our food empire has, to a degree, swallowed these ideals and regurgitated them as checklists, laws that embody a few of the appropriate details but little in the way of change. One way to fight anemic standards of "organic" or "natural" is to follow the Slow Food route. Buying, eating, and producing food is a political act, and the best way to teach people this lesson is by getting them excited about heritage charcuterie plates. If enough people embrace Slow Food's ideas along with its consumption, the modern food empire would have to adapt.

A sustainable food empire can only exist if most of its farms are smallish, diverse, and serving customers not too far away. This is called bioregionalism. But for such a model to safely feed a world population of 6 billion—to spread risk—this bioregional system has to nest within a global trading network. Global food and local food offset each other's failings. Local food is thrifty with energy and buffered from faraway disasters. Global food is economically efficient and, even more importantly, it puts mangoes and salmon on our dinner tables. We need the global system so that regions can specialize—to a degree. International trade prevents inefficient uses of land, since it's cheaper for people to buy what they can't grow effectively themselves. This combination of global and local, a nested bioregional system for want of a more sonorous term, is the best hope we have of sustaining our modern food empire.

But it's easier posited than done. The only way such a nested bioregional system could ever appear would be through legislation. Market forces are too strong to willingly give up their monocultures until it's too late. A nested bioregional system would also require the weight of an ardent consumer base behind it, wielding enough dollars to upend the economic logic of destroying the planet for the sake of cheap corn products. Again, this is easily suggested. But beliefs are changing, and not solely at a snail's pace.

It would be delightful if governments agreed that all their citizens should be entitled to a nutritious diet. That food producers should all earn a living wage. That farms should be diverse, and hence climate resilient. That regions shouldn't specialize to the point where nutrients accumulate so much that they pollute the land (a common mess wherever we raise livestock intensively) or drain away so much that they destroy it (common wherever we intensely crop). And they should agree that watering our fields with oil, essentially, is a bad idea.

Taxing inputs, transport, and energy would be an excellent step, although that's assumed to be politically suicidal. But so is ignoring the problem. And if we're serious about food security, we need to invest in the infrastructure to store enough food against a bad season or three. Because, whether we pass legislation or not, the dry years will come.

Without a popular mandate, though, laws like these won't be forthcoming. More than just a fan club for specialty yams, Slow Food is a philosophic model that we'd do well to encourage. If people directed a fraction of the energy they invest in consumption toward thinking and caring about what they eat, we wouldn't have to worry about our food empire being left on the compost heap of history. CSAs, farmer's markets, family gardens—these small steps will set us on a safer path.

That path will need farmers to raise livestock on the edges of cities, grazing them in the summer and feeding them local dry grass in winter. They'll reject the temptations of the injection and the confining pen, and when the moment comes for slaughter, they'll drive the meat a few miles into the city for market. Next door, the farmers will grow beets and grain and trees, spreading animal manure on fields to keep nutrients balanced so the crops don't break the soil. They'll favor perennial plants over annuals, since perennials usually have deeper, denser roots that tap the groundwater more efficiently. Inputs like chemical fertilizers will be too expensive to use much (and hardly needed, anyway, since the land won't begrudge its harvest). Instead of heavy pesticides, the farmers will rely on the attentions of birds, drawn to the farm by its attractive mix of flora.

Running this sort of farm will be expensive, particularly in labor costs—not a bad thing, necessarily, since it would mean lucrative jobs in the countryside. Consumers, or rather eaters, would support these farms with community-supported agricultural schemes wherein they buy a percentage of a crop or a cull in advance. People would still have to buy their bread, rice, and corn from distant plantations, and this scheme wouldn't put avocados on the tables of eaters in Glasgow or Montreal. But it would still be a revolution.

Early murmurs of such change have already sounded. In the Canadian agricultural town of Meaford, Ontario, for example, a store called the 100 Mile Market operates on the principle of natural, local sourcing, selling only foods from the nearby countryside. Its owner, Barbara Kay, retired from corporate relations to run an elk farm. When she and her husband opened 100 Mile Market to sell farm stand products during the winter months, they could hardly keep up with demand.

"It was never meant to replace the grocery store," says Kay. "We have no citrus fruits. No cleaning products." There's no orange juice, but there is local milk. No $1.99 per pound beef roasts from corporate processors, but there are grass-fed sirloins and local ice cream. Farmers, coffee roasters, beekeepers, and cheesemakers from within a short drive of Meaford place their products in the store on consignment—Kay takes a percentage for stocking them, and small producers gain access to people's shopping bags. It's a simple, efficient, and sustainable way to run a tiny food empire.

"Tiny" is the crux. "Here, there's a trust built into the food because your neighbor's growing it," says Kay. "I can say which farm your steak is from, and you can park on the side of the road and look at the animals. You know Frank, who was Santa Claus in the Christmas parade? He raised this." It's not a recipe that translates to Toronto or New York unless food prices rise considerably. Even so, the corporate titans have begun to absorb the slogans, if not always the policies, of local sourcing. Local, of course, can mean Guangzhou.

In the summer of 1992, one of the authors belted up his dungarees and took a job as a farmhand in his grandparents' cornfields. It was the summer after high school, a time when most Canadian boys braced for the riot of college life by earning a few paychecks from restaurant tables and checkout counters. The author did something less comfortable. Sunburn and mosquito spray was better than slopping a mop around the floor of a Dairy Queen.

All that summer, the rains may have fallen in Newfoundland or Burma, but they drifted clear of Ontario. The crops bent and yellowed under wrinkles of hot air, and the author's grandfather stared at the televised weather reports and paced the kitchen floor. Finally, on a sweltering July morning, grandfather, author, and a hired hand marched into the dusty grooves between the cornstalks to hoe the dirt around each plant, trying to keep it upright in earth too dry to anchor roots. Then they grabbed hold of irrigation pipes. With muscle and some quick geometry, they hauled the pipes through the toasted soil, repositioning them like artillery around the perimeter. It was a hard couple of days' work, but when the spigots turned on and a rainbow rose above the corn, the crop had been saved.

Technology may not rescue our food system, but a pair of boots and a willing mind may do the trick somehow. The entire history of agriculture—unlike that of cookery or politics—isn't about bumbling through events until someone yanks a resolution out of the mess. It's not like the happenstance inventions of cheese and alcohol, or the chain reactions of gripes and accidents that spark wars. Agriculture is about careful observation, trial and error, and torturous work. Each leap forward, from the Neolithic agricultural revolution to the invention of Californian tomatoes, was a meticulous act. We have to undertake another such job. Our tools will be education, planning, and (God help us) responsible governance. Certainly, regulation and restraint lack sex appeal. It's hard to get people excited about voting for restrictions on the use of unwholesome fertilizers, or to convince them not to buy concentrated orange juice. But hunger isn't very glamorous, either.

Six years after the author helped his grandfather rescue the cornfields, the skies above Ontario again stretched clear and bleached of clouds. By then, the author was living with his future wife in a big city, and his grandfather was too old to haul pipes. This time, the crop died before harvest. If the world as a whole is too tired, or too committed to its allegorical good life to haul the metaphorical spigot, then the world's food will burn up in our long, twenty-first-century summer.

The New Gluttons have this much right: you are what you eat. So the study of food is really part of the humanist curriculum. When our humanist hero, Francesco Carletti, finally returned to Florence in 1606, fifteen years after he had left, he went straight to the duke of Tuscany and spun his knotted yarn about Mexican fruit and the sexual mores of the king of Siam. Then, having made his report and his obsequies, Carletti lamented his outrageous bad luck, threw a few aspersions on the Dutch, and drifted back into the noisy, hand-slapping, wheedling life around the Ponte Vecchio. He died in 1636, the very year that the Japanese shogun locked away his islands from the world.

At the end of his journey, Carletti had returned to the crowded cobbles of his homeland, his nose once more primed with the old Mediterranean scents of wine and oil, bread and cheese and garlic. No matter how seasoned the traveler, the best dish, he might have thought, is one from your native soil.

And then he may have bit into a tomato.

Acknowledgments

For their generous help in seeing our manuscript through its long gestation, the authors wish to thank David Fraser, Elizabeth Fraser, Nancy Fraser, Margo Hanson, Damian Howells, Elisabeth Simelton, Rebecca Smalley, and Anne Tallontire.

Also, heartfelt thanks to Ramune Rimas for providing shelter during a particularly terrible storm.

We wish to thank Larry Weissman for his unwavering guidance through the wilds of publishing, and Leslie Meredith and Donna Loffredo at Free Press for their wisdom, patience, and belief in this book.

Much of this work was facilitated by an interdisciplinary research fellowship awarded by the Economics and Social Research Council (UK), the Economics and Social Research Council (UK)'s Centre for Climate Change Economics and Policy, and the UK's Natural Science and Environment Research Council's QUEST: Global Scale Impacts Project. Together these projects permitted Evan Fraser to escape his teaching and other academic duties to write this book. These grants also provided access to a range of scientific experts and results.

Many thanks to George and Christian for the game.

And, of course, we're grateful to our families for their support and understanding during our food empire years. Thanks especially to our patient wives, Laura Bravo, for taking the kids to Spain for six weeks, and Christine de Vuono, for helping keep everything in perspective.

Notes

THE THREE GORGES DAM

1. Before the Three Gorges was constructed, the Gezhouba Dam was built across the Yangtze River in Yichang during the 1970s and 1980s.
2. See Hongfu Yin and Changan Li, "Human Impact on Floods and Flood Disasters on the Yangtze River," *Geomorphology* 41, nos. 2–3 (2001).
3. Background to the dam can be found at the official website: China Three Gorges Project, www.ctgpc.com.
4. Y. Zong and X. Chen, "The 1998 Flood on the Yangtze, China," *Natural Hazards* 22 (2000). See page 181.
5. Philip M. Fearnside, "China's Three Gorges Dam: 'Fatal' Project or Step Toward Modernization?" *World Development* 16, no. 5 (1988).
6. A key proponent of this argument is Lester Brown; see L. Brown, *Who Will Feed China?* (Washington D.C.: World Watch, 1995).
7. The Department for International Development (UK) and the Chinese Academy of Agricultural Sciences, "Impacts of Climate Change on Chinese Agriculture, Overall Summary of Results," http://www.china-climate-adapt.org/en/document/ICCCA_overallsum mary_FINAEng.pdf. The quote is from page 2.
8. J. Qiu, "Agriculture: Is China Ready for GM Rice?" *Nature* 455, no. 7215 (2008). See in particular page 850.
9. This is a hotly debated topic. For example, both "for" and "against" arguments are discussed in R. Sherlock and J. Morrey, eds., *Ethical Issues in Biotechnology* (Oxford, UK: Rowan and Littlefield, 2002). See chapter 9 for pro-biotech arguments and chapter 10 for anti-biotech.
10. Qiu, "Agriculture: Is China Ready for GM Rice?"
11. For a general introduction to the scholarly research on "the general crisis of the seventeenth century," see G. Parker and L. Smith, eds., *The General Crisis of the Seventeenth Century* (London: Routledge, 1997).
12. The seminal account of the role of politics in creating famine is A. Sen, *Poverty and Famines* (Oxford: Clarendon Press, 1981). The following article specifically shows how politics and economics can make communities vulnerable to drought: E. Fraser, "Travelling in Antique Lands: Studying Past Famines to Understand Present Vulnerabilities to Climate Change," *Climate Change* 83, no. 4 (2007).
13. E. Anbarasan, "India Rice Export Prices up Again," BBC News, http://news.bbc.co.uk/1/hi/world/south_asia/7319589.stm.

14. "India Rice Exports Curbs Seen until Oct 2009," Reuters, http://www.flex-news-food.com/pages/19917/India/rice/india-rice-exports-curbs-seen-until-oct-2009.html.
15. P. Waldie, "From Wal-Mart Quotas to a 'Frenzy' in Vancouver, Asia's Rice Crisis Goes Global," *Globe and Mail,* April 24, 2008, http://www.theglobeandmail.com/subscribe.jsp?art=681388.
16. V. Walt, "The World's Growing Food-Price Crisis," *Time,* February 27, 2008, http://www.time.com/time/world/article/0,8599,1717572,00.html.
17. This is a quote from a speech by the president of the World Bank. See R. Zoellick, "A Challenge of Economic Statecraft," World Bank, http://web.worldbank.org/WEBSITE/EXTERNAL/NEWS/0,,contentMDK: 21711307~menuPK:34472~pagePK:34370~piPK:34424~theSitePK:4607,00.html.
18. "Record Harvest but Troubles Loom Ahead: Financial Crisis Will Hurt Agricultural Markets," UN Food and Agriculture Organization, http://www.fao.org/news/story/en/item/8271/icode/.
19. This is the argument advanced in M. Davis, *Late Victorian Holocausts: El Niño Famines and the Making of the Third World* (London: Verso, 2001). This extraordinary book outlines the relationship between the Victorian economic system and vulnerability to climate change.

CHAPTER ONE: FAIRS

1. F. Carletti, *My Voyage around the World: A Sixteenth Century Florentine Merchant*, trans. H. Weinstock (ca. 1609; London: Methuen and Co., Ltd., 1964).
2. D. Fischer, *The Great Wave: Price Revolutions and the Rhythm of History* (Oxford: Oxford University Press, 1996). See in particular section 2, "The Second Wave," on pages 65–102.
3. For a general overview of the key themes in seventeenth-century European history, see G. Parker and L. Smith, eds., *The General Crisis of the Seventeenth Century* (London: Routledge, 1997). In particular, chapter 1 provides an excellent overview of the state of Europe at this time. The final chapter provides an insight into the role of climate in precipitating this crisis.
4. There is a considerable body of scholarship devoted to explaining why Europe developed while China didn't. For example see chapters 1 and 5 in K. Pomeranz, *The Great Divergence: China, Europe and the Making of the Modern World Economy* (Oxford: Princeton University Press, 2000). In addition, see the entirety of E. Jones, *The European Miracle: Environments, Economies, and Geopolitics in the History of Europe and Asia* (Cambridge: Cambridge University Press, 2003).
5. S. Chew, *The Recurring Dark Ages: Ecological Stress, Climate Changes, and Systems Transformation* (Lanham, Md.: Altamira Press, 2006). See pages 153 and 154.
6. Anthony's story, besides being a spiritual example, has a materialistic side. As a young man, he had inherited his family's grand estate, but he may not have found reason to be grateful. Soil exhaustion throughout the empire, and in Egypt in particular, had decimated crop yields at the same time as tax rates exploded and the environment cooled. Athanasius mentions that financial pains sent some people fleeing toward religion and the desert where it was possible to stay away from being a victim of "injustice . . . or a tax collector." This theme runs deep: there seems to have been a long tradition in Egypt of running away from the heavy hand of government. The Coptic word for withdrawal is "*anacboresan,*" literally "to go up the river valley to the desert," a retreat that ancient Egyptians would make when threatened by soldiers or tax men. See the introduction and notes to Athanasius, ed.,

The Life of Antony and the Letter to Marcellinus (Mahwah, N.J.: Paulist Press, 1979). The quote is on page 64. See also footnote 95 on page 138.

7. Ibid. See also page 38 in Sing C. Chew, "Historical Social Movements, Ecological Crisis and 'Other' World Views," *Journal of Developing Societies* 24, no. 1 (2008).
8. E. C. Butler, "St. Anthony," Catholic Encyclopedia, http://www.newadvent.org/cathen/01553d.htm.
9. M. Hassett, "John Cassian," Catholic Encyclopedia, http://www.newadvent.org/cathen/03404a.htm.
10. J. Cassian, "The Twelve Books of John Cassian on the Institute of the Coenobia, and the Remedies for the Eight Principal Faults," A Select Library of Nicene and Post-Nicene Fathers of the Christian Church, second series, vol. 11, http://www.osb.org/lectio/cassian/inst/instpref.html#tp. See in particular book 4, chapter 3.
11. S. T. Loseby, "Marseille: A Late Antique Success Story?" *The Journal of Roman Studies* 82 (1992). See page 167.
12. Chew, "Historical Social Movements, Ecological Crisis and 'Other' World Views."
13. S. Lebecq, "The Role of the Monasteries in the Systems of Production and Exchange," in *The Long Eighth Century: Production, Distribution and Demand,* ed. I. Hansen and C. Wickham (Boston: Brill, 2000).
14. Ibid. The quote is on page 129.
15. G. C. Alston, "Rule of St. Benedict," Catholic Encyclopedia, http://www.newadvent.org/cathen/02436a.htm. The quote is in the third section, under "Characteristics of the Rule."
16. Quoted in E. Miller and J. Hatcher, *Medieval England: Rural Society and Economic Change 1086–1348* (London: Longman, 1978). The quote is on page xiii.
17. J. A. Raftis, "Western Monasticism and Economic Organization," *Comparative Studies in Society and History* 3, no. 4 (1961).
18. R. Hodges, *Dark Age Economics: The Origins of Town and Trade AD 600–1000*, 2nd ed. (London: New Approaches in Archaeology and Duckworth, 1989). See page 55.
19. Chew, "Historical Social Movements, Ecological Crisis and 'Other' World Views."
20. Miller and Hatcher, *Medieval England: Rural Society and Economic Change 1086–1348.*
21. See the chapter on monks in T. Jones and A. Ereira, *Medieval Lives* (London: BBC Books, 2004).
22. Quoted in Miller and Hatcher, *Medieval England: Rural Society and Economic Change 1086–1348*. The quote is on page 33.
23. Ibid.
24. The classic treatment of the medieval agricultural revolution is found in L. White, *Medieval Technology and Social Change* (Oxford: Oxford University Press, 1966). Some more recent historians argue that White overstated the importance of some elements. Nevertheless, the basic argument (that the monasteries produced an enormous surplus of food based on agricultural technology) remains intact.
25. This argument is presented in Miller and Hatcher, *Medieval England: Rural Society and Economic Change 1086–1348*. This issue is alluded to in the Bayeux Tapestry from the late eleventh century. For example, see "Britain's Bayeux Tapestry," Museum of Reading, http://www.bayeuxtapestry.org.uk/Index.htm. The bottom border of "The prisoner, scene 3" shows a peasant with a scratch plow.
26. Lebecq, "The Role of the Monasteries in the Systems of Production and Exchange."
27. A. Lucas, *Wind, Water, Work: Ancient and Medieval Milling Technology* (Boston: Brill, 2006).
28. A. Usher, *A History of Mechanical Inventions,* rev. ed. (New York: Dover Publications, 1988).
29. This argument is advanced in R. Holt, "Whose Were the Profits of Corn Milling? An

Aspect of the Changing Relationship between the Abbots of Glastonbury and Their Tenants 1086–1350," *Past and Present* 116, no. 1 (1987).

30. Ibid. See page 8.
31. Hodges, *Dark Age Economics: The Origins of Town and Trade AD 600–1000.*
32. D. Gay Wilson, "Plant Remains from the Graveney Boat and the Early History of Humulus Lupulus L. in W. Europe," *New Phytologist* 75, no. 3 (1975).
33. Ibid. See page 638.
34. There seems to be some disagreement on this date. Wilson, "Plant Remains from the Graveney Boat and the Early History of Humulus Lupulus L. in W. Europe," states that this happened in 822, while C. Bamford, *Beer: Tap into the Art and Science of Brewing* (Oxford: Oxford University Press, 2003), puts the date at 622.
35. R. Unger, *Beer in the Middle Ages and the Renaissance* (Philadelphia: University of Pennsylvania Press, 2004).
36. Bamford, *Beer: Tap into the Art and Science of Brewing.* See page 28.
37. Quoted in I. Hornsey, *A History of Brewing* (Cambridge, UK: The Royal Society of Chemistry, 2003). The quote is on page 295.
38. Hodges, *Dark Age Economics: The Origins of Town and Trade AD 600–1000.* See page 130.
39. Dagobert King of the Franks, "Grant of a Fair at St. Denis," Internet Medieval Source Book, http://www.fordham.edu/halsall/source/629stdenis.html.
40. Hodges, *Dark Age Economics: The Origins of Town and Trade AD 600–1000.*
41. There is an extensive literature on the topic of corporate concentration in the agri-food business. For example see K. Morgan, T. Marsden, and J. Murdoch, *Worlds of Food: Place, Power, and Provenance in the Food Chain* (Oxford: Oxford University Press, 2006). The statistics quoted in the text can be found on page 55.
42. In terms of nonacademic writing on the subject of the modern industrial food chain see M. Pollan, *The Omnivore's Dilemma* (New York: Penguin, 2006); A. Kimbrell, ed., *The Fatal Harvest Reader: The Tragedy of Industrial Agriculture* (Washington, D.C.: Island Press, 2002); and E. Schlosser, *Fast Food Nation* (London: Allen Lane, 2001).
43. The original treadmill theory was proposed by Cochrane in 1958. It is described and revisited in R. Levins and W. Cochrane, "The Treadmill Revisited," *Land Economics* 72, no. 4 (1996).
44. This issue is discussed in academic terms in: G. Stone, "Biotechnology and Suicide in India," *Anthropology News* 43 (2002). See page 5. This issue is also discussed regularly in the media. For example, please see: A. Malone, "The GM Genocide: Thousands of Indian Farmers Are Committing Suicide after Using Genetically Modified Crops," *The Daily Mail,* November 3, 2008, http://www.dailymail.co.uk/news/worldnews/article-1082559/The-GM-genocide-Thousands-Indian-farmers-committing-suicide-using-genetically-modified-crops.html.
45. Hodges, *Dark Age Economics: The Origins of Town and Trade AD 600–1000.* See page 47.
46. J. Russel, "Population in Europe," in *The Fontana Economic History of Europe*, vol. 1: *The Middle Ages*, ed. Carlo M. Cipolla (Glasgow: Collins/Fontana, 1972).
47. Michael A. Fullen, "Soil Erosion and Conservation in Northern Europe," *Progress in Physical Geography* 27, no. 3 (2003).
48. E. Jansen et al., "Palaeoclimate," in Working Group I, *Climate Change 2007: The Physical Science Basis,* Contribution to the Fourth Assessment Report of the Intergovernmental Panel on Climate Change, ed. S. Solomon and D. Qin, et al. (Cambridge: Cambridge University Press, 2007). See the discussion in http://www.ncdc.noaa.gov/paleo/globalwarming/medieval.html.
49. Quoted in Jones and Ereira, *Medieval Lives*. The quote is on page 114.

50. Walter Map, twelfth-century archdeacon, satirist, and critic of the Cistercians, quoted in The Cistercians in Yorkshire and the Humanities Research Institute, "The Cistercians in Yorkshire," Humanities Research Institute at the University of Sheffield, http://cistercians.shef.ac.uk/index.php.
51. The following article provides an overview of the Cistercians' "grange economy" in France: C. Berman, "Medieval Agriculture, the Southern French Countryside, and the Early Cistercians: A Study of Forty-Three Monasteries," *Transactions of the American Philosophical Society* 5, no. 5 (1986). See in particular page 10.
52. Ibid.
53. Miller and Hatcher, *Medieval England: Rural Society and Economic Change 1086–1348*. The quote is on page 33.
54. Gerald of Wales, quoted in Berman, "Medieval Agriculture, the Southern French Countryside, and the Early Cistercians: A Study of Forty-Three Monasteries." See page 7.
55. The following book provides a detailed exploration of the links between soil erosion, climate, population, and inflation: Fischer, *The Great Wave: Price Revolutions and the Rhythm of History*. See in particular page 20.
56. Ibid.
57. There have been a huge number of scientific studies done to reconstruct past climates. Using ice cores, tree rings, and lake/ocean bottom sediment analysis, scientists try to understand past temperature and rainfall patterns. These conclusions are then double-checked using computer models and confirmed using textual sources of information where possible. For example, the following study provides evidence for a European cooling in the fourteenth century: Marie-Alexandrine Sicre et al., "Decadal Variability of Sea Surface Temperatures off North Iceland over the Last 2000 Years," *Earth and Planetary Science Letters* 268, nos. 1–2 (2008).
58. See the chapter on medieval history in C. Spinage, *Cattle Plague: A History* (New York: Kluwer Academic, 2003).
59. Fischer, *The Great Wave: Price Revolutions and the Rhythm of History*. See page 35.
60. Quoted in J. Aberth, *From the Brink of the Apocalypse: Confronting Famine, War, Plague, and Death in the Later Middle Ages* (New York: Routledge, 2001). The quote is on page 14. See also A. Gransden, *Historical Writing in England* (London: Routledge, 1996), pages 6–7.
61. The original poem is attributed to T. Wright; see "Poem on the Evil Times of Edward II" (also known as "The Simonie"). This translation is quoted in Aberth, *From the Brink of the Apocalypse: Confronting Famine, War, Plague, and Death in the Later Middle Ages*. See page 11.
62. L. Bréhier, "Crusade of the Pastoureaux," Catholic Encyclopedia, http://www.newadvent.org/cathen/11539a.htm.
63. Fischer, *The Great Wave: Price Revolutions and the Rhythm of History*. See page 37.
64. A. R. Bridbury, "Before the Black Death," *The Economic History Review* 30, no. 3 (1977). See, in particular, page 401. See also D. Herlihy, "The Agrarian Revolution in Southern France and Italy, 801–1150," *Speculum* 33, no. 1 (1958).
65. Some relatively recent scholarship on the Black Death discounts the traditional theory that it was a new pathogen in Europe. See, for example, Samuel K. Cohn, Jr., "The Black Death: End of a Paradigm," *The American Historical Review* 107, no. 3 (2002). Other medical historians stick to the older theory and maintain that the plague was a new disease in Europe at the time and that it was spread by rats along the roads and trading routes of Medieval Europe. See M. McCormick, "Rats, Communications, and Plague: Toward an Ecological History," *Journal of Interdisciplinary History* 34, no. 1 (2003). Since the majority of scholarly work accepts the traditional theory, this is the perspective we have adopted in this book.

66. McCormick, "Rats, Communications, and Plague: Toward an Ecological History."
67. One of the twentieth century's preeminent rural historians suggests that following the Black Death, alternative forms of agriculture such as keeping rabbits became common across England. See J. Thirsk, *Alternative Agriculture: A History* (Oxford: Oxford University Press, 1997).
68. Fischer, *The Great Wave: Price Revolutions and the Rhythm of History*. See pages 44 and 45.
69. Plato, *Critias*, trans. Benjamin Jowett, Sacred Text Archives, http://www.sacred-texts.com/atl/critias.txt.
70. Robert Walker et al., "Ranching and the New Global Range: Amazônia in the 21st Century," *Geoforum* 40, no. 5 (2009). See the first page of the article for background to Amazonian deforestation.
71. E. M. A. Smaling et al., "From Forest to Waste: Assessment of the Brazilian Soybean Chain, Using Nitrogen as a Marker," *Agriculture, Ecosystems & Environment* 128, no. 3 (2008). See the first two sections of this paper for background on soybean production in Brazil.
72. Millennium Ecosystem Assessment, *Ecosystems and Human Wellbeing* (Washington D.C.: Island Press, 2005). See table 1 on page 7.
73. UN Food and Agriculture Organization, *Our Land Our Future* (Rome, Italy: United Nations, 1996). The quote is on page 7.
74. M. A. Stocking, "Tropical Soils and Food Security: The Next 50 Years," *Science* 302, no. 5649 (2003). See in particular figure 1.
75. R. Lal et al., "Response to Comments on 'Managing Soil Carbon,'" *Science* 305, no. 5690 (2004). See page 1567. Dominik Fleitmann et al., "East African Soil Erosion Recorded in a 300 Year Old Coral Colony from Kenya," *Geophysical Research Letters* 34, no. L04401 (2007).
76. The figures quoted here are somewhat dated and are considered by some to be controversial. Nevertheless, they represent a significant effort to quantify the economic effect of large-scale agriculture. See David Pimentel et al., "Environmental and Economic Costs of Soil Erosion and Conservation Benefits," *Science* 267, no. 5201 (1995).
77. D. Thoreau, "Walking, Part 2," The Thoreau Society, http://thoreau.eserver.org/walking2.html. The quote is from paragraph 28.

CHAPTER TWO: LARDERS

1. R. Pike, "Partnership Companies in the Sixteenth Century Transatlantic Trade: The De La Fuente Family of Seville," *The Journal of European Economic History* 34 (Spring 2005). See in particular pages 254–55.
2. Homer, *The Odyssey* (New York: Penguin Classics, 1996). See book 9, lines 45–47.
3. G. Rickman, *The Corn Supply of Ancient Rome* (Oxford: Clarendon Press, 1980). See page 51.
4. Plutarch, "The Life of Pompey," from *Parallel Lives,* Loeb Classical Library edition, 1917, Bill Thayer's Web Site, University of Chicago, http://penelope.uchicago.edu/Thayer/E/Roman/Texts/Plutarch/Lives/Pompey*.html. See chapters 24 and 25.
5. This is reviewed in Ellen Churchill Semple, "Geographic Factors in the Ancient Mediterranean Grain Trade," *Annals of the Association of American Geographers* 11 (1921).
6. Plutarch, "The Life of Pompey." See chapter 25.
7. Ibid.
8. J. K. Evans, "Wheat Production and Its Social Consequences in the Roman World," *The Classical Quarterly* 31, no. 2 (1981).

9. Chester G. Starr, Jr., "Coastal Defense in the Roman World," *The American Journal of Philology* 64, no. 1 (1943). See page 60. See also Ellen Churchill Semple, "Pirate Coasts of the Mediterranean Sea," *Geographical Review* 2, no. 2 (1916).
10. For a discussion on the legality of this legislation, see H. Stuart Jones, "A Roman Law Concerning Piracy," *The Journal of Roman Studies* 16 (1926).
11. Plutarch, "The Life of Pompey." See chapter 26.
12. For a comparison between the Roman response to the pirates and the U.S. response to the 9/11 terrorists attacks on New York, see R. Harris, "Pirates of the Mediterranean," *New York Times* online edition, September 30, 2006, http://www.nytimes.com/2006/09/30/opinion/30harris.html. Please note, however, that not everyone sees these events as similar, and drawing a parallel between this event and U.S. foreign policy post 9/11 has also come under intense criticism. See J. Emanuel, "The *NY Times* Takes a Fiction Author's Thoughts a Bit Too Seriously," Jeff Emanuel Online, http://jeffemanuel.blogspot.com/2006/10/of-all-comparisons-to-ancient-rome.html.
13. Quoted in W. Rollo, "Ostia," *Greece & Rome* 4, no. 10 (1934). The quote is on page 54.
14. A. Petronius, "The Dinner of Trimalchio," in *The Satyricon*, vol. 2, trans. W. C. Firebaugh, Project Gutenberg, http://www.gutenberg.org/files/5219/5219.txt. See chapter 38.
15. D. Thurmond, *A Handbook of Food Processing in Classical Rome* (Boston: Brill, 2006). See page 17.
16. These figures are discussed in Rickman, *The Corn Supply of Ancient Rome*. See page 5.
17. Kimberly B. Flint-Hamilton, "Legumes in Ancient Greece and Rome: Food, Medicine, or Poison?" *Hesperia* 68, no. 3 (1999).
18. Polybius, "Rome at the End of the Punic Wars," in *History*, book 6, Internet Ancient History Sourcebook, http://www.fordham.edu/halsall/ancient/polybius6.html.
19. Thurmond, *A Handbook of Food Processing in Classical Rome*. See pages 64–65.
20. J. Bakker, ed. *The Mill-Bakeries of Ostia: Description and Interpretation* (Amsterdam: J. C. Gieben,1999).
21. Apuleius, *Metamorphoses* (or *The Golden Ass*), Loeb translation, quoted in Bakker, ed., *The Mill-Bakeries of Ostia: Description and Interpretation*. The quote is on pages 7–8. Full Latin text is available; see Apvleivs, *Metamorphoseon*, The Latin Library, http://www.thelatinlibrary.com/apuleius.html.
22. Thurmond, *A Handbook of Food Processing in Classical Rome*. See page 16.
23. The first clinical description of rickets is attributed to a Roman physician called Soranus of Ephesus (ca. A.D. 98–138) who wrote,

    > *If (the infant) is eager to sit up too early and for too long a period it usually becomes hunchbacked (the spine bending because the little body has as yet no strength). If, moreover, it is too prone to stand up and desirous of walking, the legs may become distorted in the region of the thighs. This is observed to happen particularly in Rome . . . if nobody looks after the movements of the infant the limbs of the majority become distorted, as the whole weight of the body rests on the legs . . . then of necessity the limbs give in a little, since the bones have not yet become strong.*

    Quoted in Peter M. Dunn, "Soranus of Ephesus (Circa AD 98–138) and Perinatal Care in Roman Times," *Archives of Disease in Childhood, Fetal and Neonatal Edition* 73, no. 1 (1995). The quote is on page F52.
24. "California and World Olive Oil Statistics," University of California Cooperative Extension, Sonoma County, http://cesonoma.ucdavis.edu/HORTIC/california_and_world_trends.pdf.

25. Thurmond, *A Handbook of Food Processing in Classical Rome.*
26. Cato, *De Agricultura,* Loeb Classical Library edition, 1934, Bill Thayer's Web Site, University of Chicago, http://penelope.uchicago.edu/Thayer/E/Roman/Texts/Cato/De_Agricultura/C*.html. The quote is in paragraphs 64–65.
27. Thurmond, *A Handbook of Food Processing in Classical Rome.*
28. Ibid. See page 223.
29. R. Curtis, *Garum and Salsamenta: Production and Commerce in Materia Medica* (New York: E. J. Brill, 1991). See page 22.
30. Seneca, *Epistles*, XCV.25, quoted in J. Grout, "Garum," Encyclopaedia Romana, University of Chicago, http://penelope.uchicago.edu/~grout/encyclopaedia_romana/wine/garum.html.
31. Curtis, *Garum and Salsamenta: Production and Commerce in Materia Medica.* See page 1.
32. Ibid.
33. For a discussion on the role of *garum* in the Roman economy and the maritime trade see R. Thapar, "Black Gold: South Asia and the Roman Maritime Trade," *South Asia: Journal of South Asian Studies* 15, no. 2 (1992). See also R. Curtis, "In Defense of Garum," *The Classical Journal* 78, no. 3 (1983). The quote by Pliny comes from Pliny the Elder, *The Natural History,* ed. John Bostock and H. T. Riley (London: Taylor and Francis, 1855), http://old.perseus.tufts.edu/cgi-bin/ptext?doc=Perseus%3Atext%3A1999.02.0137&query=head%3D%232256]. The quote is found in book 31, chapter 43.
34. Semple, "Geographic Factors in the Ancient Mediterranean Grain Trade." See page 72.
35. Ibid.
36. These points are raised in Cedric A. Yeo, "Land and Sea Transportation in Imperial Italy," *Transactions and Proceedings of the American Philological Association* 77 (1946).
37. See Tenney Frank, "Mercantilism and Rome's Foreign Policy," *The American Historical Review* 18, no. 2 (1913).
38. Giovanna Vitelli, "Grain Storage and Urban Growth in Imperial Ostia: A Quantitative Study," *World Archaeology* 12, no. 1 (1980). See page 56.
39. This anecdote is referred to in E. Hyams, *Dionysus: A Social History of the Wine Vine* (London: Thames and Hudson, 1965). See page 90.
40. Marcus Cato, *De Agricultura,* Loeb Classical Library edition, 1934, Bill Thayer's Web Site, University of Chicago, http://penelope.uchicago.edu/Thayer/E/Roman/Texts/Cato/De_Agricultura/G*.html#104.
41. Vitelli, "Grain Storage and Urban Growth in Imperial Ostia: A Quantitative Study." See page 56.
42. Plutarch, "Caius Gracchus," The Internet Classics Archive, http://classics.mit.edu/Plutarch/gracchus.html. The quote is in paragraph 8.
43. Ibid. The quote is in paragraph 19.
44. These points are raised in Rickman, *The Corn Supply of Ancient Rome.* See page 15. See also G. Hermansen, *Ostia: Aspects of Roman City Life* (Edmonton: University of Alberta Press, 1981), page 232.
45. Rickman, *The Corn Supply of Ancient Rome.* See page 19.
46. For example, it is estimated that one-third of Rome's food supply came from Egypt. See Stephanie Mercier, "The Evolution of World Grain Trade," *Review of Agricultural Economics* 21, no. 1 (1999).
47. G. Rickman, *Roman Granaries and Store Buildings* (Cambridge: Cambridge University Press, 1971). See introduction.
48. Hermansen, *Ostia: Aspects of Roman City Life.* See page 230.
49. Soprintendenza Archeologica di Ostia Antica, "Regio II—Insula IX—Grandi Horrea

(II,IX,7)," Ostia: Harbour City of Ancient Rome, http://www.ostia-antica.org/regio2/9/9-7.htm. The quote is to the bottom of the page.

50. Rickman, *The Corn Supply of Ancient Rome*. See page 23.
51. Curtis, *Garum and Salsamenta: Production and Commerce in Materia Medica*. Please see page 1.
52. Ibid. See sections 4 and 5.
53. Pliny, *Natural History,* 31, 30, and 53, quoted in J. Donald Hughes and J. V. Thirgood, "Deforestation, Erosion, and Forest Management in Ancient Greece and Rome," *Journal of Forest History* 26, no. 2 (1982). The quote is on page 67.
54. Vitruvius, *De Architectura,* 8.1.6–7, quoted in Hughes and Thirgood, "Deforestation, Erosion, and Forest Management in Ancient Greece and Rome." See page 67.
55. Rollo, "Ostia."
56. See the following two articles for a review of this argument: N. Koepke, "Anthropometric Decline of the Roman Empire?" Paper presented at the Thirteenth Economic History Congress, Buenos Aires, 2002; and P. Enckell, E. Königsson, and L. Königsson, "Ecological Instability of a Roman Iron Age Human Community," *Oikos* 33, no. 2 (1979).
57. The following two sources provide details on this: Rickman, *The Corn Supply of Ancient Rome*, in particular chapter 2 on the grain supply of the republic; and M. Atkin, *The International Grain Trade* (Cambridge, UK: Woodhead Publishing, 1995). See pages 13–14.
58. Rickman, *The Corn Supply of Ancient Rome*. See page 12.
59. Symmachus, quoted in Hermansen, *Ostia: Aspects of Roman City Life*. The quote is on page 234.
60. S. Williams and J. Friell, *The Rome That Did Not Fall* (London: Routledge, 1999).The quote is on page 118.
61. Ibid.
62. Vitelli, "Grain Storage and Urban Growth in Imperial Ostia: A Quantitative Study." See pages 55–56.
63. Hughes and Thirgood, "Deforestation, Erosion, and Forest Management in Ancient Greece and Rome."
64. The following papers present evidence for this climatic shift: Stéphanie Desprat, María Fernanda Sánchez Goñi, and Marie-France Loutre, "Revealing Climatic Variability of the Last Three Millennia in Northwestern Iberia Using Pollen Influx Data," *Earth and Planetary Science Letters* 213, nos. 1–2 (2003); and F. McDermott, D. Mattey, and C. Hawkesworth, "Centennial-Scale Holocene Climate Variability Revealed by a High-Resolution Speleothem $\delta^{18}O$ Record from SW Ireland," *Science* 294, no. 5545 (2001).
65. R. Julia et al., "Climatic and Land Use Changes on the NW of Iberian Peninsula Recorded in a 1,500-Year Record from Lake Sanabria," *Contributions to Science* 3, no. 3 (2007). See in particular the figure on page 366.
66. L. von Mises, *Economic Policy: Thoughts for Today and Tomorrow* (Auburn, Ala.: Ludwig von Mises Institute, 1959); available online at http://mises.org/etexts/ecopol.pdf. See page 41. Also Hermansen, *Ostia: Aspects of Roman City Life*. See page 234.
67. Vitelli, "Grain Storage and Urban Growth in Imperial Ostia: A Quantitative Study." See page 60.
68. Hermansen, *Ostia: Aspects of Roman City Life*. See pages 12 and 13.
69. St. Augustine, *Confessions,* book 9, chapter 10, paragraph 23, Internet History Sourcebooks Project, http://www.fordham.edu/halsall/basis/confessions-bod.html.
70. Hermansen, *Ostia: Aspects of Roman City Life*. See pages 234–35.
71. Some key references on this topic from recent scientific publications include S. Long et al., "Global Food Insecurity: Treatment of Major Food Crops with Elevated Carbon

Dioxide or Ozone under Large-Scale Fully Open-Air Conditions Suggests Recent Models May Have Overestimated Future Yields," *Philosophical Transactions of the Royal Society B: Biological Sciences* 360, no. 1463 (2005); David S. Battisti and Rosamond L. Naylor, "Historical Warnings of Future Food Insecurity with Unprecedented Seasonal Heat," *Science* 323, no. 5911 (2009); D. Lobell and C. Field, "Global Scale Climate–Crop Yield Relationships and the Impacts of Recent Warming," *Environmental Research Letters* 2 (March 2007); and David B. Lobell et al., "Prioritizing Climate Change Adaptation Needs for Food Security in 2030," *Science* 319, no. 5863 (2008).

72. This is the opinion expressed in the most recent assessment report by the Intergovernmental Panel on Climate Change. See W. E. Easterling et al., "Food, Fibre and Forest Products," in Working Group II, *Climate Change 2007: Impacts, Adaptation and Vulnerability,* Contribution to the Fourth Assessment Report of the Intergovernmental Panel on Climate Change, ed. M. L. Parry, O. Canziani, et al. (Cambridge: Cambridge University Press, 2007).
73. Genesis 41:34–36 (New International Version).
74. "Strategic Grain Reserves—Guidelines for Their Establishment, Management and Operation," FAO Agricultural Services Bulletin 126, UN Food and Agriculture Organization, http://www.fao.org/docrep/w4979e/w4979e00.htm. The quote is found in the introductory chapter.
75. S. Devereux, "The Malawi Famine of 2002," *IDS Bulletin* 33, no. 4 (2002). See in particular pages 70–71.
76. C. Hurt, "Ag Economist: World Grain Demand Straining U.S. Supply," Purdue University, http://news.uns.purdue.edu/x/2008a/080220HurtGrain.html. The quotes are partway through the article.
77. This was the assessment of the UN Food and Agriculture Organization. See in particular page 2 in UN Food and Agriculture Organization, *November Food Outlook* (Rome, Italy: UN Food and Agriculture Organization, 2008). This document is available online at ftp://ftp.fao.org/docrep/fao/011/ai474e/ai474e00.pdf.
78. P. Abbott, C. Hurt, and W. Tyner, *What's Driving Food Prices?* Farm Foundation Issue Report, July 2008. See in particular page 48.

CHAPTER THREE: FARMS

1. For a description of the economics and banking of Seville at the time of Carletti see J. De Soto, "New Light on the Prehistory of the Theory of Banking and the School of Salamanca," *The Review of Austrian Economics* 9, no. 2 (1996).
2. The following article provides an overview of the Salamanca school: Domènec Melé, "Early Business Ethics in Spain: The Salamanca School (1526–1614)," *Journal of Business Ethics* 22, no. 3 (1999).
3. For a reference to the influence of Mercado see page 245 in R. Pike, "Partnership Companies in the Sixteenth Century Transatlantic Trade: The De La Fuente Family of Seville," *The Journal of European Economic History* 34 (Spring 2005).
4. J. Tiryakian, "A Review of: *Suma de Tratos y Contratos* by Tomás De Mercado," *History of Political Economy* 11, no. 1 (1979).
5. Quoted in Melé, "Early Business Ethics in Spain: The Salamanca School (1526–1614)." See page 179.
6. These arguments are reviewed in the following PhD thesis: S. Agir, "From Welfare to Wealth: Ottoman and Castilian Grain Trade Policies in a Time of Change" (Princeton University, 2009). See page 62.

7. Plutarch, "The Life of Sertorius," from *Parallel Lives,* Loeb Classical Library edition, 1919, Bill Thayer's Web Site, University of Chicago, http://penelope.uchicago.edu/Thayer/E/Roman/Texts/Plutarch/ Lives/Sertorius*.html. The quote is in chapter 8.
8. The following book provides an excellent and engaging discussion of the ecological impact of colonization: A. Crosby, *Ecological Imperialism: The Biological Expansion of Europe, 900–1900* (Cambridge: Cambridge University Press, 1986).
9. Ibid.
10. For a discussion on trading in the Atlantic before Columbus see D. Vinson, "The Western Sea: Atlantic History before Columbus," *The Northern Mariner* 10, no. 3 (2000).
11. Crosby, *Ecological Imperialism: The Biological Expansion of Europe, 900–1900.* See page 80.
12. James J. Parsons, "Human Influences on the Pine and Laurel Forests of the Canary Islands," *Geographical Review* 71, no. 3 (1981). See page 264.
13. Quoted in P. Lindskog and B. Delaite, "Degrading Land: An Environmental History Perspective of the Cape Verde Islands," *Environment and History* 2, no. 3 (1996). The quotes are found on page 271.
14. A. de Cadamosto, *The Voyages of Cadamosto and Other Documents on Western Africa in the Second Half of the Fifteenth Century,* trans. G. R. Crone (London: Hakluyt Society, 1937). The quote is on page 9.
15. Quoted in Crosby, *Ecological Imperialism: The Biological Expansion of Europe, 900–1900.* The quote is on page 75.
16. Quoted in Parsons, "Human Influences on the Pine and Laurel Forests of the Canary Islands." The quote is on page 263.
17. Ibid. See page 259.
18. Quoted in J. Hutchinson, "The Rain Tree of Hierro, Canary Islands (*Oreodaphne Foetens*)," *Bulletin of Miscellaneous Information (Royal Gardens, Kew)* 1919, no. 3 (1919). The quote is on page 156.
19. There is a huge literature on the Little Ice Age. The following represents just a brief sample: R. Bradley and P. Jonest, "'Little Ice Age' Summer Temperature Variations: Their Nature and Relevance to Recent Global Warming Trends," *The Holocene* 3, no. 4 (1993), see the abstract to this article; J. Grove, *The Little Ice Age* (New York: Routledge, 2001), see introduction and pages 4 and 5 in particular; T. Brook, *Vermeer's Hat: The Seventeenth Century and the Dawn of the Global World* (Toronto: Viking Canada, 2008), see page 13; and G. Parker and L. Smith, *The General Crisis of the Seventeenth Century* (London: Routledge, 1978). This whole volume summarizes the crisis of the time including presenting research on the role of sunspot activity.
20. The seminal article on the links between biodiversity and ecological resilience is David Tilman, "The Ecological Consequences of Changes in Biodiversity: A Search for General Principles," *Ecology* 80, no. 5 (1999).
21. R. Grove, *Green Imperialism: Colonial Expansion, Tropical Island Edens and the Origins of Environmentalism, 1600–1860* (Cambridge: Cambridge University Press, 1995). See page 63.
22. "Madeira Wine," http://www.madeirawine.com/html/nindex.html. In particular, see the sections on production and history.
23. Into Wine, "Madeira Wine: History of Madeira, Port of Funchal, and the Madeira Island Region," IntoWine.com, http://www.intowine.com/madeira.html?page=0%2C0. See also page 246 of J. Robinson, *Wine Course: A Guide to the World of Wine* (London: BBC, 1995).
24. W. Younger, *Gods, Men and Wine* (London: Michael Joseph, 1966). See page 81.
25. Dan Stanislawski, "Dionysus Westward: Early Religion and the Economic Geography of Wine," *Geographical Review* 65, no. 4 (1975).
26. P. McGovern, *Ancient Wine: The Origins of Viniculture* (Princeton, N.J.: Princeton University Press, 2003). See pages 241–55.

27. Yannis Hamilakis, "Food Technologies/Technologies of the Body: The Social Context of Wine and Oil Production and Consumption in Bronze Age Crete," *World Archaeology* 31, no. 1 (1999).
28. For a general discussion on the role of public authorities in producing and maintaining public goods, see E. Ostrom, "Environment and Common Property Institutions," in *International Encyclopedia of the Social & Behavioral Sciences*, ed. H. Baltus and N. Smelser (Oxford: Elsevier Science Ltd., 2001).
29. Hamilakis, "Food Technologies/Technologies of the Body: The Social Context of Wine and Oil Production and Consumption in Bronze Age Crete."
30. C. Renfrew, *The Emergence of Civilisation: The Cyclades and the Aegean in the Third Millennium B.C.* (London: Methuen, 1972).
31. Tjeerd H. van Andel, Eberhard Zangger, and Anne Demitrack, "Land Use and Soil Erosion in Prehistoric and Historical Greece," *Journal of Field Archaeology* 17, no. 4 (1990). See also J. Donald Hughes and J. V. Thirgood, "Deforestation, Erosion, and Forest Management in Ancient Greece and Rome," *Journal of Forest History* 26, no. 2 (1982).
32. E. Vermeule, *Greece in the Bronze Age* (Chicago: The University of Chicago Press, 1964).
33. While the specific role of drought in harming ancient civilizations is unknown, many scholars have suggested that drought played a significant part in the decline of the Mycenaean culture. For example see D. Kaniewski et al., "Middle East Coastal Ecosystem Response to Middle-to-Late Holocene Abrupt Climate Changes," *Proceedings of the National Academy of Sciences* 105, no. 37 (2008); and P. Betancourt, "The End of the Greek Bronze Age," *Antiquity* 50 (1976). On the other hand, some of these claims are refuted in P. I. Kuniholm, "Archaeological Evidence and Non-Evidence for Climatic Change," *Philosophical Transactions of the Royal Society of London. Series A, Mathematical and Physical Sciences* 330, no. 1615 (1990).
34. For a discussion on the evolution of civilization in Greece, see the following two sources: Dan Stanislawski, "Dark Age Contributions to the Mediterranean Way of Life," *Annals of the Association of American Geographers* 63, no. 4 (1973); and Daniel J. Pullen, "Ox and Plow in the Early Bronze Age Aegean," *American Journal of Archaeology* 96, no. 1 (1992).
35. Hughes and Thirgood, "Deforestation, Erosion, and Forest Management in Ancient Greece and Rome." The quote is on page 60.
36. For evidence of soil erosion at this time see John Bintliff, "Time, Process and Catastrophism in the Study of Mediterranean Alluvial History: A Review," *World Archaeology* 33, no. 3 (2002).
37. This hypothesis is advanced in the following two articles: C. Zerefos and E. Zerefos, "Climatic Change in Mycenaean Greece: A Citation to Aristotle," *Theoretical and Applied Climatology* 26, no. 4 (1978); and Barry Weiss, "The Decline of Late Bronze Age Civilization as a Possible Response to Climatic Change," *Climatic Change* 4, no. 2 (1982).
38. This passage from Aristotle's *Meteorologica* is quoted on page 445 of J. Neumann, "Climatic Change as a Topic in the Classical Greek and Roman Literature," *Climatic Change* 7, no. 4 (1985).
39. There is a huge literature on this. Key references include G. Peterson, "Estimating Resilience across Landscapes," *Conservation Ecology* 6, no. 1 (2002); G. Peterson, C. Allen, and C. Holling, "Ecological Resilience, Biodiversity, and Scale," *Ecosystems* 1 (1998); E. Fraser, W. Mabee, and F. Figge, "A Framework for Assessing the Vulnerability of Food Systems to Future Shocks," *Futures* 37, no. 6 (2005); S. Carpenter et al., "From Metaphor to Measurement: Resilience of What to What?" *Ecosystems* 4 (2001); and S. R. Carpenter and W. Brock, "Adaptive Capacity and Traps," *Ecology and Society* 13, no. 2 (2008).
40. C. Holling, "Understanding the Complexity of Economic, Ecological, and Social Systems," *Ecosystems* 4 (2001). The quote is on page 392.

41. These ideas are expanded on in a couple of articles written by one of the authors a number of years ago. See E. Fraser, W. Mabee, and F. Figge, "A Framework for Assessing the Vulnerability of Food Systems to Future Shocks," *Futures* 37, no. 6 (2005); and E. Fraser and W. Mabee, "Identifying the Secure City: Research to Establish a Preliminary Framework," *Canadian Journal of Urban Research* 13, no. 1 supplement (2004).
42. Holling, "Understanding the Complexity of Economic, Ecological, and Social Systems." The quote is on page 396.
43. W. Lutz, W. Sanderson, and S. Scherbov, "The End of World Population Growth," in *The End of World Population Growth in the 21st Century,* ed. W. Lutz, W. Sanderson, and S. Scherbov (London: Earthscan, 2004). The quote is on page 17.
44. A. Shvidenko et al., "Forest and Woodland Systems," in *Ecosystems and Human Well-Being: Current State and Trends,* vol. 1, ed. R. Hassan, R. Scholes, and N. Ash (Washington, D.C.: United Nations Environment Programme and Island Press, 2005). The quote is on page 587.
45. The critical documents in this body of work are the Intergovernmental Panel on Climate Change's assessment reports. Working Group I's report deals with the science of climate change. Working Group II deals with issues of climate change impacts and adaptation. See Working Group I, *Climate Change 2007: The Physical Science Basis,* Contribution to the Fourth Assessment Report of the Intergovernmental Panel on Climate Change, ed. S. Solomon, D. Qin, et al. (Cambridge: Cambridge University Press, 2007); and Working Group II, *Climate Change 2007: Impacts, Adaptation and Vulnerability,* Contribution to the Fourth Assessment Report of the Intergovernmental Panel on Climate Change, ed. M. L. Parry, O. Canziani, et al. (Cambridge: Cambridge University Press, 2007.
46. This argument is made in J. Lansing, *Priests and Programmers: Technologies of Power in the Engineered Landscapes of Bali* (Princeton, N.J.: Princeton University Press, 1991).

AN EXPERIMENT IN SURVIVAL

1. There is a considerable link between air pollution and respiratory ailments in modern China. For example, see Judith Banister, "Population, Public Health and the Environment in China," *The China Quarterly,* no. 156 (December 1998). In particular the paragraphs on pages 989–90 are relevant. The following article also describes the seriousness of these issues: Min Shao et al., "City Clusters in China: Air and Surface Water Pollution," *Frontiers in Ecology and the Environment* 4, no. 7 (2006).
2. For example see the following study: S. Long et al., "Global Food Insecurity: Treatment of Major Food Crops with Elevated Carbon Dioxide or Ozone under Large-Scale Fully Open-Air Conditions Suggests Recent Models May Have Overestimated Future Yields," *Philosophical Transactions of the Royal Society B: Biological Sciences* 360, no. 1463 (2005).
3. The following two articles provide a glimpse of these debates with regard to food production and climate change in China: Wei Xiong et al., "Climate Change and Critical Thresholds in China's Food Security," *Climatic Change* 81, no. 2 (2007); and Lin Erda et al., "Climate Change Impacts on Crop Yield and Quality with CO_2 Fertilization in China," *Philosophical Transactions of the Royal Society B* 360, no. 1463 (2005).
4. Royal Society, "Ground-Level Ozone in the 21st Century: Future Trends, Impacts and Policy Implications," *Royal Society Science Policy Report* 15, no. 8 (2008). See page 77.
5. Long et al., "Global Food Insecurity: Treatment of Major Food Crops with Elevated Carbon Dioxide or Ozone under Large-Scale Fully Open-Air Conditions Suggests Recent Models May Have Overestimated Future Yields." The quote is on page 2011.

6. "Compendium on Post-Harvest Operations," UN Food and Agriculture Organization, http://www.fao.org/inpho/content/compend/allintro.htm.
7. "FAOSTAT," UN Food and Agriculture Organization, http://faostat.fao.org.
8. P. Buck, *The Good Earth* (New York: Pocket Books, 1931). The quote is on pages 24–25.
9. V. Smil, "Nitrogen and Food Production: Proteins for Human Diets," *Ambio* 31, no. 2 (2002).
10. The following paper offers a critical examination of the economic logic behind this massive scheme: J. Berkoff, "China: The South-North Water Transfer Project—Is It Justified?" *Water Policy* 5 (2003). See also the following press release: Embassy of the People's Republic of China in the United States of America, "Background: Water Diversion Project to Relieve China's Thirsty North," December 27, 2002, People's Republic of China, http://www.china-embassy.org/eng/zt/wto/t36969.htm.
11. D. Pimentel and M. Pimentel, *Food, Energy, and Society* (Boca Raton, Fla.: CRC Press, 2008).
12. T. Malthus, *An Essay on Population*, ed. P. Appleman (New York: Norton Books, 1976).
13. The following is Ehrlich's seminal work: P. Ehrlich, *The Population Bomb* (Cutchogue, N.Y.: Buccaneer Books, 1968). He has continued to develop these themes throughout his career.
14. P. Ehrlich, A. Ehrlich, and G. Daily, "Food Security, Population, and Environment," *Population and Development Review* 19, no. 1 (1993). The quote is on page 6.
15. J. Simon, *The Ultimate Resource* (Princeton, N.J.: Princeton University Press, 1981). The quote is in chapter 5. The whole book is available for free online at http://www.juliansimon.com/writings/Ultimate_Resource.
16. L. Lim, "Chinese Rural Reforms Free Farmers from Land," *All Things Considered*, National Public Radio, November 6, 2008, http://www.npr.org/templates/story/story.php?storyId=96380759.

CHAPTER FOUR: WATER

1. For example, Carletti wrote in his journal:

   > *Then each owner makes a mark on each slave [with a brand] . . . This thing, which I remember having done under orders from a superior, causes me some sadness and confusion of conscience because truly . . . it seems to be an inhuman traffic unworthy of a professed and pious Christian . . . I beg forgiveness from His Divine Magesty, though I know that because He is aware of my intentions and my will as always feeling that business to be repugnant, such forgiveness is not required.*

   F. Carletti, *My Voyage around the World: A Sixteenth Century Florentine Merchant*, trans. H. Weinstock (ca. 1609; London: Methuen and Co., Ltd., 1964). See page 13.
2. Ibid. The quote is on page 42.
3. Ibid. The quote is on page 43.
4. Ibid. The quote is on page 58.
5. The following two articles describe the size, sophistication, and complexity of this society and its agricultural practices: W. Denevan and B. Turner, "Calculating Population and Agricultural Intensity Levels from Field Remains: A Comment on Coe's Review of 'Maya Subsistence,'" *American Antiquity* 50, no. 1 (1985); and Elizabeth M. Brumfiel et al., "Specialization, Market Exchange, and the Aztec State: A View from Huexotla [and Comments and Reply]," *Current Anthropology* 21, no. 4 (1980).

6. R. Hassig, "The Famine of One Rabbit: Ecological Causes and Social Consequences of a Pre-Columbian Calamity," *Journal of Anthropological Research* 37, no. 2 (1981). See page 178.
7. Quoted in P. Armillas, "Gardens on Swamps," *Science* 174, no. 4010 (1971).
8. See the following papers for descriptions of *chinampa* farming: V. Popper, "Investigating Chinampa Farming," *Backdirt: The newsletter of the Cotsen Institute of Archaeology at UCLA*, Fall/Winter 2000, available online at http://www.sscnet.ucla.edu/ioa/backdirt/Fallwinter00/farming.ht ml; and E. Calnek, "Pattern and Chinampa Agriculture at Tenochtitlan," *American Antiquity* 37, no. 1 (1972).
9. There is a huge literature on the link between climate, drought, and the collapse of the Maya. For example, it is argued that the Mayan civilization grew in numbers and complexity between A.D. 25 and 750, but then declined abruptly over the years from A.D. 750 to 900, when millions died during a period of drought. The following four articles represent a brief sample of this body of scholarship: James W. Webster et al., "Stalagmite Evidence from Belize Indicating Significant Droughts at the Time of Preclassic Abandonment, the Maya Hiatus, and the Classic Maya Collapse," *Palaeogeography, Palaeoclimatology, Palaeoecology* 250, nos. 1–4 (2007); R. Santley, T. Killion, and M. Lycett, "On the Maya Collapse," *Journal of Anthropological Research* 42, no. 2 (1986); Gerald H. Haug et al., "Climate and the Collapse of Maya Civilization," *Science* 299, no. 5613 (2003); and Richardson B. Gill et al., "Drought and the Maya Collapse," *Ancient Mesoamerica* 18, no. 2 (2007).
10. The role of climate is discussed in the following: Linda Manzanilla, "The Impact of Climatic Change on Past Civilizations. A Revisionist Agenda for Further Investigation," *Quaternary International* 43–44 (1997).
11. The scale of Mesopotamian trade is discussed in the following article: Christopher Edens, "Dynamics of Trade in the Ancient Mesopotamian 'World System,'" *American Anthropologist* 94, no. 1 (1992).
12. See S. Chew, "Ecological Relations and the Decline of Civilization in the Bronze Age World System," in *Ecology and the World-System,* ed. Walter L. Goldfrank, David Goodman, and Andrew Szasz (Westport, Conn.: Greenwood Publishing Group, 1999).
13. *Shi Jeng or Shih King* [*The Book of Odes* or *Book of Poetry*], trans. J. Legge. The e-book published by Project Gutenberg is available online at www.gutenberg.org/ebooks/9394.
14. For example, Harlan's seminal article on the "centers and noncenters" of agriculture suggests that Andean cultures were unique because they depended more on tubers than grasses as the mainstay of their diet. This has been confirmed by research that shows only potatoes could have provided the necessary calories and protein to support mountainous Andean cities that lacked fertile land. See J. Harlan, "Agricultural Origins: Centers and Noncenters," *Science* 174, no. 4008 (1971); and A. Morris, "The Agricultural Base of the Pre-Incan Andean Civilizations," *The Geographical Journal* 165, no. 3 (1999).
15. E. Fraser, "Social Vulnerability and Ecological Fragility: Building Bridges between Social and Natural Sciences Using the Irish Potato Famine as a Case Study," *Conservation Ecology* 7, no. 1 (2003). See page 3 for comparison of the number of people that can be supported on the same land planted with corn versus potatoes.
16. A scholarly discussion on the origins of agriculture in China can be found in Z. Jixu, "The Rise of Agricultural Civilization in China: The Disparity between Archeological Discovery and the Documentary Record and Its Explanation," *Sino-Platonic Papers* 175 (December 2006). Available online at http://www.sino-platonic.org/complete/spp175_chinese_civilization_agriculture.pdf.
17. Genetic evidence suggests, however, that there was not one but two points of domestication, as there are two subtly different varieties of emmer wheat, with slightly different genetic fingerprints. Terence A. Brown et al., "How Ancient DNA May Help in

Understanding the Origin and Spread of Agriculture [and Discussion]," *Philosophical Transactions: Biological Sciences* 354, no. 1379 (1999).

18. This is reported in Xiaoqiang Li et al., "Early Cultivated Wheat and Broadening of Agriculture in Neolithic China," *The Holocene* 17, no. 5 (2007).
19. See: Jixu, "The Rise of Agricultural Civilization in China: The Disparity between Archeological Discovery and the Documentary Record and Its Explanation."
20. For descriptions of early Chinese agriculture and how it contributed to the development of civilization, see the chapter on China in F. Fernandez-Armesto, *Civilizations* (London: Macmillan, 2000). For reference specifically to agriculture in the loess plateau of China, see Ping-Ti Ho, "The Loess and the Origin of Chinese Agriculture," *The American Historical Review* 75, no. 1 (1969).
21. Quoted in S. Dalley, *Myths from Mesopotamia: Creation, the Flood, Gilgamesh, and Others* (Oxford: Oxford University Press, 1998). The quote is on page 9.
22. In addition to Dalley, *Myths from Mesopotamia: Creation, the Flood, Gilgamesh, and Others,* for a background to flood myths, see chapter 3 (in particular pages 66–67) in K. Armstrong, *A Short History of Myth* (Edinburgh: Canongate, 2005).
23. For a description of the biological and cultural effects of the Neolithic revolution on human health see Clark Spencer Larsen, "Biological Changes in Human Populations with Agriculture," *Annual Review of Anthropology* 24 (1995). The following text provides an overview of similar issues: T. McMichael, *Human Frontiers, Environments and Disease* (Cambridge: Cambridge University Press, 2001). See also G. Lenski and J. Lenski, *Human Societies: An Introduction to Macro-Society*, 6th ed. (New York: McGraw-Hill, 1978); and D. Shard, "The Neolithic Revolution: An Analogical Overview," *Journal of Social History* 7, no. 2 (1974).
24. For the argument on agriculture's relation to the inception of warfare, see R. O'Connell, *Ride of the Second Horseman: The Birth and Death of War* (Oxford: Oxford University Press, 1995). In particular, pages 53–68 and 85–103 are relevant. See also P. Nolan, "Toward an Ecological-Evolutionary Theory of the Incidence of Warfare in Preindustrial Societies," *Sociological Theory* 21, no. 1 (2003).
25. Edens, "Dynamics of Trade in the Ancient Mesopotamian 'World System.'"
26. J. Hendon, "Archaeological Approaches to the Organization of Domestic Labor: Household Practice and Domestic Relations," *Annual Review of Anthropology* 25 (1996).
27. While there is some debate on the extent to which hunter-gatherer communities were fully egalitarian and economically cooperative, the research remains pretty conclusive that they were *more* egalitarian and cooperative than the cultures based on complex irrigation that flourished in ancient China and Mesopotamia. The following article reviews many of these debates: S. Steadman, "Heading Home: The Architecture of Family and Society in Early Sedentary Communities on the Anatolian Plateau," *Journal of Anthropological Research* 60, no. 4 (2004).
28. E. Boulding, "Familial Constraints on Women's Work Roles," *Signs* 1, no. 3 (1976).
29. The following article (and the replies) review possible theories to account for the origins of agriculture and highlight the extent to which these theories are controversial among anthropologists: David Rindos et al., "Symbiosis, Instability, and the Origins and Spread of Agriculture: A New Model [and Comments and Reply]," *Current Anthropology* 21, no. 6 (1980).
30. Boulding, "Familial Constraints on Women's Work Roles."
31. K. Wittfogel, *Oriental Despotism* (London: Vintage, 1981).
32. M. Elvin, *The Retreat of the Elephants: An Environmental History of China* (London: Yale University Press, 2004). The quote is on page 11.

33. Armstrong, *A Short History of Myth*. See in particular chapter 3.
34. This quick sketch of the history of the Fertile Crescent is a huge simplification. Details notwithstanding, key themes from this time include salination, drought, political invasion, and decline. Interested readers can refer to the following sources: for a discussion on the links with climate change, see J. Neumann and S. Parpola, "Climatic Change and the Eleventh-Tenth-Century Eclipse of Assyria and Babylonia," *Journal of Near Eastern Studies* 46, no. 3 (1987); for a basic background on Sumer, see chapter 2 in particular in H. Crawford, *Sumer and the Sumerians,* 2nd ed. (Cambridge: Cambridge University Press, 2004); for a discussion of Sumerian myths see Armstrong, *A Short History of Myth*; in terms of discussions on the role of salination in Mesopotamian history, see T. Jacobsen and R. Adams, "Salt and Silt in Ancient Mesopotamian Agriculture," *Science* 128, no. 3334 (1958).
35. Chew, "Ecological Relations and the Decline of Civilization in the Bronze Age World System."
36. Ibid.
37. Quoted in T. Jacobsen, *Salinity and Irrigation Agriculture in Antiquity; Diyala Basin Archaeological Projects: Report on Essential Results, 1957–58* (Malibu, Calif.: Undena Publications, 1982). The quote is on page 11.
38. Neumann and Parpola, "Climatic Change and the Eleventh-Tenth-Century Eclipse of Assyria and Babylonia." The quote is on page 161.
39. E. Parker, *Ancient China Simplified* (London: Chapman & Hall, 1908).
40. Quoted in Cho-yun Hsu, *Han Agriculture,* ed. Jack L. Dull (Seattle: University of Washington Press, 1980). The quote is on page 188.
41. Elvin, *The Retreat of the Elephants: An Environmental History of China*. The quotes are on page 104.
42. Hsu, *Han Agriculture.*
43. Ibid.
44. Ibid. The quote is on page 215.
45. Ibid. The quote is on page 217.
46. Elvin, *The Retreat of the Elephants: An Environmental History of China*. See page 19.
47. United Nations, *The Millennium Development Goals Report,* United Nations, http://www.un.org/millenniumgoals/2008highlevel/pdf/newsroom/MDG_Report_2008_ENGLISH.pdf. See page 40, in particular the map of the world.
48. Taikan Oki and Shinjiro Kanae, "Global Hydrological Cycles and World Water Resources," *Science* 313, no. 5790 (2006). The quote is on page 1068.
49. P. Lawrence, J. Meigh, and C. Sullivan, "The Water Poverty Index: An International Comparison," *Keele Economics Research Papers* 2002/19 (2002). See in particular the table on page 11.
50. M. F. W. Slegers and L. Stroosnijder, "Beyond the Desertification Narrative: A Framework for Agricultural Drought in Semi-Arid East Africa," *Ambio* 37, no. 5 (2008). See in particular the figure on page 376.
51. M. A. Stocking, "Tropical Soils and Food Security: The Next 50 Years," *Science* 302, no. 5649 (2003).
52. E. Simelton, E. D. G. Fraser, M. Termansen, P. M. Forster, and A. J. Dougill, "Typologies of Crop-Drought Vulnerability: An Empirical Analysis of the Socio-Economic Factors That Influence the Sensitivity and Resilience to Drought of Three Major Food Crops in China (1961–2001)," *Environmental Science & Policy Special Issue* 12, no. 4 (2009). See the map showing wheat sensitivity (figure 3b).
53. Panmao Zhai et al., "Changes of Climate Extremes in China," *Climatic Change* 42, no. 1 (1999).

54. E. Fraser, "Travelling in Antique Lands: Studying Past Famines to Understand Present Vulnerabilities to Climate Change," *Climate Change* 83, no. 4 (2007). See in particular the third case study.
55. A very good study on the Ethiopian famine is E. Meze-Hausken, "Migration Caused by Climate Change: How Vulnerable Are People in Dryland Areas?" *Mitigation and Adaptation Strategies for Global Change* 5, no. 4 (2000).
56. Z. W. Kundzewicz et al., "Freshwater Resources and Their Management," in Working Group II, *Climate Change 2007: Impacts, Adaptation and Vulnerability,* Contribution to the Fourth Assessment Report of the Intergovernmental Panel on Climate Change, ed. M. L. Parry, O. F. Canziani, et al. (Cambridge: Cambridge University Press, 2007). See in particular pages 183–84.
57. R. V. Cruz et al., "Asia. Climate Change 2007," in Working Group II, *Climate Change 2007: Impacts, Adaptation and Vulnerability,* Contribution to the Fourth Assessment Report of the Intergovernmental Panel on Climate Change, ed. M. L. Parry, O. F. Canziani, et al. (Cambridge: Cambridge University Press, 2007). The whole chapter is relevant.
58. Charles J. Vorosmarty et al., "Global Water Resources: Vulnerability from Climate Change and Population Growth," *Science* 289, no. 5477 (2000).
59. W. E. Easterling et al., "Food, Fibre and Forest Products," in Working Group II, *Climate Change 2007: Impacts, Adaptation and Vulnerability*, Contribution to the Fourth Assessment Report of the Intergovernmental Panel on Climate Change, ed. M. L. Parry, O. F. Canziani, et al. (Cambridge: Cambridge University Press, 2007).
60. Kundzewicz et al., "Freshwater Resources and Their Management."
61. The baseline 1995 estimate comes from N. Arnell, "Climate Change and Global Water Resources: SRES Scenarios and Socio-Economic Scenarios," *Global Environmental Change* 14, no. 1 (2004). The high value is calculated in J. Alcamo, M. Flörke, and M. Märker, "Future Long-Term Changes in Global Water Resources Driven by Socio-Economic and Climatic Change," *Hydrological Science Journal* 52, no. 2 (2007). Both figures are reviewed and cited in Kundzewicz et al., "Freshwater Resources and Their Management."
62. Discussions on the link between water and war can be found in N. Myers, "Environmental Refugees in a Globally Warmed World," *Bioscience* 43, no. 11 (1993); L. Brown, *Outgrowing the Earth: The Food Security Challenge in an Age of Falling Water Tables and Rising Temperatures* (New York: W. W. Norton, 2005); and S. Postel and A. Wolf, "Dehydrating Conflict," *Foreign Policy* (Sept./Oct. 2001). See also G. Dyer, *Climate Wars* (Toronto: Random House Canada, 2008). Myers and Brown both present quite pessimistic views on this subject. Postel and Wolf tend to provide a more optimistic assessment.
63. G. Barton, trans., "Inscription of Entemena #7," in *The Royal Inscriptions of Sumer and Akkad* (New Haven, Conn.: Yale University Press, 1929). See pages 59–63.
64. Ibid.
65. Postel and Wolf, "Dehydrating Conflict."
66. A. Hoekstra, ed., *Virtual Water Trade: Proceedings of the International Expert Meeting on Virtual Water Trade*, Value of Water Research Report Series No. 12 (Delft, The Netherlands: IHE Delft, 2003). See page 13.
67. These statistics are quoted in Hoekstra, ed., *Virtual Water Trade: Proceedings of the International Expert Meeting on Virtual Water Trade.* See page 13 of the introduction in particular, but the whole volume should be of interest.
68. Ibid. See figures on page 18.
69. Dennis Wichelns, "The Role of 'Virtual Water' in Efforts to Achieve Food Security and Other National Goals, with an Example from Egypt," *Agricultural Water Management* 49, no. 2 (2001). See page 131.

70. Development Concepts and Doctrine Centre (DCDC), *The DCDC Strategic Trends Programme,* UK Ministry of Defence, http://www.mod.uk/NR/rdonlyres/4DFA218B-7B49-4EDB-82BD-770928C6334F/0/20071218_strat_trends_prog_U_DCDCIMAPPS.pdf. The quote is on page 8.
71. "National Security and the Threat of Climate Change Briefing Report," Center for Naval Analyses. Available online at http://securityandclimate.cna.org/report/CNA_NatlSecurityAndTheThreatOfClimateChange.pdf. The quotes are on slides 22 and 26.

CHAPTER FIVE: DIRT

1. F. Carletti, *My Voyage around the World: A Sixteenth Century Florentine Merchant*, trans. H. Weinstock (ca. 1609; London: Methuen and Co., Ltd., 1964). The quote is on page 37.
2. These statistics are available online at www.potato2008.org/en/world/index/html.
3. Data on agricultural production is available from "FAOSTAT," UN Food and Agriculture Organization, http://faostat.fao.org/default.aspx.
4. For a background note on the importance and role of nitrogen in farming, see California Fertilizer Foundation, "Plant Nutrients—Nitrogen," California Foundation for Agriculture in the Classroom, http://www.cfaitc.org/Commodity/pdf/Nitrogen.pdf.
5. This argument is made in a number of places including V. Smil, "Nitrogen and Food Production: Proteins for Human Diets," *Ambio* 31, no. 2 (2002).
6. J. von Liebig, *Chemistry in Its Application to Agriculture and Physiology* (Philadelphia: Wiley and Putnam, 1847). The quote is on page 34.
7. Smil, "Nitrogen and Food Production: Proteins for Human Diets."
8. F. Haber, "The Synthesis of Ammonia from Its Elements: Nobel Prize Lecture," Nobel Prize Institute, http://nobelprize.org/nobel_prizes/chemistry/laureates/1918/haber-lecture.pdf. The quote is on page 327.
9. California Fertilizer Foundation, "Plant Nutrients—Nitrogen."
10. Los Alamos National Labs Chemistry Division, "Nitrogen," Periodic Table of the Elements website, http://periodic.lanl.gov/elements/7.html.
11. California Fertilizer Foundation, "Plant Nutrients—Nitrogen."
12. V. Smil, *Enriching the Earth: Fritz Haber, Carl Bosch, and the Transformation of World Food Production* (Cambridge, Mass.: MIT Press, 2001). See in particular chapter 8.
13. S. Ruschenberger, *Three Years in the Pacific: Including Notices of Brazil, Chile, Bolivia, Peru* (Philadelphia: Carey, Lea & Blanchard, 1834). The quote is on pages 343–44.
14. Quoted in Dan O'Donnell, "The Lobos Islands: American Imperialism in Peruvian Waters in 1852," *Australian Journal of Politics & History* 39, no. 1 (1993). The quote is on page 39.
15. R. Jameson, "On the Guano or Modern Coprolite," in R. Jameson, ed., *The Edinburgh New Philosophical Journal: Exhibiting a View of the Progressive Discoveries and Improvements in the Sciences and the Arts* (Edinburgh: Adam Black, 1831–32). The quote is on page 127.
16. Quoted in W. Matthew, "A Primitive Export Sector: Guano Production in Mid-Nineteenth-Century Peru," *Journal of Latin American Studies* 9, no. 1 (1977). The quote is on page 36.
17. A. Usher, "Soil Fertility, Soil Exhaustion, and Their Historical Significance," *The Quarterly Journal of Economics* 37, no. 3 (1923). See page 406.
18. D. Helms, "Soil and Southern History," *Agricultural History* 74, no. 4 (2000). See page 727.
19. Ruschenberger, *Three Years in the Pacific: Including Notices of Brazil, Chile, Bolivia, Peru.* The quote is on page 344.
20. Matthew, "A Primitive Export Sector: Guano Production in Mid-Nineteenth-Century Peru." See page 37.

21. W. Jordan, "The Peruvian Guano Gospel in the Old South," *Agricultural History* 24, no. 4 (1950). See page 214.
22. Ibid. See page 215.
23. G. W. Peck, *Melbourne, and the Chincha Islands: With Sketches of Lima, and a Voyage Round the World* (New York: Charles Scribner, 1854). The quote is on pages 214–15.
24. Quoted in Jordan, "The Peruvian Guano Gospel in the Old South." The quote is on page 219.
25. Ibid., quoted on page 216.
26. See page 77 in *The Journal of the Seventy-First Annual Convention of the Protestant Episcopal Church in Maryland* (Oxford: Oxford University Press, 1854).
27. Jordan, "The Peruvian Guano Gospel in the Old South."
28. M. Fillmore, "State of the Union Address," Project Gutenberg, http://infomotions.com/etexts/gutenberg/dirs/etext04/sufil11.htm.
29. Kenneth E. Shewmaker, " 'Untaught Diplomacy': Daniel Webster and the Lobos Islands Controversy," *Diplomatic History* 1, no. 4 (1977).
30. O'Donnell, "The Lobos Islands: American Imperialism in Peruvian Waters in 1852."
31. Quoted in J. Spengler, "Malthus and World Hunger," *Proceedings of the Academy of Political Science* 30, no. 3 (1971). The quote is on page 131.
32. Quoted in D. Charles, *Between Genius and Genocide: The Tragedy of Fritz Haber, Father of Chemical Warfare* (London: Pimlico, 2006). The quote is on page 82.
33. A. Rimas and E. D. G. Fraser, *Beef: The Untold Story of How Muscle, Meat and Milk Shaped the World* (New York: William Morrow/HarperCollins, 2008). See in particular chapters 1, 2, and 3.
34. Although controversial, this argument is advanced by R. O'Connell in his exploration of the origins of warfare. See pages 53–68 and 85–103 in R. O'Connell, *Ride of the Second Horseman: The Birth and Death of War* (Oxford: Oxford University Press, 1995). The interested reader may also enjoy the following article that critically explores this and a number of other theories on the origins of warfare: I. J. N. Thorpe, "Anthropology, Archaeology, and the Origin of Warfare," *World Archaeology* 35, no. 1 (2003). See also the discussion on the origins of farming and warfare in chapter 4 of this volume.
35. Keith L. Manchester, "Man of Destiny: The Life and Work of Fritz Haber," *Endeavour* 26, no. 2 (2002). See page 64.
36. Charles, *Between Genius and Genocide: The Tragedy of Fritz Haber, Father of Chemical Warfare*. See pages 24–25.
37. Ibid. The quote is on page 28.
38. Ibid. See page 65.
39. See chapter 5 of D. Stoltzenberg, *Fritz Haber: Chemist, Nobel Laureate, German, Jew* (Philadelphia, Penn.: Chemical Heritage Press, 2004).
40. Hague Convention, "Convention (II) with Respect to the Laws and Customs of War on Land and Its Annex: Regulations Concerning the Laws and Customs of War on Land," 1899, published on the ICRC website, http://www.icrc.org/ihl.nsf/FULL/150?OpenDocument. See article 21.
41. Manchester, "Man of Destiny: The Life and Work of Fritz Haber." See page 65.
42. Haber, "The Synthesis of Ammonia from Its Elements: Nobel Prize Lecture." The quote is on page 339.
43. California Fertilizer Foundation, "Plant Nutrients—Nitrogen."
44. Smil, *Enriching the Earth: Fritz Haber, Carl Bosch, and the Transformation of World Food Production*. See chapter 8, in particular pages 160–61.
45. Ibid. See page 184.
46. Ibid. See chapter 9.

47. These figures are quoted in T. Young and J. Karkoski, "Green Evolution: Are Economic Incentives the Next Step in Non-Point Source Pollution Control?" *Water Policy* 2, no. 3 (2000). See pages 151–52.
48. Smil, *Enriching the Earth: Fritz Haber, Carl Bosch, and the Transformation of World Food Production*. See chapter 9.
49. S. Romero, "Peru Guards Its Guano as Demand Soars Again," *New York Times* online edition, http://www.nytimes.com/2008/05/30/world/americas/30peru.html?_r=2&pagewanted=1&partner=rssnyt&emc=rss&oref=slogin.
50. Ibid.
51. R. J. M. Crawford and J. Jahncke, "Comparison of Trends in Abundance of Guano-Producing Seabirds in Peru and Southern Africa," *South African Journal of Marine Science* 21, no. 1 (1999). See also P. Muck and D. Pauly, *Monthly Anchoveta Consumption of Guano Birds, 1953 to 1982* (Makati, Philippines: ICLARM, 1987).
52. Romero, "Peru Guards Its Guano as Demand Soars Again."
53. V. Smil, "Detonator of the Population Explosion," *Nature* 400 (1999). The quote is on page 415.

CHAPTER SIX: ICE

1. F. Carletti, *My Voyage around the World: A Sixteenth Century Florentine Merchant*, trans. H. Weinstock (ca. 1609; London: Methuen and Co., Ltd., 1964). The quote is on pages 52 and 53.
2. Ibid. The quote is on page 53.
3. E. F. Binkerd and O. E. Kolari, "The History and Use of Nitrate and Nitrite in the Curing of Meat," *Food and Cosmetics Toxicology* 13, no. 6 (1975). See page 656.
4. J. Smith, "The Iceman Cometh," *World Trade* 19, no. 8 (2006).
5. Ibid., quoted on page 62.
6. Ibid.
7. J. Parton, *Captains of Industry* (Boston: Houghton, Mifflin, and Company, 1890). See page 68.
8. Ibid. The quote is on page 69.
9. Barry K. Goodwin, Thomas J. Grennes, and Lee A. Craig, "Mechanical Refrigeration and the Integration of Perishable Commodity Markets," *Explorations in Economic History* 39, no. 2 (2002).
10. Ibid. See page 156.
11. C. Russell, *The Greatest Trust in the World* (New York: Arno Publishing, 1905; reprinted 1975). The quote is on page 11.
12. Ibid. The quote is on page 26.
13. R. Aduddell and L. Cain, "Public Policy Toward 'The Greatest Trust in the World,'" *The Business History Review* 55, no. 2 (1981).
14. H. Ford, *My Life and Work* (Garden City, N.Y.: Garden City Publishing Company, 1922); e-book published by Project Gutenberg, 2005, http://www.gutenberg.org/dirs/etext05/hnfrd10.txt. See chapter 16, "Railroads."
15. Ibid.
16. For background to this, see Peter Jackson, Neil Ward, and Polly Russell, "Mobilising the Commodity Chain Concept in the Politics of Food and Farming," *Journal of Rural Studies* 22, no. 2 (2006).
17. S. McClurg, *Water and the Shaping of California* (Berkeley, Calif.: Water Education Foundation and Heyday Books, 2000). See page 95.
18. J. Connor and W. Shiek, *Food Processing: An Industrial Powerhouse in Transition* (New York: Wiley-Interscience Publications, 1997). See pages 157–61.

19. Ibid.
20. McClurg, *Water and the Shaping of California.*
21. The following article describes different "food regimes" that help explain U.S. agricultural history: H. Friedmann and P. McMichael, "Agriculture and the State System: The Rise and Decline of National Agricultures, 1870 to the Present," *Sociologia Ruralis* 29, no. 2 (1989). See in particular pages 95–96.
22. Ibid. See page 106.
23. S. Stoll, *The Fruits of Natural Advantage: Making the Industrial Countryside in California* (Berkeley: University of California Press, 1998). See page 38.
24. H. Seftel, "Government Regulation and the Rise of the California Fruit Industry: The Entrepreneurial Attack on Fruit Pests, 1880–1920," *The Business History Review* 59, no. 3 (1985). See in particular pages 370–71.
25. See Stoll, *The Fruits of Natural Advantage: Making the Industrial Countryside in California*, and W. Friedland, "The Global Fresh Fruit and Vegetable System: An Industrial Organization Analysis," in *The Global Restructuring of Agro-Food Systems*, ed. P. McMichael (Ithaca, N.Y.: Cornell University Press, 1994). See in particular pages 174–75.
26. Some of the background to this is provided by S. Latham, "Marketing Cooperatives: A Model for Output Decisions of the Cloverdale Lettuce and Vegetable Cooperative" (master's thesis; University of British Columbia, 1992). See pages 5–8.
27. Friedland, "The Global Fresh Fruit and Vegetable System: An Industrial Organization Analysis." See page 213.
28. W. Friedland, A. Barton, and R. Thomas, *Manufacturing Green Gold: Capital, Labour, and Technology in the Lettuce Industry* (London: Cambridge University Press, 1981).
29. Ibid. See page 38.
30. Ibid.
31. C. Francis et al., "Impact of Sustainable Agriculture Programs on U.S. Landgrant Universities," *Journal of Sustainable Agriculture* 5, no. 4 (1995).
32. Friedland, Barton, and Thomas, *Manufacturing Green Gold: Capital, Labour, and Technology in the Lettuce Industry.*
33. Friedmann and McMichael, "Agriculture and the State System: The Rise and Decline of National Agricultures, 1870 to the Present."
34. T. Young and J. Karkoski, "Green Evolution: Are Economic Incentives the Next Step in Non-Point Source Pollution Control?" *Water Policy* 2, no. 3 (2000).
35. J. Hunt et al., "Patterns of Aquatic Toxicity in an Agriculturally Dominated Coastal Watershed in California," *Agriculture, Ecosystems and the Environment* 75, no. 1–2 (1999). The figures and quote come from the abstract and section 1 of the paper.
36. For example, the following paper represents just one of countless studies on the effects of "non-point" pollution, or pollution that is not emitted from a single place such as a factory: K. Loague et al., "A Case Study Simulation of DBCP Groundwater Contamination in Fresno County, California; 1. Leaching through the Unsaturated Subsurface," *Journal of Contaminant Hydrology* 29, no. 2 (1998).
37. N. Kuminoff et al., *The Measure of California Agriculture, 2000* (Davis, CA: University of California Agricultural Issues Center, 2000). See page 40.
38. McClurg, *Water and the Shaping of California.* See page 105.
39. J. Soule and J. Piper, *Farming in Nature's Image* (Washington D.C.: Island Press, 1992). See page 26.
40. McClurg, *Water and the Shaping of California.* See page 105.
41. For a study on how this has pertained to farming in Canada, see A. Winson, *The Intimate Commodity* (Guelph, Ont.: Garamond Press, 1992). See pages 139–41.

42. W. Butler and C. Wolf, "California Dairy Production: Unique Policies and Natural Advantages," in *Dairy Industry Restructuring: Research in Rural Sociology and Development*, vol. 8, ed. H. Schwarzweller and A. Davidson (Amsterdam: JAI, 2000). See pages 141–43.
43. Friedland, Barton, and Thomas, *Manufacturing Green Gold: Capital, Labour, and Technology in the Lettuce Industry*, and D. Goodman and M. Redcliffe, *Refashioning Nature: Food, Ecology and Culture* (London: Routledge, 1991).
44. Stoll, *The Fruits of Natural Advantage: Making the Industrial Countryside in California*. See page 62.
45. D. Allen and D. Lueck, "Family Farm Inc.," *Choices* (1st quarter 2000).
46. Arguments about the problems of complexity are presented by Joseph Tainter. See Joseph A. Tainter, *The Collapse of Complex Societies* (Cambridge: Cambridge University Press, 1988); and Joseph A. Tainter, "Sustainability of Complex Societies," *Futures* 27, no. 4 (1995).
47. *Ford, My Life and Work*. See chapter 16, "Railroads."
48. W. Friedland and E. Pugliese, "Class Formation and Decomposition in Modern Capitalist Agriculture: Comparative Perspectives," *Sociologia Ruralis* 29, no. 2 (1989). See page 154.
49. K. Morgan, T. Marsden, and J. Murdoch, *Place, Power and Provenance in the Food Chain* (Oxford: Oxford University Press, 2006). See page 60.
50. A. Smith, *An Inquiry into the Nature and Causes of the Wealth of Nations: A Selected Edition* (Oxford: Oxford University Press, 1998). See chapter 5.
51. J. Clay, *World Agriculture and the Environment* (Washington, D.C.: Island Press, 2004). See page 138.
52. M. F. Neves, "The Brazilian Orange Juice Chain," in *Commodity Market Review* (Rome: UN Food and Agriculture Organization, 2008), pp. 85–100.
53. W. Friedland, "Agrifood Globalization and Commodity Systems," *International Journal of Sociology of Agriculture and Food* 12 (2004), http://www.ijsaf.org/archive/vol12/abstracts/vol12_abstract_friedland.html.
54. Neves, "The Brazilian Orange Juice Chain."
55. C. Considera, "Building a Leniency and Amnesty Policy: The Brazilian Experience," *The International Journal of Competition Policy and Regulation* (June/July 2001).
56. "Brazil Orange Juice Probe Goes On," BBC News, http://news.bbc.co.uk/1/hi/business/6176178.stm.
57. Neves, "The Brazilian Orange Juice Chain." See page 91.
58. See the chapter on orange juice in Clay, *World Agriculture and the Environment*.
59. J. Donovan and B. Krissoff, "The U.S. Orange Juice Industry in the FTAA," in *U.S. Agriculture and the Free Trade Area of the Americas*, USDA Agricultural Economic Report No. AER-827, ed. M. Burfisher (Washington D.C.: USDA Economic Research Service, 2004). See page 85.
60. Clay, *World Agriculture and the Environment*.
61. The industry's reply to the allegation that it was using child labor was presented on ABECITUS, "Commitment to Eradicate Child Labor in Citriculture," ABECITUS website, http://www.abecitrus.com.br/english/social_comp_us.html. [At the time of printing, this web page was unavailable.]

STORM CLOUDS

1. Susan M. Walcott and Clifton W. Pannell, "Metropolitan Spatial Dynamics: Shanghai," *Habitat International* 30, no. 2 (2006). See page 200.

2. For a background on the history of Shanghai see "City Profile: Shanghai," *Cities* 16, no. 3 (1999).
3. Travel China, "Taihu Lake (Tai Lake)," TravelChina.com, http://www.travelchinaguide.com/attraction/jiangsu/wuxi/taihu_lake.htm.
4. Satellite images of the bloom are available at a NASA website. See J. Beitler, "Cleaner Water from Space," NASA, http://nasadaacs.eos.nasa.gov/articles/2008/2008_algae.html.
5. Personal communication. See also Xiaodong Wu et al., "Horizontal Distribution and Transport Processes of Bloom-Forming Microcystis in a Large Shallow Lake (Taihu, China)," *Limnologica—Ecology and Management of Inland Waters* 40, no. 1 (2010).
6. L. Guo, "Doing Battle with the Green Monster of Taihu Lake," *Science* 317, no. 5842 (2007). See page 1166.
7. Q. Yanfeng, "Taihu Lake Water Safety Fears Remain," *China Daily* online edition, updated May 30, 2008, http://www.chinadaily.com.cn/china/2008-05/30/content_6722842.htm.
8. This point is made in J. Dongmei, Z. Yuanfang, and L. Genfa, "The Roles of Countrywomen in Controlling Non-Point Source Pollution," *Chinese Journal of Population, Resources and Environment* 4, no. 2 (2006).
9. Geying Lai, Ge Yu, and Feng Gui, "Preliminary Study on Assessment of Nutrient Transport in the Taihu Basin Based on SWAT Modeling," *Science in China Series D: Earth Sciences* 49, no. 1 (2006).
10. H. Y. Guo, X. R. Wang, and J. G. Zhu, "Quantification and Index of Non-Point Source Pollution in Taihu Lake Region with GIS," *Environmental Geochemistry and Health* 26, no. 2 (2004).
11. Ying-Xin Xie et al., "Assessment of Nitrogen Pollutant Sources in Surface Waters of Taihu Lake Region," *Pedosphere* 17, no. 2 (2007). See page 206.
12. Most Chinese scholars we've talked to agree that while this is an interesting interpretation of the origins of these characters, it probably isn't completely accurate.

CHAPTER SEVEN: BLOOD

1. C. Corn, *The Scents of Eden* (New York: Kodansha International, 1998). See page 13.
2. F. Carletti, *My Voyage around the World: A Sixteenth Century Florentine Merchant*, trans. H. Weinstock (ca. 1609; London: Methuen and Co., Ltd., 1964). The quote is on page 189.
3. Corn, *The Scents of Eden*. See chapter 2.
4. Carletti, *My Voyage around the World: A Sixteenth Century Florentine Merchant*. The quote is on page 193.
5. Ibid. The quote is on page 194.
6. There are many English translations of *The Sensible Cook*. One online version includes excerpts from P. Rose, *The Sensible Cook. Dutch Foodways in the Old and the New World* (Syracuse, N.Y.: Syracuse University Press, 1998). See http://www.kookhistorie.nl/.
7. These spices and the Spice Islands are described in an early nineteenth-century source: J. Bigland and J. Morse, *A Geographical and Historical View of the World: Exhibiting a Complete Delineation of the Natural and Artificial Features of Each Country: And a Succinct Narrative of the Origin of the Different Nations, Their Political Revolutions, and Progress in Arts, Sciences, Literature, Commerce & Etc. The Whole Comprising All That Is Important in the Geography of the Globe, and the History of Mankind* (Philadelphia: Thomas B. Wait and Co., 1811). See pages 405–6.
8. H. Cook, *Matters of Exchange: Commerce, Medicine, and Science in the Dutch Golden Age* (New Haven, Conn.: Yale University Press, 2007). See page 181.

9. J. van Goor and F. van Goor, *Prelude to Colonialism: The Dutch in Asia* (Hilversum, Netherlands: Uitgeverij Verloren, 2004). See pages 78–79. Note that some sources spell Verhoeff as Verhoeven.
10. This scene is described in Corn, *The Scents of Eden*. See pages 140–41.
11. R. Seavoy, *Origins and Growth of the Global Economy: From the Fifteenth Century Onward* (Westport, Conn.: Greenwood Publishing Group, 2003). See pages 29–43.
12. Coen, quoted in A. G. Frank, *Reorient: Global Economy in the Asian Age* (Berkeley: University of California Press, 1998). The quote is on pages 281–82.
13. One of the best books on the culture of the Netherlands at this time is S. Schama, *The Embarrassment of Riches: An Interpretation of Dutch Culture in the Golden Age* (New York: Vintage Books, 1987).
14. Quoted in Cook, *Matters of Exchange: Commerce, Medicine, and Science in the Dutch Golden Age*. The quote is on page 183.
15. Quoted in J. Tracy, *The Political Economy of Merchant Empires: State Power and World Trade, 1350–1750* (Cambridge: Cambridge University Press, 1997). See page 4.
16. Cook, *Matters of Exchange: Commerce, Medicine, and Science in the Dutch Golden Age*. See pages 187–88.
17. Quoted in Tracy, *The Political Economy of Merchant Empires: State Power and World Trade, 1350–1750*. The quote is on page 4.
18. O. Prakesh, "The Great Divergence: Evidence from Eighteenth Century India," European Union. Paper presented at the Seventh GEHN Conference at Istanbul, September 11–12, 2005. Available online at http://eurindia.pc.unicatt.it/english/public_results/publications/The%20Great%20Divergence_GEHN%20Sept%20%202005.pdf. See page 10. This paper has been quoted by permission of the author.
19. T. Oxley, "The Banda Nutmeg Plantations," in *Journal of the Indian Archipelago and Eastern Asia*, ed. J. Logan (Singapore: Jacob Baptist, 1856).
20. A. Gutierrez, "Codifying the Past, Erasing the Future: NAFTA and the Zapatista Uprising of 1994," *Hastings West-Northwest Journal of Environmental Law and Policy* 4, no. 2 (1996). See pages 143–44.
21. C. Bijoy, "Zapatista Declaration," *Economic and Political Weekly* 29, no. 25 (1994). The quote is on page 1490.
22. This was reported in T. Golden, "Mexican Troops Battling Rebels; Toll at Least 57," *New York Times*, January 3, 1994. See page A1.
23. Gutierrez, "Codifying the Past, Erasing the Future: NAFTA and the Zapatista Uprising of 1994." See page 147.
24. Ibid.
25. North American Free Trade Agreement, "Chapter 7: Agriculture and Sanitary and Phytosanitary Measures," available online at the Foreign Affairs and International Trade Canada website, http://www.international.gc.ca/trade-agreements-accords-commerciaux/agr-acc/nafta-alena/texte/chap07a.aspx?lang=en#Article703.
26. S. Zahniser and W. Coyle, "U.S.-Mexico Corn Trade During the NAFTA Era: New Twists to an Old Story," USDA Electronic Outlook Report FDS-04D-01 (Washington, D.C.: USDA Economic Research Service, May 2004).
27. See discussion on swidden agriculture in H. Lamprecht, *Silviculture in the Tropics* (Eschborn, Germany: GTZ, 1989).
28. M. Ganz, *Rebels: Into Anarchy—and Out Again* (New York: Dodd, Mead and Company, 1920). The quote is on page 246.
29. D. Frank, "Housewives, Socialists, and the Politics of Food: The 1917 New York Cost-of-Living Protests," *Feminist Studies* 11, no. 2 (1985).

30. "Blame Food Speculators; Baltimore Merchants Say Supplies Are Held in Cars," *New York Times,* February 24, 1917. The quote is on page 3.
31. Ganz, *Rebels: Into Anarchy—and Out Again.* The quote is on page 260.
32. Ibid. The quote is on page 251.
33. Frank, "Housewives, Socialists, and the Politics of Food: The 1917 New York Cost-of-Living Protests."
34. This scene is described by E. Thompson, "The Moral Economy of the English Crowd in the Eighteenth Century," *Past and Present* 50 (1971). See page 82.
35. Ibid., quoted on page 99.
36. Ibid. The quote is on page 89.
37. A. Smith, *An Inquiry into the Nature and Causes of the Wealth of Nations: With a Commentary* (n.p.: Plain Label Books, 1835). See page 346. This edition is available as an ebook online at http://books.google.co.uk/books?id=jKr4NWJERbIC&printsec=frontcover&source=gbs_navlinks_s#v=onepage&q=&f=false.
38. For a good review of the issue of "food deserts," see S. Furey, C. Strugnell, and H. McIlveen, "An Investigation of the Potential Existence of 'Food Deserts' in Rural and Urban Areas of Northern Ireland," *Agriculture and Human Values* 18, no. 4 (2001).
39. N. Wrigley, " 'Food Deserts' in British Cities: Policy Context and Research Priorities," *Urban Studies* 39, no. 11 (2002). See page 2029.
40. Ibid. See page 2031.
41. Thompson, "The Moral Economy of the English Crowd in the Eighteenth Century." The quote is on page 87.
42. J. Archer, *Social Unrest and Popular Protest in England: 1780–1840* (Cambridge: Cambridge University Press, 2000). See page 3.
43. Frank, "Housewives, Socialists, and the Politics of Food: The 1917 New York Cost-of-Living Protests." See page 263.
44. There are a number of papers written on this subject. For example, see B. Meggers, "Archaeological Evidence for the Impact of Mega-Niño Events in Amazonia during the Past Two Millennia," *Climatic Change* 28 (1994); and R. Grove, "The Great El Niño of 1789–93 and Its Global Consequences: Reconstructing an Extreme Climate Event in World Environmental History," *The Medieval History Journal* 10, nos. 1–2 (2007).
45. Grove, "The Great El Niño of 1789–93 and Its Global Consequences: Reconstructing an Extreme Climate Event in World Environmental History." See pages 77–78.
46. Ibid. See pages 83–86.
47. Ibid., quoted on page 84.
48. L. Tilly, "The Food Riot as a Form of Political Conflict in France," in *Social Mobility and Modernization: A Journal of Interdisciplinary History Reader*, ed. R. Rotberg (Cambridge, Mass.: MIT Press, 2000). See page 179.
49. Reuters News Agency, "U.N. agencies weigh response to food crisis," Reuters, http://www.reuters.com/article/idUSSP15678520080428.
50. "Rising Food Prices Cause Riots," BBC News, http://news.bbc.co.uk/player/nol/newsid_7330000/newsid_7335900/7335974.stm?bw=bb&mp=wm&asb=1&news=1&ms3=22&ms_javascript=true&bbcws=2#.
51. "IMF Helping Countries Respond to Food Price Crisis," International Monetary Fund, http://www.imf.org/external/pubs/ft/survey/so/2008/NEW060308A.htm. The quote is found in the section titled "Not a global food shortage."

CHAPTER EIGHT: MONEY

1. F. Carletti, *My Voyage around the World: A Sixteenth Century Florentine Merchant*, trans. H. Weinstock (ca. 1609; London: Methuen and Co., Ltd., 1964). The quotes are on pages 99 and 100.
2. R. Fortune, *Three Years' Wanderings in the Northern Provinces of China* (London: J. Murray, 1847). The quote is on pages 391–92.
3. Ibid. See page 393.
4. C. Carrico, "Dancing Goats, Coffee Houses, and the Chic of Araby," *Molecular Interventions* 3, no. 1 (2003). See pages 40–41.
5. B. Rajan, *Under Western Eyes* (London: Duke University Press, 1999). See page 2.
6. The following provides an engaging, accessible, and well-researched history of this enterprise: J. Keay, *The Honourable Company* (London: Harper Collins, 1991).
7. V. Forman, "Transformations of Value and the Production of 'Investment' in the Early History of the English East India Company," *Journal of Medieval and Early Modern Studies* 34, no. 3 (2004). See pages 611 and 612.
8. Ibid., quoted on page 621.
9. J. Lancaster, "Account by James Lancaster on His Far East Voyage," Quoted in *Empire: A 90 Part History of the British Empire by the British Broadcasting Corporation*, episode 15, BBC Radio 4, October 14, 2005. Lancaster's original was written about the year 1605.
10. J. Crawfurd, "On the History and Migration of Cultivated Plants Producing Coffee, Tea, Cocoa, Etc.," *Transactions of the Ethnological Society of London* 7 (1869). See pages 197–206.
11. F. Denys, *Tea for the British* (London: Chatto and Windus, 1973). See page 29.
12. "Robert Montgomery Martin," *Oxford Dictionary of National Biography*, Oxford University Press, http://0-www.oxforddnb.com.wam.leeds.ac.uk/view/article/18208 (subscription required for full text).
13. R. Martin, *The Past and Present State of the Tea Trade of England* (London: Parbury, Allen, and Co., 1832). The quote is on page 196.
14. Mrs. John Sherwood, *Manners and Social Usages* (n.p.: Plain Label Books, 1887). Available online through Project Gutenberg at http://www.gutenberg.org/dirs/etext05/7msus10.txt. The quote is on page 245.
15. Martin, *The Past and Present State of the Tea Trade of England*. The quote is on page 196.
16. Forman, "Transformations of Value and the Production of 'Investment' in the Early History of the English East India Company." See in particular the discussion on pages 612–13 with regard to this point and the early history of the Honourable Company.
17. Keay, *The Honourable Company*. See page 359.
18. P. Tuck, *Britain and the China Trade 1635–1842* (Oxford: Clarendon Press, 1926; facsimile (London): Routledge, 2000). See in particular appendix S.
19. Commissioner Lin, "Letter to Queen Victoria," Internet Modern History Sourcebook. Available online at http://www.fordham.edu/halsall/mod/1839lin2.html.
20. Carletti, *My Voyage around the World: A Sixteenth Century Florentine Merchant*. The quote is on page 199.
21. P. Wickramagamage, "Large-Scale Deforestation for Plantation Agriculture in the Hill Country of Sri Lanka and Its Impacts," *Hydrological Processes* 12 no. 13–14 (1999). See pages 13–14.
22. M. Davis, *Late Victorian Holocausts: El Niño Famines and the Making of the Third World* (London: Verso, 2001). See pages 61–62.

23. J. T. Headley, *The Travels of General Grant* (Philadelphia, 1881), page 444. Quoted in Davis, *Late Victorian Holocausts: El Niño Famines and the Making of the Third World.* The quote is on page 5.
24. Ibid., quoted on page 94.
25. Ibid., quoted on page 418.
26. Digby (1849–1904) was a journalist and editor in India. His book, *Prosperous British India* (1901), argued that India's wealth was being drained by the UK government.
27. D. Forbes, *Christmas: A Candid History* (Berkeley: University of California Press, 2007). See page 64.
28. S. Connolly, ed., *The Oxford Companion to Irish History* (Oxford: Oxford University Press, 2004). See page 480.
29. One of the best histories of Ireland is R. F. Foster, *Modern Ireland* (New York: Penguin Books, 1988).
30. See page 13 in J. Mokyr, *Why Ireland Starved* (London: George Allen & Unwin, 1987). Also see the chapter on the famine in Foster, *Modern Ireland.*
31. M. Daly, *The Famine in Ireland* (Dublin: Dublin Historical Association, 1986). See also C. Kinealy, *The Great Calamity* (Dublin: Gill & MacMillan, 1994).
32. Cormac Ó Gráda, *The Great Irish Famine* (London: Macmillan, 1989).
33. Quoted in A. Bourke, *The Visitation of God? The Potato and the Great Irish Famine* (Dublin: Lilliput Press, 1993). The quote is on page 32.
34. Ó Gráda, *The Great Irish Famine.*
35. A. Hollis and A. Sweetman, "Microfinance and Famine: The Irish Loan Funds during the Great Famine," *World Development* 32 (2004).
36. G. B. Shaw, *Man and Superman* (London: Constable, 1911).
37. The quote can be found in N. Borlaug, "Nobel Lecture: The Green Revolution, Peace, and Humanity," The Nobel Foundation, http://nobelprize.org/nobel_prizes/peace/laureates/1970/borlaug-lecture.html.
38. L. Gao, "The Conservation of Chinese Rice Biodiversity: Genetic Erosion, Ethnobotany and Prospects," *Genetic Resources and Crop Evolution* 50, no. 1 (2003). See the full article, but the discussion on page 29 is particularly relevant.
39. Karl Hammer and Gaetano Laghetti, "Genetic Erosion—Examples from Italy," *Genetic Resources and Crop Evolution* 52, no. 5 (2005). See in particular figure 1 on page 630.
40. K. Kiritani, "Pest Management in Rice," *Annual Review of Entomology* 24, no. 1 (1979). See in particular the discussion on page 282.
41. Ibid.
42. Janet Hemingway, Linda Field, and John Vontas, "An Overview of Insecticide Resistance," *Science* 298, no. 5591 (2002).
43. Kiritani, "Pest Management in Rice." See page 284.
44. For a review of the ways that habitat can be managed to provide enhanced pest resistance, see Douglas A. Landis, Stephen D. Wratten, and Geoff M. Gurr, "Habitat Management to Conserve Natural Enemies of Arthropod Pests in Agriculture," *Annual Review of Entomology* 45, no. 1 (2000).
45. These developments are reviewed in T. Clarke, "China Leads GM Revolution," *Nature* online edition, January 25, 2002, http://cmbi.bjmu.edu.cn/news/0201/86.htm.
46. J. Qiu, "Agriculture: Is China Ready for GM Rice?" *Nature* 455, no. 7215 (2008). See page 850.
47. C. Holling, "Understanding the Complexity of Economic, Ecological, and Social Systems," *Ecosystems* 4 (2001). The quote is on page 396. See also the edited book that summarizes this body of research: L. Gunderson and C. S. Holling, eds., *Panarchy: Understanding Transformations in Human and Natural Systems* (Washington, D.C.: Island Press, 2002).

48. This argument is expanded on in E. Fraser, W. Mabee, and F. Figge, "A Framework for Assessing the Vulnerability of Food Systems to Future Shocks," *Futures* 37, no. 6 (2005).
49. E. Fraser, "Social Vulnerability and Ecological Fragility: Building Bridges between Social and Natural Sciences Using the Irish Potato Famine as a Case Study," *Conservation Ecology* 7, no. 1 (2003).

CHAPTER NINE: TIME

1. For a biography of Dekker and an introduction to his work and time, see University College London's Department of Dutch, "Multatuli Study Pack," University College London, http://www.ucl.ac.uk/dutch/self_study_packs/english_language/multatuli/index.html.
2. R. Edwards, "Translator's Introduction," in *Max Havelaar* (Amherst: University of Massachusetts Press, 1982). See page 8.
3. M. Davis, *Late Victorian Holocausts: El Niño Famines and the Making of the Third World* (London: Verso, 2001). See page 94.
4. Multatuli, *Max Havelaar, or, the Coffee Auctions of the Dutch Trading Company* (Amherst: University of Massachusetts Press, 1982). The quote is on page 73.
5. Ibid.
6. P. A. Toer, "Best Story: The Book That Killed Colonialism," *New York Times*, April 19, 1999. See page 6112 of the NewYork Edition. This is also available online at http://www.nytimes.com/1999/04/18/magazine/best-story-the-book-that-killed-colonialism.html?pagewanted=1.
7. This statistic comes from page 3 of Ten Thousand Villages' annual report, which is available online at http://www.tenthousandvillages.com/pdf/Annual_Report%202009.pdf.
8. For a background history to the Fair Trade movement, see the introduction and chapter 1 in D. Jaffee, *Brewing Justice: Fair Trade Coffee, Sustainability, and Survival* (Los Angeles: University of California Press, 2007).
9. "Understanding the WTO: The Basics—The Uruguay Round," World Trade Organization, http://www.wto.org/english/thewto_e/whatis_e/tif_e/fact5_e.htm.
10. "Understanding the WTO: The Agreements—Agriculture: Fairer Markets for Farmers," World Trade Organization, http://www.wto.org/english/thewto_e/whatis_e/tif_e/agrm_3e.htm.
11. There are many critics of the global food trading system. One of the most articulate and vehement voices is Vandana Shiva. For example, see V. Shiva, *Monocultures of the Mind* (London: Zed Books, 1993).
12. This list of characteristics is an amalgamation of the most common elements that appear in various Fair Trade standards. It was drawn from Jaffee, *Brewing Justice: Fair Trade Coffee, Sustainability, and Survival*. See page 2.
13. Information on this label and its standards are available from the Max Havelaar Foundation website, http://www.maxhavelaar.ch/en/maxhavelaar/.
14. According to Fairtrade Labelling Organizations International, which administers Europe's Fair Trade market:

    In 2007 Fairtrade sales amounted to approximately €2.3 billion worldwide, a 47% year-to-year increase over 2006. At the end of 2008 there were 872 Certified Producer Organizations in 58 developing countries. That represents more than 1.5 million pro-

ducers, about 7.5 million people, including dependents, who are benefiting directly from Fairtrade.

This quote comes from the FAQ section of www.fairtrade.net and is available online at http://www.fairtrade.net/faqs.html?&no_cache=1.

15. For information on the relation between TransFair and Starbucks, please see TransFair USA, "Starbucks, TransFair USA and Fairtrade Labelling Organizations International Announce Groundbreaking Initiative to Support Small-Scale Coffee Farmers," Organic Consumers Association, http://www.organicconsumers.org/articles/article_15377.cfm.
16. The following articles provide a nice history of these developments and the key elements of this debate: D. Reed, "What Do Corporations Have to Do with Fair Trade? Positive and Normative Analysis from a Value Chain Perspective," *Journal of Business Ethics* 86, no. 1 (2009), and P. Edward and A. Tallontire, "Business and Development: Towards Re-Politicisation," *Journal of International Development* 21, nos. 819–833 (2009).
17. For information on Starbucks' commitment to fair-trade purchasing, see TransFair USA, "Starbucks, TransFair USA and Fairtrade Labelling Organizations International Announce Groundbreaking Initiative to Support Small-Scale Coffee Farmers," Organic Consumers Association, http://www.organicconsumers.org/articles/article_15377.cfm.
18. The quote is from "Starbucks Shared Planet: Ethical Sourcing," Starbucks corporate website, http://www.starbucks.com/sharedplanet/ethicalInternal.aspx?story=fairTrade.
19. Jaffee, *Brewing Justice: Fair Trade Coffee, Sustainability, and Survival*. See in particular chapter 7, pages 199–231.
20. Ibid. See page 210.
21. Edward and Tallontire, "Business and Development: Towards Re-Politicisation." See also A. Tallontire, "Top Heavy? Governance Issues and Policy Decisions for the Fair Trade Movement," *Journal of International Development* 21 (2009).
22. See page 1005 in Tallontire, "Top Heavy? Governance Issues and Policy Decisions for the Fair Trade Movement."
23. Personal communication with Anne Tallontire, University of Leeds, UK.
24. This quote comes from the application form for Fairtrade applications and can be found at "Application Form for Fairtrade Applications," Fairtrade Labelling Organizations International, http://www.flo-cert.net/_admin/userfiles/file/Applications/GN%20Scope%20Check%20Application%20Form%20FO%2010%20en.doc.
25. C. Dolan, "Virtual Moralities: The Mainstreaming of Fairtrade in Kenyan Tea Fields," *Geoforum* 41, no. 1 (2010). See also P. Bahra, "Tea Workers Still Waiting to Reap Fairtrade Benefits: Premium Paid for Ethical Goods May Not Be Passed On," *The Times* (London), January 2, 2009. Available online at http://www.timesonline.co.uk/tol/news/uk/article5429888.ece.
26. R. Carson, *Silent Spring* (London: H. Hamilton, 1962).
27. E. Lockeretz, *Organic Farming: An International History* (Wallingford, UK: CABI, 2007). See page 4.
28. Ibid.; see chapter 9.
29. J. Guthman, "Regulating Meaning, Appropriating Nature: The Codification of California Organic Agriculture," *Antipode: A Radical Journal of Geography* 30, no. 2 (1998). See page 140.
30. J. Guthman, *Agrarian Dreams: The Paradox of Organic Farming in California* (Berkeley: University of California Press, 2004). See in particular chapter 6, which begins on page 110.
31. For more information, the U.S. Biodynamic Farming and Gardening Association's website can be found at http://www.biodynamics.com/aboutus.
32. Lockeretz, *Organic Farming: An International History*. The quote is on page 40.

33. C. Dimitry and C. Greene, "Recent Growth Patterns in the U.S. Organic Foods Market," U.S. Department of Agriculture, http://www.ers.usda.gov/Publications/AIB777/. See the summary of this report.
34. National Agriculture Library, "Organic Production/Organic Food," U. S. Department of Agriculture, http://www.nal.usda.gov/afsic/pubs/ofp/ofp.shtml.
35. For a formal comparison of the similarities in how the Fair Trade and organic certification bodies have come into being, see Daniel Jaffee and Philip Howard, "Corporate Cooptation of Organic and Fair Trade Standards," *Agriculture and Human Values* (in press).
36. E. Aguilera, "Aurora Organic Dairy under Scrutiny: Lawsuits Claim That Products from the Dairy Misrepresented the Lifestyle and Treatment of Its Cows," *Denver Post*, January 27, 2008. This article is available online at http://www.denverpost.com/commented/ci_8083332?source=commented-business.
37. Quoted in: S. Raabe, "Mega-Dairy Aurora Organic Admits It's an Intensive Confinement Organic Feedlot," *Denver Post*, January 16, 2005. Available on line at http://www.organicconsumers.org/Organic/aurora012405.cfm.
38. "Aurora Organic Dairy Signs Consent Agreement with USDA's Agricultural Marketing Service," U.S. Department of Agriculture, http://www.usda.gov/wps/portal/!ut/p/_s.7_0_A/7_0_1OB?contentidonly=true&contentid=2007/08/0228.xml.
39. "Aurora Factory Farm Photos," Cornucopia Institute, http://www.cornucopia.org/horizon-factory-farm-photo-gallery/aurora-factory-farm-photo-gallery/.
40. See this news story: M. Adams, "Aurora Organic Dairy Corporation Hit by Class Action Lawsuits Over 'Organic' Milk Labels," Natural News, http://www.naturalnews.com/022133.html.
41. See news story: S. Raabe, "Aurora Dairy, Feds Agree on Organics Decree," *Denver Post*, August 30, 2007. Available online at www.denverpost.com/business/ci_6753940.
42. C. Skrzycki, "USDA Trying to Put Loophole in Organic Dairy Rules out to Pasture," *Washington Post*, November 4, 2008.
43. For a review of the organic dairy industry see E. DuPuis, "Not in My Body: rBGH and the Rise of Organic Milk," *Agriculture and Human Values* 17 (2000).
44. F. Buttel, "The Recombinant BGH Controversy in the United States: Toward a New Consumption Politics of Food?" *Agriculture and Human Values* 17, no. 3 (2000). See in particular page 7.
45. Guthman, "Regulating Meaning, Appropriating Nature: The Codification of California Organic Agriculture." See in particular page 143.
46. Guthman, *Agrarian Dreams: The Paradox of Organic Farming in California*. The quote is on page 111.
47. A good text on sustainable agriculture is J. Soule and J. Piper, *Farming in Nature's Image* (Washington D.C.: Island Press, 1992).
48. "USDA Publishes Proposed Rule to Clarify Pasture Provisions of Organic Regulations," U.S. Department of Agriculture, http://www.ams.usda.gov/AMSv1.0/ams.printData.do?template=printPage&navID=&page=printPage&dDocId=STELPRDC5073342&dID=102368&wf=false&docTitle=USDA+Publishes+Proposed+Rule+to+Clarify+Pasture+Provisions+of+Organic+Regulations.
49. A. Meneley, "Extra Virgin Olive Oil and Slow Food," *Anthropologica* 46, no. 3 (2004). See pages 167–68.
50. B. Pietrykowski, "You Are What You Eat: The Social Economy of the Slow Food Movement," *Review of Social Economy* 62, no. 3 (2004). See pages 311–12.
51. "The Slow Food Manifesto," Slow Food International, www.slowfoodludlow.org.uk/docs/manifesto.html.

52. Pietrykowski, "You Are What You Eat: The Social Economy of the Slow Food Movement." See page 314.
53. C. Fischler, "Food, Self and Identity," *Social Science Information* 27, no. 2 (1988). See page 275.
54. C. Petrini, *Slow Food Nation: Why Our Food Should Be Good, Clean, and Fair* (New York: Rizzoli Ex Libris, 2007). See page 173.

CONCLUSION: THE NEW GLUTTONY AND TOMORROW'S MENU

1. One somewhat pessimistic study on food security that tries to assess the effect of more than two degrees of warming: David S. Battisti and Rosamond L. Naylor, "Historical Warnings of Future Food Insecurity with Unprecedented Seasonal Heat," *Science* 323, no. 5911 (2009).
2. The following study tries to model the effect of climate change and ozone pollution: S. Long et al., "Global Food Insecurity: Treatment of Major Food Crops with Elevated Carbon Dioxide or Ozone under Large-Scale Fully Open-Air Conditions Suggests Recent Models May Have Overestimated Future Yields," *Philosophical Transactions of the Royal Society B: Biological Sciences* 360, no. 1463 (2005).
3. Mark W. Rosegrant and Sarah A. Cline, "Global Food Security: Challenges and Policies," *Science* 302, no. 5652 (2003).
4. Roy Darwin, "Climate Change and Food Security," *Issues in Food Security,* Agriculture Information Bulletin Number 765-8, June 2001, http://www.ers.usda.gov/publications/aib7658/aib765-8.pdf.
5. Josef Schmidhuber and Francesco N. Tubiello, "Global Food Security under Climate Change," *Proceedings of the National Academy of Sciences* 104, no. 50 (2007). See in particular page 19706.
6. Ibid.
7. X. Yinlong et al., "Statistical Analyses of Climate Change Scenarios over China in the 21st Century," *Advances in Climate Change Research* 2, Supplement 1 (2006).
8. S. Postel, "Entering an Era of Water Scarcity," *Ecological Applications* 10, no. 4 (2000). See page 942. See also page 1035 in Robert B. Jackson et al., "Water in a Changing World," *Ecological Applications* 11, no. 4 (2001).
9. H. Yang and A. Zehnder, "China's Regional Water Scarcity and Implications for Grain Supply and Trade," *Environment and Planning A* 33, no. 1 (2001). See page 82.
10. Liu Changming and Zhang Shifeng, "Drying up of the Yellow River: Its Impacts and Counter-Measures," *Mitigation and Adaptation Strategies for Global Change* 7, no. 3 (2002). See page 1573.
11. This scenario is presented in G. Dyer, *Climate Wars* (Toronto: Random House Canada, 2008). See chapter 2.
12. Ibid. The quote is on page 62.
13. For example, the following paper tries to calculate the effect of climate change on grain prices but doesn't try to predict anything as specific as how, say, U.S. exports might be affected: M. L. Parry et al., "Effects of Climate Change on Global Food Production under SRES Emissions and Socio-Economic Scenarios," *Global Environmental Change* 14, no. 1 (2004).

Index

ABOUT THE AUTHORS

Evan D. G. Fraser is an adjunct professor of geography at the University of Guelph in Ontario, Canada, and a Senior Lecturer at the School of Earth and Environment at the University of Leeds in the UK. His research is on farming, climate change, and the environment. He has worked in the UK, Thailand, Belize, British Columbia, and Ontario, and has published many scholarly research articles, book chapters, and policy briefs on environmental issues for senior politicians. He lives in the Yorkshire Dales with his wife and three children.

Andrew Rimas is a journalist in the Boston area. He is the managing editor at *The Improper Bostonian* magazine and has worked as an associate editor and staff writer at *Boston* magazine. His work has frequently appeared in those publications and in *The Boston Globe*, as well as *The Boston Globe Magazine, Ottawa Citizen,* and other publications. Along with Evan D. G. Fraser, he is the coauthor of *Beef: The Untold Story of How Milk, Meat, and Muscle Shaped the World.*